Women in the
Japanese workplace

Women in the Japanese workplace

Mary Saso

CARL A. RUDISILL LIBRARY
LENOIR-RHYNE COLLEGE

Hilary Shipman
London

© Mary Saso 1990

Publication of this book has been assisted by a grant from the Japan Foundation.

All rights reserved. No part of this book may be reproduced or transmitted in any form or by any means, without permission in writing from the publisher.

First published 1990 by
Hilary Shipman Limited
19 Framfield Road
Highbury
London N5 1UU

HD
6197
.527
1990

1 5 7061

Sept. 1992

British Library Cataloguing in Publication Data
Saso, Mary
    Women in the Japanese workplace.
    1. Title
    331'.4

ISBN 0-948096-18-7
          0-948096-19-5

Cover design by David Bennett
Calligraphy by Tsugiko Saso

Typeset by Florencetype Ltd, Kewstoke, Avon
Printed and bound by Biddles Limited
Guildford & King's Lynn

Contents

Figures and tables

Figures

Tables

Foreword

Exceptional non-mommy-track careerist desired by DWCM, 56, Yale, Harvard degrees, who's stable, decent, optimistic, happy, athletic, fit, amusing, spiritual, pro-feminist and supportive . . .

It is likely, Mary Saso makes clear, to be a long time before Japan has large numbers of pro-feminist, supportive equivalents of this immodest DWCM (who, I should explain to those unaccustomed to the code language of the New York Review of Books personal columns, is a divorced, white, Christian – read 'non-Jewish' – male). Nor does Japan have a lot of non-mommy-track careerist women – i.e., women who have consciously opted either not to have children or at least not to give time to mothering on a scale which would materially affect their chances in career competition with men. There are already some such to be found, especially in the public sector – in education, medicine, central and local government administration – and also in the research and development (R and D) departments (rarely in any other department) of private corporations. Their numbers are increasing, and the likelihood of their actually getting career advancement – actually becoming headmistresses and hospital managers and laboratory directors – is, if only glacially, improving.

But it is clear that Mary Saso would join those American women who object vigorously to the whole concept of an institutionalized division between mommy-track careers and severely-reduced-mothering careers. She would prefer – what she describes as 'rational' in Chapter 10 – a world in which we all take more of our potential affluence in the form of increased leisure, so that parenting can become shared parenting for both men and women. The time it consumes would be taken from the hours otherwise spent playing golf or decorating the house or collecting stamps, not out of time claimed by the workplace (or home workstation), where men and women could then at last compete on an equal footing. They could make not just dual career families, but dual parent families too, as she neatly puts it.

Japanese men may not be very good at doing the laundry, but they are often quite enthusiastic about playing with their children, she says, so we are not without hope. If, indeed, Japan were to be a pioneer in this regard, that would be good news for Japan's worried competitors. But it doesn't seem likely. Everywhere one looks in the advanced industrial countries, the story seems to be the same. International competition is intensifying with the cheapening of communications and transport. Every nation is obsessed with its 'competitiveness'. At the same time, a higher proportion of the jobs that survive – or are created by – the development of technology, are responsible and intellectually non-trivial jobs capable of giving intrinsic satisfaction. And as corporations increasingly complain about not being able to get enough people bright enough to do those jobs well, there is increasing pressure on those who can. Hence, at present, there are more signs of Japanese male corporate workaholism spreading – first to co-opted Japanese women and then to the middle classes of other countries – than of Japan coming to appreciate the pleasures of what is still in that country somewhat disparagingly called *maihomu-shugi* ('my home-ism').

And, of course, dedicated workaholism in Japan has very special implications for the relation between the sexes because of the Japanese employment system. 'Equal pay for equal work' is hardly a useful rallying cry for women when the whole pay system is based on incremental-scale career wages, not payment for job functions, so that a 25-year-old man with seven years' service and a 45-year-old man with 27 could be doing the same job but be paid a widely different wage. In the circumstances it was sensible that the 1986 Equal Employment Opportunity Law did not bother reiterating the (pretty empty) equal pay provisions of the post-war Labour Standards Law, but concentrated, instead, on promotion opportunities – on provisions which were aimed to secure that women should be put on the same career tracks and enjoy the same career wage trajectories as men.

Provisions which, however, were purely exhortatory were not reinforced by any penal provisions and, Mary Saso shows, seem to have had very little effect on actual practice, particularly in the private sector. The consequence is that the male–female wage differentials, which she analyses carefully – with due allowance for all the statistical quirks and pitfalls which beset this kind of exercise – remain larger in Japan than elsewhere. And, reflecting the nature of the large corporation employment system the spheres of women's employment remain highly segregated; there remains a good deal of work on family farms and in other commercial and manufacturing family enterprises – for the most part not separate from the family residence; about a quarter of the total work-force in fact. Then there is the 'office lady' work for junior-college graduates, and shopfloor or counter-side work for high-school graduates, in the larger 'permanent employment' organizations. They are on incremental scales made to look like those of men, but their 'career' is expected to end with marriage or the birth of their first child, and there is very little alternative provision for those who choose not to marry or to remain childless. Finally, and of increasing numerical importance, there is the wide range of jobs offered in the secondary labour market, very largely paid at rate-for-the-job market rates, or at most on very gently sloping age-wage scales, a lot of them, especially in the large firms, part-time jobs – though part-time can mean up to 35 hours a week.

What this segmented pattern actually means in terms of options and opportunities for individual women is well brought out by the statistical comparison between Japan and

Britain which the book deploys. The author believes, as I confess I do not, all those influential people in Japan who say that the Japanese large-corporation 'lifetime employment system' is going to change. If it does, as she suggests, the likelihood is that British and Japanese patterns will converge, since there seems to be very little fundamental difference in attitudes to work and to motherhood between the two countries.

Mary Saso is what I would call a Stage I feminist. That is to say that she will allow the possibility that personality differences partly explain why few women in the factories she studied were appointed as supervisors, and does not insist, as a Stage II feminist would, that it is all the result of oppressive male conspiracies, albeit sometimes covered with a veneer of crocodile concern expressed in schemes of maternity leave and paternity leave, workplace child-care facilities and the rest. But she will not allow even the theoretical possibility that in either the British or the Japanese population (she doesn't talk about other gene pools) these personality differences might have some physiological base and not be solely the result of cultural conditioning. That to me is a bit of a limitation, and her lack of agnostic curiosity on that score prevents her from telling us what (if anything) Japanese psychologists are discovering about the roots of gender differences.

But, unlike most feminists of either stage of commitment, she is not disproportionately preoccupied with the problems of that minority of women who are qualified for, and seek, professional careers, either on the mommy-track or off it. Her fieldwork, which she presents in a fresh and lively way, was concerned mostly with women in manual jobs – in jobs, anyway, whether clerical or manual, that do not require a lengthy training, and where interruption for some years of child-rearing has only nominal seniority-score implications for career advancement, and very few implications for substantive work ability, or for cumulated experiential wisdom, or for cumulated work achievement. Instead of concentrating on the 'typical' British and the 'typical'

Japanese workplace, she has the interesting idea of comparing Japanese, Irish, Welsh and English women all under different forms of Japanese management. She offers a lot of arresting detail, about wages and job tenures, about training, about union involvement and about attitudes – with sidelong glances at the wider problems of Japanese investment in the United Kingdom, and at the reasons why British men are less happy under Japanese management than British women. But for me the most striking of her observations was that British women seem to get more positive satisfaction out of the work itself, and find more positive enjoyment in the work environment, than Japanese women doing comparable jobs in Japan.

Altogether a fascinating book, and one to be wholly recommended not only for the wealth of information which it contains, but also for the decent and humane values which inform the author's judgements.

Ronald Dore
Director
Japan-Europe Industry Research Centre
Imperial College, London

Acknowledgements

Because I am one of the band of women working freelance, often as a homeworker, I am indebted to family members who have encouraged me, supported me and given me practical assistance. My husband, Hiroo Saso, has not only entertained and taken over a lot of the care of the children, but also translated my questionnaires into Japanese and at the same time suggested additional questions and lines of inquiry. While I was visiting companies in Britain and Ireland, my parents, Pat and Margaret Sellars, took the children under their care and encouraged me to devote more time to research. The examples of my working mother and also my mother-in-law, who is a self-employed teacher of calligraphy, first clearly showed me that working women were not at all a phenomenon characteristic of those with few family responsibilities or of the West.

I have benefited from discussions with researchers in the field of Japanese labour, notably Machiko Osawa, Kazuo Koike and Marga Clegg. Their comments and advice along with those of staff at the Japan Institute of Labour have supplemented the academic angle. Hiromi Asano as a public servant in the Ministry of Labour is expected to work long hours, but she gave me her time to find out how particular statistical series were defined and to iron out apparent discrepancies in the data as well as supplying me with a mound of relevant material on legislation and surveys. I would not have been as aware of the difficulties faced by British working mothers without the information and thoughtful comments provided by Cilla Farquhar. Susan Yamada took a critical look at the text and pointed out many of the ambiguities and infelicitous expressions. And the editors – Hilary Macaskill and Michael Shipman – were not content merely to revise and approve, but gave me plenty of encouragement at each stage.

Staff at Denki Roren (Japanese Federation of Electrical Machine Workers' Unions) introduced me to Japanese trade union policies on women and gave me plenty of background material. Material and advice were also willingly supplied by the staff of the national development agencies concerned with informing prospective Japanese investors about Ireland and Wales; in particular Richard Ryan gave me important information, which corrected some common misconceptions about Ireland's investment climate. I am grateful to the employees of NEC Corporation and of Matsushita Electric Company, in Japan, Ireland and Wales, who never displayed any tedium, despite my persistent enquiries and requests to observe work on the shop floor. Most of all, I cannot forget all those working women who frankly responded to my questions and expressed support for my work.

Introduction

Ever since Japan came to the attention of the West in the middle of the nineteenth century, there has been a tendency among both Japanese and overseas observers to focus on what appears to be quaint to Western eyes. This tendency has been particularly evident in the case of studies of Japanese working women. We have heard a lot about the long apprenticeship of geisha and about the tea-pouring careers of 'office ladies'. While quaint stereotypes are interesting to read about and convenient to judge, they are neither enlightening nor helpful when any wider implications are to be considered.

The sorts of implications which are the concern of this book fall into two main categories. The ways in which the treatment of working women is changing and their response to those changes within Japan provide an important example of the extent to which women are – or are not – integrated into industrial and post-industrial societies. The other main implication concerns the way in which Japanese manufacturing facilities locating in Europe may transfer overseas their employment practices with respect to women. By and large Japanese manufacturers overseas, apart from car and power-shovel factories, are mostly employing women on the shop floor. The assembling of televisions, integrated circuits and other types of electronic goods provides employment predominantly for women.

In attempting to avoid the quaintness trap – often unfortunately set by diligent sociologists and social anthropologists – I have employed various devices, which in their own way may be just as guilty of manipulation. At the outset, therefore, I will outline my approach here so that it may be assessed before the results appear.

The first simple principle involved was to use comparisons whenever possible. There is little justification in bemoaning the subordinate position of Japanese women in the workplace without finding out how British and Irish women are treated in similar circumstances. Another principle was not to rely only on dry data, but to see how the statistics related to actual cases of working women. In studying individual workers, however, an unavoidable bias became evident. Unless a large-scale survey is undertaken with a randomly selected sample of the population being compulsorily interviewed, those relatively few women who agree to be interviewed by an author working on her own are almost inevitably unrepresentative. And when the Japanese woman is confronted with a foreign interviewer (even one who speaks Japanese), she may be inclined, perhaps culturally, towards giving the answers she believes are being sought.

I tried to mitigate this bias in two ways, neither of which may have been wholly effective. Rather than only relying on introductions to potential interviewees through friends, I also sought the impersonal assistance of personnel officers to select employees for interviews, which of course does mean that another sort of bias was introduced. Secondly, in order to avoid the possible tendency of a small-scale interviewer asking leading questions and perhaps seeking titillating information, I based the interviews on a questionnaire. Ideally there should be a good balance of both open response questions and those with answers to be selected. The latter allow a better and more systematic comparison to be made, but the former may reveal more honest and revealing responses. There are, however, many pitfalls associated with carrying out such opinion surveys, because of the impossibility of obtaining exact translations of each question and their interpretation in different cultures. The questionnaires which I compiled, therefore, have not been used to make quantified comparisons between the working conditions and attitudes of Japanese, British and Irish women.

Because those I interviewed were not selected by any statistically respectable sampling method – their respectability may instead be enhanced by being known as 'case studies' – I have had to rely on officially produced statistical series to confirm or make overall judgements. The result may not be as picturesque as in those studies generating their own data, but the size of my samples, apart from their non-respectability, did not permit me to provide any conclusive evidence without resorting to other sources.

Even though I have confined my subject to working women, the sources across Japan, Britain and Ireland from which I could get information and the possible topics of interest are numerous. Therefore I have had to place limits on what I should discuss in the light of the concerns of those reading this book. The potential readership belongs to two main groups: those who are interested in the personnel practices of overseas Japanese manufacturing plants and those who are concerned about the role of working women in an industrialized country. The latter topic inevitably extends to an examination of how women and men can integrate their working lives with child-rearing. What I found hopeful was that the post-industrial society in both Japan and the West could offer more scope for resolving this important issue of integrating economic and social roles.

After all that I have written above about avoiding the trap of taking a quaint look at Japanese working women, I now wish to quote what appears to be a quaint example of how the Japanese themselves – or at least the powers that be – view working women. In June 1988, the Ministry of Education, during its regular screening of proposed textbooks for schools, instructed that a passage dealing with working conditions for women should be revised. The original reference, which said that working hours should be shortened in order to improve working conditions for women, was deleted; and in its place was inserted the following: 'If women are to continue to work on equal terms with men, women's self-awakening is required in such fields as work morale and ethics.' (*The Japan Times*, 1 July 1988)

The original passage was a fairly innocuous suggestion which merely recognized the fact that, in the face of the long working hours taken on by Japanese workaholics, women with the additional burden of household and family tasks find it wellnigh impossible to work on equal terms with men. The revision is a far more loaded piece of prose in which it is presumed that a woman does already work on equal terms with a man and that, if she does not, the failure is only due to her own lack of work consciousness. Thus this example of how men view working women is not merely quaint, but actually very alarming. One of the tasks of this book will be to demonstrate how mistaken is this official view. That task has already been begun by women in Japan such as the Hataraku Fujin no Kai (an organisation for middle-aged working women), whose 1987 survey results gathered in *Obasan wa Okota-zo* (We're Really Angry) show that Japanese women are neither passive nor unaware that they cannot work on equal terms with men. The translation of one short passage (p.280) will be sufficient to demonstrate their awareness and their strong will:

> Looking from the bottom of present-day society we can easily see how its structure has a design full of contradictions and discrimination, within which women are ingeniously contained. Whatever changes occur, we want in our lives to take pride in our determination to see and speak about society, even from the lowliest perspective. The working women's association has been in action for 20 years to seek the realization of truly equal opportunities for women and men in society and we shall steadily continue on that path, since our greatest wish is to focus the power of middle-aged working women in changing society.

1 | Setting the scene in Japan and the British Isles

Two similar, but contrasting, scenes of women at work are particularly vivid in my mind. The stage for both scenes is an NEC – 'computers and communications' – plant. The much larger plant (Tamagawa) is surrounded by railway lines in the highly industrialized city of Kawasaki, which is squashed between Tokyo and Yokohama; the smaller one (Ballivor) lies incongruously in a rather remote Irish village. Even though the locations are so different in character many of the young Japanese women at NEC's Tamagawa plant are originally from rural areas, but now they live in company dormitories, whereas their Irish counterparts continue to live on family-run farms in sparsely populated County Meath. Most of the young Japanese women only expect to work at NEC for half a dozen years, whereas the Irish women in NEC's Ballivor plant do not intend to give up their employment with NEC so quickly.

On the shop floor in the two plants it would be hard to distinguish between the Japanese women and the Irish women; they are all peering through microscopes and operating similar machines for the production of integrated circuits. Their space-age balaclavas and coveralls are identical, but are their attitudes and expectations at all similar? Why do the Japanese women working at NEC appear to be less attached to the labour force? What is their view of paid work compared to that of Irish and British women working at Japanese factories? Do they all have job security, training and promotion opportunities to compensate for their highly disciplined work environment? Are the young Japanese women at NEC representative of all

1

Japanese working women? And how do work patterns for Japanese women differ from those for their Irish and British counterparts? These are just a handful of the issues which will be considered in this book. First, though, in order to begin to answer the last comparative question I shall examine the position of all women in the labour force in both Japan and Britain, with some comments about Ireland insofar as the participation patterns there differ from Britain.

The subjective view

Whenever anything is written in general about Japanese women and work, the following approach is popular. First, there are expressions of outrage both because the average wage differential by sex is so wide and also, ironically, because women apparently choose to stay at home rather than seek poorly paid employment. And there is the comforting conclusion that in this respect Japan is 20 years behind the West, but it is slowly catching up. This glib approach seems to suggest both a slightly superior smugness on the part of Western commentators and also an assurance that employment conditions for women can only continue to improve. But such complacent conclusions rest mostly on subjective impressions of progress. Even when bits of data are thrown in for support of the contention that the more women are working the more they are emancipated, agreement would be foolhardy without first checking both the long-term trends and the conditions under which women are working.

In trying to avoid the dangers of a subjective approach, therefore, I shall begin by examining comprehensive data and legislation both to make comparisons between Japan and the British Isles and also to see whether there have been any real changes over time. Even the use of hard data, however, requires some subjective judgements, because often the definitions used in collecting the data are not compatible; and even the simplest measures may sometimes show great variety depending on the source. A great deal of caution is needed, therefore, in making a direct comparison between countries. Still it should be possible to come to some conclusions about overall trends, which in the following chapters will be examined in more detail and assessed with respect to the lives of individual working women. Ultimately I intend to judge whether the trends and attitudes concerning women working are converging between Japan and the West and whether the overall direction is one of improvement. And I shall be considering the implications, in particular, for women shop-floor workers of Japanese companies in Britain and Ireland.

Participation in the labour market

Whether a woman has some kind of job or else is registered as unemployed, her willingness to engage in remunerative work – as opposed to the demanding, but unpaid, domestic labour of child care and housework – is shown by her participation in the labour force. I shall begin, therefore, in surveying the overall data on working women with the simplest straight comparison of participation rates for women's economic activity in different countries. Table 1.1 shows overall average rates for women between 15 and 64 years of age, while Figure 1.1 displays the age profiles for Japanese, British and Irish women, where in each age group the rate is measured by the percentage of all women in that group engaging in paid work.

It should be remarked that the participation rates are likely to be underestimates, because the self-employed workers who are evading taxes may deny that they are engaged in economic activity. In both the British Isles and Japan it is immediately evident just from talking with friends that many women participate in the hidden economy. In Ireland such opportunities are limited, but women in the rural areas are working on farms and in small family

TABLE 1.1 *Female labour force participation rates*

	1965	1975	1982	1985	1987
Ireland*	—	34.5	37.6	36.6	37.2
Japan	55.7	51.7	55.9	57.2	57.8
UK	50.0	55.1	57.0	60.2	62.0

Notes:
1. Rates measured as economically active women, including those acknowledged to be unemployed, as a percentage of all women aged between 15 and 64 years.
2. * In the case of Ireland, 1987 should be read as 1986.

Source: OECD, *Labour Force Statistics*.

enterprises without pay. British women often provide unreported hairdressing, cleaning and child-minding services, while in Japan there are fairly significant remunerative opportunities for women, especially in tutoring and in other individual services, such as addressing envelopes in a fine script. The scope of demand for clandestine labour in Japan is quite astonishing. And unlike elsewhere the pay for such work tends to be relatively high – as could be testified by English teachers from overseas who are continually requested to engage in private tutoring. Even more than in Britain, the Japanese tend to feel that cash payments for such services are nothing to do with the tax office. Nor would many of the women involved be willing to admit that they were 'participating in the labour force'. Therefore I would argue that the resulting underestimation of participation rates is probably greater in Japan than in Britain, although the extent of concealed employment cannot by its very nature ever be measured accurately.[1]

While remembering that those in 'grey' employment are not being measured – unless as unemployed members of the labour force – Table 1.1 shows few distinctions between Japan and the United Kingdom (UK); but it displays a substantially lower rate of economic activity for women in Ireland, which reflects not just the persistence of certain values and a relatively large agricultural sector, but also high levels of unemployment. Since women in Ireland are now

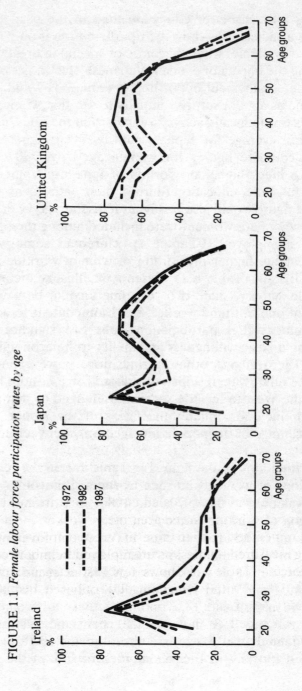

FIGURE 1.1 *Female labour force participation rates by age*

Ireland

Japan

United Kingdom

1972
1982
1987

Source: OECD, Employment Outlook, 1988.

receiving a much better education than in the past, there could be a radical growth in their participation if only more jobs were available, which becomes of special interest when I examine the impact of overseas Japanese electronics plants on female employment opportunities (Chapters 7 and 8). It may come as a great surprise initially to see that women are almost as economically active in Japan as in the UK. Indeed the overall average for Japan would be even higher if we were to compare figures for women aged over 20 years, because a much higher proportion of Japanese women are still in full-time education during their late teens. The Japanese figure would also be higher if discouraged workers, most of whom are women, were included among the figures for the unemployed (Chapter 4). Moreover some would argue that the higher proportion of women working part-time in Britain (Table 6.1) presents an illusory picture of economic activity, since two part-timers could be working instead of one full-time worker; but I am content to accept the argument that participation rates are significant in indicating a basic willingness and ability to be economically active. There is one other qualification, however, which works the other way; in Japan the labour force is more likely than in the West to include some women aged 65 and over, and their inclusion inflates the figure of the labour force as a percentage of the population aged only between 15 and 64 years.

If we then look at the figures in Table 1.2 on the relative proportions of women and men workers, it becomes clear that it was only in the 1970s and 1980s in Britain that the proportion of working women out of all workers, including part-timers, rapidly rose to over 40 per cent from only 35.6 per cent in 1970. Similarly in the USA the working women's proportion out of all workers was as low as around 30 per cent in 1950 and, after rising steadily, only reached 40 per cent in the mid-1970s.[2]

Nor was this US figure of 40 per cent historically unprecedented. In Japan as recently as 1960 women accounted for 40.7 of the labour force, while in the same

TABLE 1.2 *Labour force composition (percentages)*

	1950	1960	1970	1975	1981	1985	1987
Japan:							
women	38.4	40.7	39.3	37.3	38.7	39.7	39.9
men	61.6	59.3	60.7	62.7	61.3	60.3	60.1
Britain:							
women	28.2	32.0	35.6	38.8	40.4	41.6	42.3
men	71.8	68.0	64.4	61.2	59.6	58.4	57.7

Sources: ILO, *Economically Active Population* 1950–2025, Opportunities Commission, *Women and Men in Britain, A Research Profile*. Management and Coordination Agency, *Rodoryoku Chosa*.

year just under 30 per cent of women aged over 15 years were full-time housewives – a much lower proportion than the peak of 37 per cent in 1975. (In the late 1980s barely 30 per cent of adult Japanese women are full-time housewives.) Such relatively high rates of labour participation by Japanese women have not been immediately evident to Westerners, because a substantial portion of women's economic activity has been outside the large companies – especially in small companies or in family enterprises including farms.

To sum up, in the West we have generally seen a steady rise in the proportion of working women, while in Japan the trend has been much more erratic since 1945. In the 1950s relatively more Japanese women than in the West were economically active, but between 1960 and 1975 the proportion working declined, because rapidly rising levels of prosperity during the 1960s encouraged Japanese women initially to enter further education and later to stay at home and concentrate on rearing their children. Since 1975, however, there has been more symmetry between Japan and Britain as increasing numbers of middle-aged women have sought part-time work in both countries – though to a lesser extent in Japan.

This pattern becomes clearer by looking at Figure 1.1 which shows the proportion of working women in different age groups. The most strikingly visual points in both the graphs for Japan and Britain are the overall increases in participation in just 15 years and the diminution in the M shape of a bimodal distribution. The rates for Japan and Britain at the two peaks, where women are employed or seeking work before and after taking care of young children, are rather similar, with the edge going to Britain in the case of middle-aged women. Since in Japan a much larger proportion of young women are students and the bimodal distribution is more pronounced than in Britain, the initial low participation rate of less than 20 per cent, as compared to around 70 per cent of young British women, and the later deeper trough depresses the overall average participation rate for all age groups.

Incidentally, the bimodal distribution in Figure 1.1 is particularly characteristic of Japan and Britain. In many other developed countries, including Ireland, only one peak in women's economic activity occurs (usually somewhere in the twenties age group), while in the USA and the Scandinavian countries the M profile has been replaced by a plateau of around 80 per cent participation for women aged between 20 and 55 years of age. It should be remarked that the high plateau is a recent phenomenon, apart from in the case of Finland, since it was only in the 1970s that there was a rapid acceleration in the number of American women with young children seeking work. Meanwhile in Norway and Sweden the opportunities for part-time work and the provisions for child-care leave have become so favourable as to encourage mothers with young children to remain in the labour force.

The questions which spring to mind here are whether there will be a further convergence between Japan and Britain and whether the trend of increased participation in the labour force – along with the trough between the two peaks being filled in so that a plateau appears – will continue, or come to a halt as appears to be happening in Japan. The final answers must wait until the final chapter, but in the meantime it is worth pointing out that the bimodal distribution does not simply indicate that most women leave the labour force just once when they bear children. Indeed until a longitudinal cohort study, which follows women through their working life, is introduced in Chapter 2, we cannot really conclude anything from a distribution recorded for all women at one point in time.

Indeed, rather than just considering participation rates, the nature of a woman's participation in the labour market needs to be discussed, because there are greater differences between Japan and Britain than are immediately evident from the above data. These differences spring primarily from the substantial presence in Japan of self-employed and unpaid family workers in what may be characterized as an informal sector.

Japan's informal sector

If you were to wander down any of the back streets and alley-ways which create minor mazes within Tokyo or one of Japan's other apparently thoroughly modernized and industrialized cities, you would gradually become aware that there are all sorts of small enterprises half-concealed within private homes. Handwritten sign boards show that lessons are available in not only music, English and mathematics, but also in flower arranging, calligraphy and other traditional arts, all of which are mostly taught by women. It should, however, be remarked that in the traditional arts very few of the women teachers attain the position of an official, let alone leader, in the 'schools'; the high-status positions are almost all held by the few male teachers who engage in these arts.

But leaving aside the important question of vertical segregation by gender until Chapter 3, if you continue further down the narrow streets you are more immediately aware of the numerous small neighbourhood stores, where usually a wife and her husband are working side by side. And, perhaps most remarkably, but less visible – except when the manufactured parts are being laid out on the street in preparation for packing – there are the tiny factories, which are dependent on the work of part-time working women in addition to family members. The small shops and factories are often managed jointly by the wife and husband, with all family members helping in both the enterprise and in household work. In such a case I have seen the still-young grandfather prefer to leave the shop management to his wife and grown-up children while he takes the toddlers to the local park.

Family labour was also a significant feature of pre-industrial Britain. During the seventeenth century both the wife and her husband were thought to be mutually dependent, without the notion of the husband supporting his wife. Now, however, the relevant International Labour Office (ILO) statistics indicate that in the case of Britain there are no working women in the category of family employment, compared to 19.3 per cent of all Japanese working women, including those in agriculture (Table 2.1). The problem is partly one of definition, as workers in family businesses often prefer to call themselves self-employed. But even then the ILO figures suggest that only just over 6 per cent of British working women are self-employed, compared to 12 per cent of Japanese. Despite the low figure in Britain this is a topic which will be taken up in Chapter 6, because of the importance of new forms of working, including self-employment, for women.

Wide wage differentials due to variety of factors

One reason why self-employment remains as a fairly popular option for Japanese women is that their promotion prospects and average wages in paid employment are relatively low. The overall wage differentials between female and male employees, however, need to be carefully analysed before jumping straight to the conclusion that there is direct wage discrimination. But, first, let us just see what has been the

TABLE 1.3 *Women's average earnings as a percentage of men's*

	1970	1975	1980	1985	1987
Britain					
a. weekly gross	54.5	61.5	64.8	65.9	66.3
b. hourly	63.1	72.1	73.5	74.0	73.6
Japan					
a. monthly gross*	50.9	55.8	53.8	51.8	52.3
b. monthly scheduled	56.1	61.4	58.9	59.6	60.5

Notes:
1. British data are from a survey of all full-time employees aged 18 and over. The Japanese surveys cover employees in private enterprises, excluding those working less than 35 hours a week, and until 1975 the monthly scheduled earnings data included some public companies.
2. The second rows (b) refer to payments exclusive of overtime.
3. *Monthly gross cash payments are averages, including special payments, notably annual bonuses, in private enterprises with 30 or more employees.

Sources: Britain – Department of Employment, *New Earnings Survey, Part A.* Japan – Ministry of Labour, *Maitsuki Kinro Tokei Chosa* and *Chingin Kozo Kihon Tokei Chosa.*

size of the differential measured as the average (mean) wages for working women as a percentage of the average for men.[3]

The construction of Table 1.3 shows a few of the problems that arise in trying to compare average wage differentials, the most obvious of which is the fact that men with fewer or negligible household duties customarily work more overtime (and more scheduled hours, especially in Japan), thereby boosting their gross wages. Less obvious, but even more important in an international comparison, is the coverage of the surveys from which the data are drawn. In Britain the most favourable employment conditions for women are usually found in the public sector, which is not adequately incorporated in the Japanese surveys. An additional factor widening wage differentials in Japan is that scheduled wages include various generous family and housing allowances which are controversially only paid by the company to the 'household head' or higher earning partner. Such factors may help a little to explain some part of the wider differentials in Japan. On the other hand it should also be remarked that the above data only refer to employees, thereby excluding the numerous women who are self-employed or 'unpaid' workers in family enterprises. The average pay differentials in the case of Japan (and to a lesser extent in Britain) would certainly be exacerbated even further if 'industrial homeworkers', who are usually female and work for low piece-rates in their own homes, could be included in the differential calculation.

What is most disturbing about Table 1.3 is that since 1975 the average wage differential between women and men in Japan has widened quite significantly, while in Britain the differential has narrowed, though spasmodically since 1980. The question of why differentials have widened in Japan will have to be taken up in Chapter 3; it should just be mentioned at this point that one of the major reasons is the way in which continuous length of service substantially affects wage rates in Japan with the result that middle-aged women who re-enter the labour market are heavily penalized. But there does also appear to have been direct wage discrimination even in the case of casual jobs. Gail Lee Bernstein (1983, p.81) found that in a rural community in the early 1970s there were clear pay differentials between the sexes for most seasonal jobs except for public works projects and rice transplanting.

Overall differentials should not only be measured by the single figure of the arithmetic average (mean), which is simply the sum of all wages in the sample divided by the number of wage earners. Since the distribution of earnings is positively skewed, with the bulk of wage earners in the lower to middle-income brackets and relatively few earning considerably higher wages, there is a significant difference between the median wage – below which level the wages of 50 per cent of wage earners lie – and the mean (in ascending order). It is arguable that the median wage is a more representative measure than the mean, which gives undue weight to the highest earnings in the distribution. Ranking wage groups in order to find the median, moreover, permits a view of the wage distributions and accompanying differentials. In Table 1.4, therefore, not only the median wages, but also the upper/lower deciles and quartiles of earnings, which show the wage levels above/below which lie the wages for 10 per cent and 25 per cent of wage earners, are displayed along with their percentage differences.

While it is clear from Table 1.4 that the pay differentials are wider at the upper levels of the range, this is a pattern which is consistent to both Britain and Japan, which suggests that female manual workers at the lower end of the pay distribution are being penalized – whether directly or indirectly – less severely for their sex than non-manual

TABLE 1.4 *Range of earnings and medians in Britain and Japan, 1987*

	Britain Weekly pay excluding overtime (£)			Japan Scheduled monthly pay (1,000 yen)		
	male A	female B	% diff. B/A×100	male D	female E	% diff. E/D×100
Highest decile	325.6	222.8	68.4	398.3	228.9	57.5
Upper quartile	237.5	172.4	72.6	309.2	174.2	56.3
Median	*176.4*	*129.5*	*73.4*	*236.5*	*139.0*	*58.8*
Lower quartile	135.5	101.3	74.8	178.5	115.9	64.9
Lowest decile	108.8	84.2	77.4	143.1	98.8	69.0
As percentage of the corresponding median						
Highest decile	184.6	172.0		168.4	164.6	
Lowest decile	61.7	65.0		60.5	71.1	

Notes:
Britain – gross weekly earnings excluding overtime pay for full-time employees on adult rates.
Japan – standard monthly wages for full-time employees in all sizes of company and all industries, excluding agricultural and government workers.
Sources: Britain – Department of Employment, *New Earnings Survey, Part B.* Japan – Ministry of Labour, *Chingin Kozo Kihon Tokei, Part 1.*

workers. The distribution of pay in Japan within each category of female and male appears to be a little more egalitarian, or less skewed, than in Britain, as crudely shown by the median and highest decile being a little less far apart. Nonetheless the difference between the median pay for women and men is much wider than in Britain, which actually results in the overall distribution of pay being more skewed in Japan than in Britain.

It would be too facile simply to conclude that the appreciably wider wage differentials in Japan are indicative of a state of underdevelopment or of a conspiracy against women. One particularly important reason for a lower ratio of female to male pay in Japan is the fact that a substantial proportion of Japanese women are in low-paying manual occupations, which is indicated by the lowest decile being closer to the median in Japan than in Britain, because relatively more Japanese than British women are employed in manufacturing as production workers (Chapter 3). Since manual wages in both Japan and Britain are on average lower than non-manual wages, the average pay ratio by gender in Japan is pulled down in comparison to Britain where a higher proportion of women are found in clerical and other non-manual occupations. Moreover the relative importance of public sector employment for British women – as will be seen later in Table 3.2 – where pay differentials are narrower than in the private sector, helps to narrow the overall differential compared to Japan.

In addition there are various factors, some of which may be argued to be socially or economically legitimate rather than purely discriminatory, which help to explain why differentials persist in both Japan and Britain. The two major factors are the persistence of occupational segregation and the temporary withdrawal of women from the labour market in order to bear and rear children. As will be seen in Chapter 3, the latter factor has a particularly significant impact on relative pay in Japan, although the issue of occupational segregation is, interestingly, less clear-cut.

In concluding this section it is worth mentioning that, in spite of equal pay legislation leading to relatively higher-priced female labour in Britain and a narrowing of the wage differential by sex, employment has contracted for men, but not for women. Female employment in Britain, according to figures from the Equal Opportunities Commission, expanded by 9.0 per cent between 1976 and 1987. During the same period in Japan, labour force data show that the total number of women employees grew by 34.2 per cent. The wide discrepancies between the figures for Japan and Britain for women's employment growth are indicative of several factors, one of which is the radical structural change in Japanese women's economic activity (Chapter 2) and another is the fact that overall employment in Britain fell by almost 6 per cent during the same period. These are important points to consider again in the final chapter concerning the future of employment in the post-industrial society.

Protective legislation as an excuse for discrimination

Equal pay legislation has been in effect in Japan since 1947, so the persistence of wage differentials by sex suggests that there is indirect discrimination or labour market bias accounting for women's lower pay. Therefore it could be argued that all the legislation directed towards equal pay and equal opportunity is of no account. In the case of Britain Table 1.3 indicates, however, that equal pay legislation has evidently had a dramatic effect, especially between 1970 and 1975. But Zabalza and Tzannatos (1985, p.2) argue that any further gains would be doubtful without any erosion of the persistent occupational segregation. Although the overall narrowing of the differential in Britain since 1980 appears to have been somewhat better than their analysis suggested, the yearly trend is much more erratic with a slight widening of percentage differentials occurring in 1982, 1984 and 1987. Certainly the equal value amendment seems to have not yet had any impact on average differentials, although the 1987 local authority manual workers settlement, which has resulted in a dramatic upward shift in earnings for low-paid caring jobs, should ultimately narrow the wage differential between women and men in the manual category.

The apparent success of British legislation makes it worth finding out to what objectives the legislative framework, which also reflects some of society's preoccupations, has been directed, in order to clarify the issues facing working women. As is the general practice throughout this book, the focus will tend to be on Japan while indicating what are the relevant discrepancies with legislation in the British Isles. In this way the contrasts may be better revealed, especially when looking at how the relevant legislation has developed over time.

Since Britain's industrial revolution occurred around 135 years before Japan's, legislation designed to regulate women's working hours and employment conditions was established earlier in Britain. Thus the Factory Bill of 1844 anteceded Japan's 1911 Factory Act by almost 70 years, but both provided similar protection such as a maximum working day of 12 hours for women. While part of the rationale for protection may have been altruistic, the main motivation was to ensure that the health and morals of the country's mothers should not be damaged. Thus the protection was directed at those women working in the textile factories rather than all the Japanese women who were working long and strenuous hours in the rice fields. The women who have 'stayed at home' on the labour-intensive farms and in family businesses are economically highly active, but they have received little legislative attention. Lacking recognition for their work in these informal sectors has reinforced the myth that Japanese women are primarily housewives.

The rapid social and legislative changes under the guidance of the American occupation after the Pacific War permitted the establishment of relatively comprehensive legislation to protect working women, which went well beyond legislative provisions in most other countries at that time. But the apparent progressiveness and egalitarian nature of the 1947 Labour Standards Law and Civil Code should not close our eyes to the way in which laws, especially those implemented in the exceptional circumstances of the

American occupation of Japan, may not be compatible with the prevailing social values. Even now, in what some may consider to be a more enlightened age with respect to women's rights, a cynic could argue that the state is only concerned with the national interest. Indeed, the Ministry of Labour in its policies for 1988 to 1993 states that maternity protection measures are necessary not only for the health of the women themselves but also for the healthy growth of the next generation. (A less cynical view might merely applaud the congruence of interests between working women and the state.)

It is arguable, moreover, that the original 1947 Labour Standards Law has ultimately been to the disadvantage of working women because it gave employers an excuse for their evident reluctance to promote women. Its provisions were tantamount to raising the price of female labour and to permitting discriminatory practices. Thus employers could assert that any promotion of women to executive level positions would be inefficient because of night work (from 10pm to 5am) being prohibited except for certain professions, overtime being restricted to six hours per week and two hours each day, and menstrual leave being permitted, not to mention the provision for 12 weeks' maternity leave. The Labour Standards Law's recognition of the necessity of permitting maternity leave was relatively early when compared with similar provisions established in Britain's 1975 Employment Protection Act and Ireland's 1981 maternity leave legislation. Later when many of the other protective provisions were eased at the time of the Equal Employment Opportunity Law in 1986, maternity leave was lengthened to 14 weeks.[4]

The original 1947 Labour Standards Law in Japan attracted the charge of engendering discrimination by excessively favouring protection, especially 'protection of motherhood'. But in any case its provisions for maternity leave were not widely adhered to in the mass of small companies and family businesses. In particular, the provision for one or two days' paid menstrual leave a month was fairly nominal; it really only applied to women in strenuous work, notably nursing, most of whom never took the right, partly because of embarrassment. Concerning the prohibition on women working at night, in fact many women with young children would have preferred night work as their husbands could look after the children, but the legislators were more concerned about the possible dangers for a young girl's morals in working in a factory at night than about the convenience of working mothers.

Thus one of the primary objectives of the Labour Standards Law was to ensure that working women would not neglect any of the household and child-rearing responsibilities. Legislation directed to enabling working women to combine the two roles was later on strengthened and supplemented with a few additional regulations, notably the Working Women's Welfare Law in 1972 and a Child-Care Leave Bill in 1975 to allow nurses and teachers to take up to one year's unpaid leave after a child's birth. At the same time major companies were encouraged to set up similar schemes, though with very limited success. Eventually in 1986 the government agreed to make a lump sum payment per re-employed woman. Yet, in spite of the fairly liberal legislative conditions now designed so as not to deter women from continuing their careers after the birth of a child, social attitudes have – as we shall see later – led mothers to abandon their careers in favour of taking on low-status positions either as part-time workers or in the secondary sector of small companies, where average wages are considerably lower than in Japan's major companies.

There has been plenty of evidence to show that while the 1947 legislation was extensive, its application has been limited to the bare bones, in particular with regard to equal pay. The Civil Code and Labour Standards Law did include as early as 1947 a provision for equal wages regardless of sex, but only for clearly equivalent jobs. Japan has yet to recognize the principle of comparative worth as has been belatedly seen in the UK's 1984 equal value amendment to the Equal Pay Act and Ireland's 1987 Employment Equality

Act. Consequently, apart from the case of youths initially hired on the same terms, the Japanese law appears to have had a minimal impact, because the wage gap between women and men has been exacerbated by the designation of different titles for identical jobs. And since women's lower pay has been justified by giving them a position different in name only or by failing to promote them, the wage gap widens considerably with age (Chapter 3). Such ruses did not have to be employed in Britain where equal pay legislation was not implemented until the mid-1970s, when the obviously discriminatory system in collective agreements of setting female wages at a certain percentage of male wages could be almost instantly eliminated. (Another factor in the success of Britain's anti-sex discrimination legislation is the way in which many wage agreements are centralized.) Thus Britain's tardiness was rewarded by a clear narrowing of wage differentials.

Britain has also been singled out by the Organisation for Economic Cooperation and Development (OECD) in its *Employment Outlook* of 1988 (p.166) as one of the few countries which has promoted affirmative action measures by granting state subsidies to companies engaging in preferential treatment programmes. Most Japanese would look at such measures with amazement, and indeed it is arguable that treatment which undermined meritocracy – upon which much value is placed in Japan – would only alienate the opinion of society. Thus legislation may be better directed towards ensuring that both parents feel responsible for the rearing of their children and towards facilitating flexible employment opportunities – topics to which I shall return in later chapters.

In Japan the correction of the anomaly, whereby legislative protection was partly responsible for continued discrimination against working women, was intended in the implementation of an Equal Employment Opportunity Law in April 1986 accompanied by partial revisions to the original Labour Standards Law, and then followed by a new, highly controversial Labour Standards Law in April 1988.

The effectiveness and desirability of these two laws will be assessed in Chapter 4 in the light of the rest of the book's evidence. At this point, therefore, a brief look at the main provisions will suffice.

At first glance the Equal Employment Opportunity Law appears to have an exemplary bunch of provisions, which call upon companies to ensure equal access in recruitment, promotion and job assignment opportunities as well as forbidding discriminatory treatment in employees' training and welfare benefits and in retirement and dismissal policies. The latter set of prohibited practices could be classified as direct discrimination, as defined in Britain's Sex Discrimination Act of 1975, while the former group concerns indirect discrimination. The new 1988 Labour Standards Law continues the trend of removing much of the protection for working women concerning hours worked. It also permits the company to impose flexible working hours according to production needs with the overt aim of shortening total working hours. Since, however, it is the employer who can require women employees to work more hours on certain days, the imposition of flexible hours is considered to be deleterious for working mothers.

In conclusion, legislation prior to 1986 in Japan was more concerned with ensuring that women should harmonize their working and family lives than that they should be free of discrimination in the workplace. Similarly in Britain women's freedom to work and mobility in the labour market were constrained by the plethora of protective legislation concerning dangerous work and working after childbirth, at least up until the 1975 enforcement of the Equal Pay Act and the Sex Discrimination Act. And some of the remaining discriminatory provisions in Britain, which are cloaked in the guise of protection – such as not permitting women to become miners – are now being abolished so as to bring British legislation in line with the European Community (EC). It is worth remarking that in itself the relatively extensive protection since 1947 for working women in Japan is an indication that the often quoted Confucian precept that women should be literally just *ryosai kembo* (good wives and wise mothers) has been adhered to only as an ideal, while daughters and wives have in practice been expected to contribute to the household income despite their meagre earnings.

Comparisons within companies

Looking at legislation along with general tables and charts about the female labour market, as I have attempted to do in this chapter, tells us next to nothing about the attitudes of women in different countries and their actual working conditions. But, unless the samples were very large, it would be considered illegitimate to look randomly at Japanese and British or Irish individuals in order to make generalized comparisons about their working conditions and attitudes, because there is such a great variety within each country. Nevertheless, in the case of Japanese companies with subsidiaries overseas, fairly direct comparisons should be possible. Therefore, as well as women working in small companies in Japan, I sought to interview women in similar positions employed by the same company in Japan and the British Isles. A few distortions in this technique of matched pairs are inevitable, because the overseas plant is relatively recently established and much smaller in terms of total employment than the same company's plants in Japan. Another important point to bear always in mind is that the Japanese manufacturing companies with subsidiaries in Europe are invariably the 'top' companies where employment conditions are particularly good. Therefore, even though a substantial part of this book is devoted to a narration stemming from discussions with women working for Matsushita and NEC, I have attempted to put their relatively privileged postion in perspective by first examining the overall position of Japanese working women and, particularly, the conditions for women who are part-timers in small businesses or who are self-employed.

Notes

(1) Some attempts have, however, been made: OECD (1986), *Employment Outlook*, pages 66 to 79.

(2) Kessler-Harris (1982), pages 301 to 312, gives a figure of 29 per cent for 1950, but Koizara (1987), page 19, provides an estimate of 33.9 per cent in the same year.

(3) Other more complicated ways of measuring relative pay have been undertaken, for example, in Zabalza (1985), annex 4. But for this book, where econometric models are not being used, the mean and the median are reasonably adequate, though a long way from perfect, estimates.

(4) Details in English on maternity benefits and protection for pregnant and nursing women workers may be found in: Japan Institute of Labour (1986), pages 22 to 23. There will be further discussion of the topic of maternity provisions in Chapter 5 of this book.

2 | Women's working patterns in Japan

Women's rights did not become severely constrained in Japan until the fifteenth century, when the development of the feudal system reinforced the prevailing Confucian morality requiring wives to be subservient to their husbands. (The written characters for husband literally mean 'master'.) Nor has the influence of the feudal era been wholly erased by Japan's rapid industrialization and its subsequent radical modernization after the 1945 defeat in the Pacific War. Some observers like to point out that Japanese personnel policies are based on feudalism, especially the paternalistic attitude of management and the attention paid to status. And status is linked to gender, since there is still some adherence to the severe requirements for feminine modesty laid down in 1672 in the neo-Confucian *Onna Daigaku* (learning for women), despite the promulgation in 1898 of a more liberal *Shin Onna Daigaku* (new learning for women) by Yukichi Fukuzawa – a male scholar.

The extent to which feudalism generally remains is controversial. The consequent status of women in Japan has been likened by Alice Cook (1984, p.15) to the position of women in Ireland in terms of rights and expectations in employment. She states that Ireland and Japan out of all the OECD countries are 'the most resistant to sex equality' and that 'a long tradition has produced strongly established anti-egalitarian customs that unions have not seriously challenged'. In terms of employment rights such a comparison does not stand up to the legislative evidence we have seen in Chapter 1, but expectations tell a different story, because of the patterns under which women have participated in the process of Japan's industrialization as we shall now see.

Historically poor working conditions

When textile factories began to be established from about the middle of the nineteenth century, it was young unmarried women from the rural areas who provided a cheap labour force. Women were employed in manufacturing to a greater extent than in many other industrialized countries at that time and Sharon L. Sievers (1983, p.57) has concluded from her research of the period that women underpinned Japan's industrial revolution. Whereas in Britain during the late nineteenth century 62 per cent of textile workers were female, in Japan around the turn of the century 83 per cent of textile workers (and over 60 per cent of all factory workers) were women, which has prompted Gary Saxonhouse (Patrick ed., 1976) to examine the reasons for the overwhelming dependence of mills on a transient female work-force. As industry diversified, men chose to enter a variety of industrial occupations and women were left to work on the farms. Thus women became confined to a more limited range of jobs, which laid the basis for occupational segregation, while at the same time they were not given the chance to acquire specialized industrial skills.

The women in the textile factories worked under appalling conditions and lived in crowded dormitories, so it was no wonder that they only stayed in employment for a few years. In any case the young women, some of whom were barely teenagers, worked under one-year contracts, which were made between their fathers and mediators from the factories. Under the contract system loans were given to poverty-stricken rural families as an advance on the daughters' wages in return for which the women agreed to work under any conditions for up to five years. Thus the daughters were effectively put into bonded labour for the benefit of their fathers and the company owners. The conditions of employment for women in factories have improved substantially in line with the protective legislation discussed in Chapter 1. But some aspects have not changed; the young Japanese women I met at NEC generally still live in dormitories and they envisage working at NEC itself for no longer than about six years – only until they get married.

Thus was established the pattern, which continues even now, of employing young women in a structure defined by the family on a short-term basis with the result that they fail to reach supervisory positions. This practice of short-term employment is quite contrary to the better-known conditions, which evolved at a later stage in response to labour shortages, of permanent employment and seniority promotion for a minority of regular male workers in large Japanese companies. Women remain as apparently peripheral workers who do not fit into the preferred employment conditions. It should be emphasized, however, that preference does not indicate prevalence; even among male workers in large companies there are subcontracted, seasonal and temporary workers to whom permanent employment and seniority wages and promotion do not apply. Indeed commentators on Japanese labour markets, such as Rodney Clark (1979) and Kazuo Koike (1988), now take some pains to stress that permanent employment and seniority-based wages are both limited in their scope and a recent development of the early to mid-twentieth century. Nor within their limited range are these practices unique to Japan. Nonetheless, even though such employment conditions may not be widespread, the popular perception of their existence is important, as has been noted by Masahiko Aoki (1984, p.6). Therefore, since women have been largely excluded from permanent employment systems, their integration in the labour force appears to be peripheral.

Being young and from the still feudalistic rural areas of Japan, women in the factories were not inclined to protest their conditions, especially since they were only employed for a few years. In spite of such factors, women did go on a local strike at the Amamiya silk mill as early as 1886 – the first recorded workers' strike in Japan. Subsequently, women textile workers organized walkouts and strikes, most of which were partially successful. Yet women workers were ultimately more or less ignored by labour organizers in Japan, who in effect failed to acknowledge their early and important contribution to industrial action.

Conditions in the textile factories tended to deteriorate as Japan sought to make its products competitive internationally during the early part of the twentieth century, with the result that Japanese women were probably working under worse conditions than elsewhere. Even when the 1911 Factory Act was implemented in 1916, it was too loosely structured in that it only covered women working in places with more than 15 employees, for whom the protection was just a working day or night of no more than 12 hours. The Factory Act's inadequacies must have angered some of the otherwise rather quiescent working women. A mass rally of textile workers, which was organized in 1919 by the women's section of the labour group, Yuaikai (Friendship Society), was moved to send a resolution concerning the suffering of Japanese working women to the ILO. Such labour activities in Japan did take place relatively late, due to both Japan's own late emergence as an industrialized nation and also the hangover of feudalistic notions of a 'benevolent' authority. The Yuaikai could not be considered to have been a fully fledged union, nor was its women's section formed until 1915; yet in Britain the Women's Protective and Provident League, under which several women's unions were established, had been formed as early as 1874.

Nor has this rather late start in union activities by working women yet been rectified. Their initial short length of service followed by a return to work on a part-time basis – often in non-unionized smaller companies – has tended to keep women out of the union mainstream. Even in the large, unionized companies women do not play an active part in the union. Some observers may argue that this pattern primarily reflects Japanese women's passivity or their lack of spare time to attend union meetings. The latter factor plays some part, but union officials – both female and male – at Denki Roren (Japanese Federation of Electrical Machine Workers' Unions) told me that the major reason was that the Japanese working world was a male-centred society. The implication is that women are on the fringes of working life, despite their relatively high level of labour force participation. One should nonetheless beware of relying on a culturalist interpretation for Japanese women's lack of activity in unions; the involvement of British and Irish women in union affairs at the plants which I visited is also fairly negligible. This topic of union relevance to women, therefore, merits further discussion in later chapters.

Women working not necessarily as paid employees

The major way in which Japanese women have been economically active, even though they continue to be an insignificant force in the mainstream of Japanese companies, is through their working in family enterprises or on their own as teachers or as entrepreneurs; the numerous small shops and factories and the independent instructors of traditional crafts, music and languages have already been remarked upon (Chapter 1). The significance of the role of women in such enterprises has persisted in spite of Japan's modernization. Indeed as a result of both the rapidity of industrialization in Japan and also of the post-war desolation, pre-industrial enterprises have remained viable and have been able to become part of the strengthening service sector. I regard this pattern to be a variation on the usual manifestations of the late development effect, which is generally concerned with the way in which a late starter can leapfrog over certain kinds of technology. The thesis developed by Ronald Dore (1973, p.12) to apply to labour relations in large Japanese companies shows that the late development effect also permits the avoidance of anachronistic patterns of social organization. Now in this manifestation of the effect with respect to pre-industrial enterprises, rather than a leapfrog over technology or patterns of social organization taking place, the relative lateness and rapidity of Japan's industrialization have actually failed to embrace all the pre-modern economic sectors insofar as in some households the family economy has persisted and informal labour markets outside the large companies have continued to offer employment to substantial numbers. Ultimately these sectors continue to be appropriate for the needs of married working women and, it is arguable, have become compatible with the post-industrial economy.

In addition, the emerging modern service sector, which appears once a country has reached a certain standard of living, has been providing new opportunities for resourceful women entrepreneurs in fashion, flower arranging, and in opening their own dress shops, bars or coffee houses. Similar trends are evident in Britain with the success of women entrepreneurs in 'niche-retailing', such as the Sock Shop chain. This kind of enterprise does not require such a large amount of capital as may be denied to a woman. Thus the number of women entrepreneurs in industrialized countries is becoming significant, despite the greater barriers they face in obtaining capital than men. Data from Ireland indicate, moreover, that 'high female incomes are more frequent in self-employment than in dependent employment' (OECD, 1988, p.162).

Particularly in Japan many women have calculated that since the company employment system gives undue importance to length of service and overtime, in both of which factors women are penalized, their abilities are better directed towards entrepreneurship. Census figures show remarkable increases since 1970 in the numbers of self-employed women who have professional expertise, including accountants, editors and sportswomen. Japanese women who are self-employed may have lost their supposed passivity through economic necessity as two of my acquaintances who have set up their own businesses in flower arrangement and in running a coffee house are divorcées, who are relatively rare in Japan. But the direction of causation is just as likely to be running the other way in that these women's spirits could not be contained within marriages where their role was to be subservient to the 'master'. (The entertaining question of whether the division of labour and power in the Japanese household is more inegalitarian than in the West will be pursued in Chapter 5.)

And so, because of emerging women entrepreneurs and because of the persistence of family businesses which have been bypassed by modernization, both modern and traditional enterprises, in which Japanese women are working, continue to be prevalent in the back alley-ways of Japan's cities. At the same time there has also been a remarkable movement over the past two decades as young women have chosen not to work on their family-run farms and, to a certain extent, in their family businesses, but have instead moved into outside paid employment. Table 2.1 shows that in 1960 the proportion of working women in both categories was roughly the same, but by 1987 less than 20 per cent were left in family businesses, while over 68 per cent were classified as paid employees. It is worth noting, however, that this movement appears to be far less rapid and significant if the agricultural sector is excluded.

Thus the overall decline in the labour force participation rate of women between 1960 and 1975 masks a radical change in the structure of women's employment since the early 1960s when self-employed women and those in family businesses were more numerous than paid employees in Japan. Evidently, during the transitional phase, the number of women ceasing to count themselves as working in family businesses was not fully compensated by the number becoming employees, so the female participation rate dropped. But if the growth in the number of female employees is considered alone – by almost 52 per cent between 1960 and 1975 – the conception of Japanese women 'staying at home' in increasing numbers becomes quite invalid.

TABLE 2.1 *Japanese women: status of employment*
(percentage of all working women, 1960–1987)

	Self-employed		Family business		Employees	
1960	15.8	(17.5)	43.4	(21.4)	40.8	(61.1)
1965	14.5	(14.7)	36.8	(17.9)	48.6	(67.4)
1970	14.2	(13.3)	30.9	(16.9)	54.7	(69.6)
1975	14.3	(12.3)	25.7	(16.4)	59.8	(71.1)
1980	13.7	(12.6)	23.0	(15.3)	63.2	(71.9)
1985	12.5	(12.0)	20.0	(13.5)	67.2	(74.3)
1987	12.0	(11.5)	19.3	(13.2)	68.4	(75.0)

Notes:
1. The majority of industrial homeworkers, who work mostly in the field of light manufactures for piece rates, are included in the category of 'self-employed'; the rest are in 'family business'.
2. 'Family business' includes unpaid family workers.
3. Bracketed figures are for women in non-agricultural occupations.

Source: Ministry of Labour, *Fujin Rodo no Jitsujo.*

While the proportion of working women who are self-employed or in family businesses at home has declined during the past three decades in Japan, in Britain an opposite trend has appeared in the 1980s during which self-employment for all workers has grown by around 5 per cent each year, though the recorded levels are still well below the figures in Japan. Just as has always been the case in Japan, self-employment is becoming a significant option for married British women (Chapter 6).

Therefore the structure of employment status between Japan and Britain will probably converge, because the pace of change towards paid employment in Japan as shown in Table 2.1 is unlikely to continue at the same rate as in the past three decades. Indeed there may be a slight reversal in the trend with higher proportions opting to be self-employed or in family businesses, as the yen appreciation has worsened employment prospects in the exporting industries and, moreover, as middle-aged women increasingly find that the informal labour market is more flexible and appropriate for their needs. Self-employment, apart from family businesses, for Japanese women is already displaying a resilience in the face of radical social and economic changes in their working lives, since there was only a 1.3 percentage point decline in their proportion (excluding agriculture) between 1975 and 1985 compared to a 5.2 percentage point decline in the preceding decade. Moreover, older women are having to take over the highly demanding, dominant role on the labour-intensive farms as men and youths choose to work, sometimes seasonally, in the factories which are appearing on green-field sites in the rural areas of Japan. One of the characteristic sights for anyone travelling outside the cities is that of middle-aged and elderly women wearing baggy trousers and large sun hats, who are bent over working in the rice fields. Farming women indeed defy all trends in that also they are often in paid employment for part of the year, when they take on seasonal or part-time jobs, not only in factories, but also on construction sites. Gail Lee Bernstein (1983, p.87) found that almost every woman in a farming village on the island of Shikoku had some kind of part-time job in addition to all her arduous farmwork. The exceptions were those mothers with small children and the elderly.

Decline followed by increase in participation rates

A second important trend since the 1960s is the way in which the bimodal distribution by age of women's participation in the labour market shown in Figure 1.1 developed from a single peak in 1960. In that year, as can be seen in Table 2.2, 70.8 per cent of Japanese women aged 20 to 24 years were economically active with a sharp drop to around 55 per cent in the subsequent age groups; and there was only a small climb to 59 per cent for women aged over 35 years. Within the space of ten years, however, women's tendency to leave the labour market after the age of 25 years and their later re-entry caused the 25 to 29 year participation rate to fall dramatically to 45.5 per cent and the 40 to 50 year rate to

TABLE 2.2 *Changes in Japanese women's economic activity rate by age and over time*

	Overall rate	Age (years)									
		15– 19	20– 24	25– 29	30– 34	35– 39	40– 44	45– 49	50– 54	55– 59	60– 64	65 & over
1960	54.5	49.0	70.8	54.5	56.5	59.0		59.0*		46.7*		25.6
1965	50.6	35.8	70.2	49.0	51.1	59.6		60.2*		45.3*		21.6
1970	49.9	33.6	70.6	45.5	48.2	57.5	62.8	63.0	58.8	48.7	39.1	17.9
1975	45.7	21.7	66.2	42.6	43.9	54.0	59.9	61.5	57.8	48.8	38.0	15.3
1980	47.6	18.5	70.0	49.2	48.2	58.0	64.1	64.4	59.3	50.5	38.8	15.5
1985	48.7	16.6	71.9	54.1	50.6	60.0	67.9	68.1	61.0	51.0	38.5	15.5
1987	48.6	16.6	73.6	56.9	50.5	61.3	68.4	68.4	61.8	50.8	38.5	15.4

Notes:
1. Rates measured as economically active women as a percentage of all women in each age group.
2. *In 1960 and 1965, rates apply to an aggregated 40- to 54-year-old age group and to a 55- to 64-year-old age group.

Source: Management and Coordination Agency, *Rodoryoku Chosa*.

rise to around 63 per cent. Consequently – with the additional factor of a higher proportion of young women staying in education during their late teens – the average age of women working in non-agricultural enterprises with at least five employees jumped from the mid-twenties in 1960 to the mid-thirties by 1979, according to the Ministry of Labour's regular report on the situation of working women (*Fujin Rodo no Jitsujo*, 1988, Table 29).

During the war years Japanese women, just as in the West, took over men's jobs in the factories and mines. Even though most women suddenly lost these jobs in the late 1940s – the national railways dismissed tens of thousands of women in a single day – the post-war reconstruction and the absolute desolation of many households required women to be economically active during the 1950s. Subsequently the two factors of rapidly rising levels of prosperity in the 1960s and a decline in the farming population as agriculture became less labour-intensive permitted more and more women to stay at home to take care of their small children. Consequently women's participation rate in the labour force declined and the bimodal shape became most marked in the early 1970s. Married women who were still having to work in the 1960s and 1970s period dreamt of being just a housewife. The perceptive remark of Bernstein (1983, p.168) to the effect that, 'The idea of women's liberation, if it means anything at all, means freedom from the economic uncertainties and physical drudgery of farming' is a sentiment which would also have applied to the women working under miserable conditions in small shops and factories.

Every year, meanwhile, more young women have been entering higher education, notably two-year colleges. Thus the overall average decline in the female participation rate was caused by both the allure of being a full-time housewife and by the desire for education. In addition, the severe economic recession in the early 1970s appears to have led to some middle-aged women leaving or being discouraged from entering the labour force. The combination of these factors resulted in the overall participation rate reaching rock bottom in 1975. Subsequently this trend was radically reversed in the late 1970s, when renewed growth and a need for a more flexible labour force after the economic upheaval of the first oil shock in 1973/74 led employers to encourage middle-aged women to return to work as part-timers. And married women themselves increasingly sought part-time work as their families' living standards no longer rose at the dizzying rates experienced in the 1960s.

These trends become clearer if we follow the participation of women in each age group as they grow older through a cohort analysis as displayed in Table 2.3. By following the upward diagonals, which show the changes in age-specific rates, we can see that those women who were still at school in the 1950s have throughout most of their adult lives had similar rates of participation in each age group to women who were already 30 years old in the 1950s. Therefore, even though the overall participation rate declined in the 1960s and 1970s, there has been a basic stability in the level of women's economic activity. The major exception is the case of women who were in their child-bearing years between 1965 and 1975.

TABLE 2.3 *Participation rates for selected cohorts of Japanese women 1950–1975*
(percentage of women in each birth cohort reported to be economically active in census reference period)

Age in 1950 (yrs)	1950	1955	1960	1965	1970	1975	1980	1985
–10–6						22.6	71.1	54.1
– 5–1					35.7	66.8	49.4	49.2
0–4				37.6	70.8	43.5	46.5	57.9
5–9			49.6	69.7	45.1	43.2	55.5	65.8
10–14		50.1	69.4	46.5	47.3	52.8	61.8	65.9
15–19	46.9	68.2	50.2	48.0	56.3	59.7	62.3	59.8
20–24	64.0	51.9	51.4	58.3	63.6	61.9	58.7	49.9
25–29	48.4	49.6	55.1	62.1	64.6	58.6	50.7	37.9
30–34	50.2*	53.5	56.8	62.6	60.9	50.9	38.8	15.2

Note:
* In 1950, rate applies to an aggregated 30- to 39-year-old age group.
Source: Management and Coordination Agency, *National Census.*

Any recent marked generational change in attachment to the labour force has only appeared for those who were not yet born in 1950: the first two rows of Table 2.3. But the change is quite striking. Thus women born around 1960 have higher levels of economic activity in their twenties than women who were born just ten years earlier. A more detailed cohort analysis would demonstrate that the rate of withdrawal from the labour force for child-rearing was dropping during the 1970s with each successive cohort and the rate of re-entry for middle-aged women was rising, which has been corroborated by the clear diminution of the bimodal participation pattern (Figure 1.1). Although this trend is still rather concealed, the primary reason appears to be a change in the labour force attachment of better-educated women, since other women have in any case almost always been working, whether on the farms or in small factories and shops. One further piece of evidence is the recent rapid yearly gain in the percentage of college graduates who are obtaining regular paid employment, rather than just settling for *arubaito* (irregular employment covering a whole range of temporary jobs). Now almost the same percentage of women as men is obtaining regular employment on graduation (*Fujin Rodo no Jitsujo*, 1988, p.56). The overall consequence has been that in the 1980s more women in all age groups, except for those aged under 20 years and those aged over 55 years, have been participating in the labour force.

Changes in social perceptions

The question of whether a woman with a higher education after leaving school is more likely to pursue a career is particularly interesting in Japan because of the way that her motivation for receiving a college education has – at least until recently – differed from her counterparts in most Western countries. It is also an important issue in terms of predicting overall trends because almost 35 per cent of young Japanese women receive a higher education. In the other OECD countries a higher education has usually been associated with a stronger attachment to work and a career; in general the more educated a woman, the longer is her participation in the labour market because of both higher earnings and greater expectations along with the provision of more intrinsically rewarding jobs. When such women in the West do leave the labour force during their child-bearing years, they are more likely to return; and they can then find employment in relatively well-paid clerical and professional jobs in the service sector.

Japanese women and their families, in contrast, have originally looked upon a higher education as a means to obtain a better lifestyle, not through a career, but rather through meeting and marrying a man with bright prospects of becoming an executive in a large company. The aspiring executive would prefer to wed a better-educated woman, who would then be expected to devote herself to furthering the education of their children in the notorious role of a *kyoiku mama* (a mother obsessed with her children's education). Machiko Osawa (1988) has demonstrated that there has been an inverse relationship between female education and paid employment because of the belief that education primarily raised a woman's productivity at home insofar as she could promote her children's education both by assisting with their homework and by being willing to take them to music, swimming and cram schools.

Indeed this factor of the children's education was a major contributor to the popularity of the ironically modern notion of the desirability of women being full-time housewives, which only really became a feasible option for a lot of families from the late 1950s. One of the women I know who is a full-time housewife has chosen that option not only because she saw and rejected the drudgery of her mother's life working in a family-run dry cleaners, but also because she wanted to give as much attention as possible to her children's education. Now, however, the changing social perception of working women, which has been largely led and nourished by the powerful mass media, have encouraged some of the better-educated young women to seek a career. But, even where a woman has graduated from a four-year university, as opposed to a two-year college where the emphasis is often on home economics, she is likely to have graduated in a subject which is of little vocational use to her. Nor has there yet been any striking change in this pattern of education for women. The proportions of women studying for an arts degree has remained at over 35 per cent since the 1960s, and there has only been a slight increase in those studying for a science or engineering degree from around 3 per cent to just under 5 per cent (*Fujin Rodo no Jitsujo*, 1988, Table 42).

The above observations are not intended to deny that some female university graduates have chosen to take up a career. When women have been ambitious enough and willing to devote themselves to the long hours and severe competition of public employment or a profession, they have risen within the Japanese system, which is to some extent 'gender-blind' in relying on competitive examinations. But since this book is concerned with the 'average' working woman and the number of successful women in professions and the bureaucracy is relatively few, I shall not discuss their position in detail. It is my contention, however, that professional women in Japan have tended to enjoy a relatively high status and to experience much less discrimination than women working in other jobs. Thus the kinds of changes examined in this chapter are of little relevance to the position of teachers and other professionals who have been working in another sphere altogether.

In almost all other cases four-year university female graduates, who are only one-third of the women attending college, have been penalized in the initial job hunting arena or *shuushoku senso* (recruitment war), because the employers' expectation has been that they would only be working a couple of years before getting married and having a baby, whereas two-year college graduates would have several more years to offer. This perception is gradually changing, along with the other changes outlined below; but a conservative attitude towards women, in particular, is very hard to shift. Japanese commentators like to write of there being a 'wave' of interest in women's employment. That seems to indicate only a superficial change in attitudes; and, indeed, there is usually some kind of an undertow to a fairly big wave.

One other factor discouraging educated women from seeking a career, which was socially sanctioned until the late 1970s, was the practice in many, usually major, companies of pressuring a better-educated woman to leave once she married, through the less than subtle *kata-tataki* (tap on the shoulder). There was an economic rationale on both sides. The company did not have to continue paying rising seniority wages to a worker whose position was often at worst merely decorative and at best was a largely unskilled clerical position, while the young woman herself in many cases received a lump-sum early retirement payment and unemployment benefit for a certain period – in effect a wedding dowry from the company. A special system for the retirement of women employees upon their marriage or giving birth was operated as recently as 1977 by 7.4 per cent of surveyed companies (Yamaguchi, 1986, p.17). By 1981 the percentage had dropped to 2 per cent and now the system is outlawed, though it may still be operating informally insofar as a woman could feel obliged to leave because of custom or a disapproving atmosphere. (The functional reasons for *kata-tataki* will be considered further in the discussion on internal labour markets in Chapter 9.)

Although this practice in certain workplaces is still customary, companies would no longer admit to exerting any pressure on newly wed women in the present climate of accepted opinion; and, indeed, a fairly radical change in the way in which the value of better-educated women employees is assessed does appear recently to have occurred. The computer giants, NEC and Fujitsu, are actively recruiting women to be trained as software engineers, not only because of a shortage of programmers but also because women are no longer always viewed as being fickle employees who will soon leave the company.

Once an educated woman has exited from the labour force, it would hardly be worth her while returning after the early child-rearing years as most of the jobs available for re-entrants are poorly paid, unskilled positions in retailers and in small manufacturing companies. Thus re-entry is generally associated with downward occupational mobility into work not requiring special skills. One major reason for there being poor prospects for re-entrants is that the seniority principle, which depends upon continuous years of service, is upheld and indeed is further reinforced by job advertisements which place an upper age limit, often between 25 and 35 years old, on entry into a position. One woman wrote in sorrow to the *Asahi Shimbun* newspaper (24 May 1989) about her fruitless search for a worthwhile job:

'Forty, huh? The only job for you would be washing dishes.' That was the kind of answer I got wherever I called . . .

Compared to young people we take our jobs seriously . . . and above all many women in their forties these days are still youthful, eager and charming; so why is it that this country tends to judge women not by their personality or ability, but by their age?

As will be examined later (Chapter 5), some major companies are now on paper giving special consideration to women who had previously been their employees, but the scope of such schemes is very limited. And even where a women is already qualified and trained as a nurse or a teacher, it is considered more prudent for her to continue to work, with only a short break for maternity leave, rather than to exit from the labour force and have to go through the cumbersome re-entry procedures to her profession after several years. Incidentally professional Japanese women have tended to marry men in the same professions. One reason is that the woman's job is less likely to have to take second place when both husband and wife are in identical jobs. Thus a dentist couple and a lawyer couple, whom I know, can make better compromises over who should collect the children from the nursery. Moreover there is the possibility of setting up a joint practice, just like a traditional family business.

For an educated Japanese woman who does not have professional qualifications, her career has become that of being a highly motivated and efficient mother. She reads journals and watches deadly serious television programmes about bringing up and educating children. But her diligence is waning because of attacks on the *kyoiku mama* with the result that there is now a lot of interest in the issue of underemployed full-time housewives or what could be called 'at-a-loose-end homemakers'. Indeed it is middle-aged women who most value the non-pecuniary social benefits of work, because their social lives have so far been restricted to chatting on the street after taking out the rubbish or to rather formal meetings at their children's schools. Because of such social factors, which crop up at various points in my discussion, the notion is at last taking hold that a woman

FIGURE 2.1 *Changes in Japanese women's life cycle*

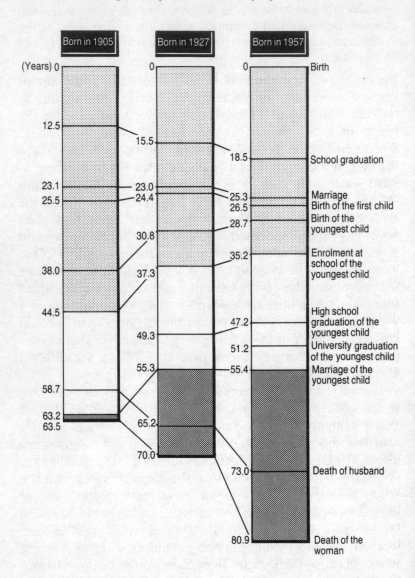

Born in 1905	Born in 1927	Born in 1957	
(Years) 0	0	0	Birth
12.5	15.5		
		18.5	School graduation
23.1	23.0		
25.5	24.4	25.3	Marriage
		26.5	Birth of the first child
		28.7	Birth of the youngest child
	30.8		
38.0	37.3	35.2	Enrolment at school of the youngest child
44.5			
	49.3	47.2	High school graduation of the youngest child
		51.2	University graduation of the youngest child
	55.3	55.4	Marriage of the youngest child
58.7			
63.2	65.2		
63.5			
	70.0		
		73.0	Death of husband
		80.9	Death of the woman

Source: Japan Institute of Labour, *Problems of Working Women.*

does not only work because she or her family needs the money, but because work is personally self-fulfilling and enlarges her social contacts.

There has, moreover, been a dramatic change, as shown in Figure 2.1, in the life cycle of most Japanese women since the 1950s. And the change has occurred more rapidly and in a much more fundamental way than in the West. Accompanied by the almost uniform trend towards a two-child family, the average woman's life expectancy has greatly increased. Consequently, whereas the woman born in 1905 could expect only 18 years of relative freedom between her youngest child entering school and her own death, her granddaughter must find ways of occupying a similar period of almost 45 years, 15 years of which are admittedly as a senior citizen. Such a radical change in the average life cycle of women over a short space of time – the implications of which have been reinforced by dramatic changes since 1945 in the educational system for girls and in people's lifestyles – means that there is a very clear distinction, especially in their expectations and attitudes, between different generations of Japanese women. Corroborative evidence for this clear impression on how life cycles and younger women's attitudes towards their role have changed is provided by a wealth of empirical detail from a large-scale survey carried out by the Economic Planning Agency (1987).

It is not only demographic changes, as clarified in the above model life cycles, which have permitted women to consider working for a longer period or re-entering the labour force. Hours devoted to housework have been cut because small Japanese homes are now crammed with relatively cheap, labour-saving devices. Nor need shopping be a burden since competition in the retail sector has led to some shops being open 24 hours a day and to supermarkets in convenient locations always being fully stocked. There are also economic-pull factors impelling women to seek paid work because of discrepancies between household income and household needs (Chapter 4). Moreover, household

41

monetary needs tend to increase more than proportionately to a rise in per capita income levels because of the substitution of market-produced for home-produced goods. And then of course the cycle enlarges as the rising consumer demand for market-produced goods and services leads to an expanded employer demand for female labour.

This cycle, which springs from the monetarization of the household economy, has occurred particularly rapidly in Japan, along with the dramatic change from an agricultural to an industrialized economy. Even now the popularity of magazines and television means that commercial advertisements for goods which displace home production quickly pervade every home and make the goods highly desirable and acceptable. In Japan, in particular, the commercial sector is highly competitive so that there is a constant – and some would say insidious – bombardment of special offers and 'new' goods. The resulting changes in consumption have not been reversed in Japan by any desire for going 'back to the land' or subsistence production. In the case of one rare couple in Japan who have chosen a subsistence life, the wife is a Canadian whose ideal of a rural idyll has not been dented by memories of Japanese rural life in the pre-war period. Japanese women know only too well from the tales of their mothers how hard life can be on a farm. Consequently the controversial issue has arisen of farmers going to the Philippines to find brides who are willing to take on the burden of unpaid family labour in Japanese agriculture.

Ironically enough, the fairly recent notion that a woman's place should be in the home has been somewhat contradictory of the value that Japanese in general place on paid employment and the working environment. Thus the image which the Japanese themselves like to present to the West of homogeneity and shared values can be very misleading when considering such issues as how attached women are to the labour force. In general the Japanese are wont to argue that women have minimal loyalty and commitment to their jobs because their primary concern is their family: an argument which slides over the point that concern for the family has led women to work hard in order to supplement family income. (In the pre-modern era even *samurai* women from the now abandoned aristocracy would discreetly engage in weaving and other piece-work.) In any case the famous company loyalty of male workers has been fostered by the bonus system rather than being part of a distinctive work ethic. For both women and men, therefore, economic motivation primarily determines their degree of work attachment, which is an obvious but often overlooked fact.

From rice fields to supermarkets

The above mentioned irony in which society values the working world, but proposes that women should stay at home might be explained by an elaborate theory of patriarchy; or it may simply be that the occupations in which working women generally find themselves are considered to be of too low a status for the middle class, in which the vast majority of the Japanese believes themselves to be. Thus a very low value is attached to women's jobs not only by society, but also by the participating women themselves. Nor have the changes in occupational structure, which have been a striking part of Japan's modernization, been accompanied by a much greater spread of occupations for women or an upgrading of the kinds of jobs in which they usually find themselves.

The issue of occupational segregation, along with that of the consequent wage differentials, will be discussed in more detail in Chapter 3; at this point I would just like to look at the major sectoral trends over time. Even since as recently as 1960 there has been a radical shift in women's jobs from agriculture – the main primary industry – to manufacturing and ultimately to employment in the tertiary sector, which is defined to include services, trade, restaurants, financial institutions and the civil service. In Japan's modern tertiary sector the demand for women's employment is especially buoyant in information services, restaurants, insurance and welfare services. The notion is becoming popular that service industry jobs are peculiarly appropriate for women because they have a sense of fashion and can provide a 'personal touch'. It should be remarked that the latter reason is perhaps tantamount to acknowledging that women are better able to take on a servile role. Thus many apparently white-collar jobs in the service industry should really be dubbed 'pink-collar' insofar as they would be steered clear of by most men.

TABLE 2.4 *Trends in proportions of Japanese working women between main sectors*
(percentage composition in each year)

	Primary (Agriculture, forestry, fishing)	Secondary (Mining, manufacturing, construction)	Tertiary (Services, trade, restaurants)
1960	43.1	20.2	36.7
1965	32.5	23.1	44.4
1970	26.2	26.0	47.8
1975	18.4	25.7	55.7
1980	13.2	28.2	58.4
1985	10.6	28.3	60.8
1987	9.9	27.1	62.7

Source: Ministry of Labour, *Fujin Rodo no Jitsujo.*

It may be a revelation to some readers looking at Table 2.4 that in 1960 the 43.1 per cent of Japanese women workers in agricultural occupations was higher than the comparable figure in Ireland of 15.3 per cent, gleaned from the ILO's *Economically Active Population 1950–2025*. The explanation lies in the fact that the relative importance of the roles of women and men as agricultural workers is reversed between the two countries. Thus, in 1960, only 26.3 per cent of Japanese men were working in the primary sector –

mainly agriculture – which was appreciably less than the 43.8 per cent of Irish men in the same sector. The data still seem surprising. It is possible that many of the Irish women who are working on family-run farms do not value their work highly enough or are reluctant to admit to working in the fields. In Japan in the 1960s, meanwhile, women's work was acknowledged to be essential in the agricultural sector.

The other significant difference between the trends in Japan and most other OECD countries lies in the way in which Japan's secondary sector, notably manufacturing, continued to gain in importance in the distribution of working women right up until 1984, when the proportion appears to have peaked at 28.4 per cent. In contrast, the relevant proportion for British women has declined steadily over the past four decades. Consequently, especially because of the opportunities for part-time employment in Britain in the areas of health and education, the proportion of British working women in the tertiary sector, which in 1980 had already reached over 75 per cent, is still much higher than in Japan. Of course, there have been Japanese women working in services for a long time; the most famous are the geisha and bar hostesses, but despite their fame they are relatively few and, unfortunately, they fit well within the framework of women serving men. It was only in 1980 that the service industry – strictly defined to exclude the civil service, the wholesale and retail trade and restaurants – began to account for a larger number of women employees than manufacturing (*Fujin Rodo no Jitsujo*, 1988, Table 11). Thus even now the overall pattern of employment for Japanese women – with over 27 per cent in manufacturing and less than 63 per cent in the tertiary sector – is at odds with both Britain and Ireland, where the proportions are respectively only around 20 per cent and well over 70 per cent. In fact up to the mid-1980s Japan was the only exception to the general rule among OECD countries that the weight of manufacturing in female employment was declining.[1]

One reason for Japan's uniqueness in this respect at least is the relative strength of her manufacturing industry in export markets. Therefore the usual labour productivity gains in manufacturing, as opposed to services, have contributed to larger output without employment displacement. It remains to be seen whether trade friction and other factors will dilute this strength and consequently push up unemployment rates from the present low levels of 2.6 per cent for women and 2.5 per cent for men in 1988. It is also worth mentioning at this point that not only is there a significant number of discouraged female workers not appearing in the unemployment data (Chapter 4), but also the official Japanese unemployment figure is reckoned to be an underestimate. Unlike Britain where the registered unemployed are measured, the unemployment rate in Japan is estimated from a survey of households. If a surveyed woman asserts that she is actually seeking work in the survey week and has not worked at all during the past week, then she is counted as unemployed. Thus the Japanese unemployment rate does not include those who wish to work longer hours nor those who did seek work sometime in the past four weeks, which is the usual standard in OECD countries.

Nonetheless, not only is the official unemployment rate for Japanese women quite low, but also only around 22 per cent of those who are unemployed have suffered an involuntary loss of employment with the comparable figure for unemployed men being over 41 per cent in 1987. The figure for those unemployed women who have voluntarily chosen to quit their previous place of employment is fairly high at around 42 per cent.[2] (And, oddly enough, in a society where men employees are thought to be totally loyal to their company, the figure for voluntary quitters among unemployed men reaches 27 per cent.)

Women working longer in one company

It is, in any case, not surprising that older women are more likely to quit their jobs than men when their promotion prospects are so much more restricted and when they have time and travel constraints in getting to work because of their children's needs. Rather than comparing quit rates, therefore, the question of whether women are actually more fickle employees than men is better answered by looking at length of service figures for continuous employment in one company only for those aged under 30 years. The congruity of the figures for employees in their twenties is striking. In fact by 1987 young women had slightly longer average years of service than men; for those aged between 25 and 29 years the average for women was 5.5 years as opposed to 5.4 years for men. And this is despite the contention of one woman lawyer that sexual harassment is one cause of women quitting workplaces (*The Japan Times*, 15 October 1989).

FIGURE 2.2 *Trends in distribution of Japanese women employees by length of service*
(percentages in all industries)

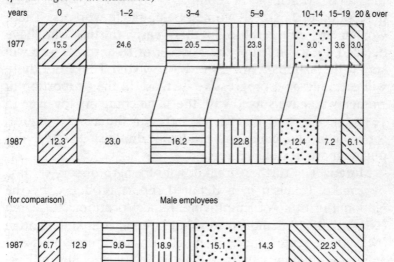

Source: Ministry of Labour, *Chingin Kozo Kihon Tokei Chosa*.

And when we look at the distribution by length of service for all age groups in Figure 2.2, the trend towards women giving longer, continuous years of employment with the same company becomes quite clear, in spite of the average length of continuous service for all women employees being just 7.1 years in 1987, compared to 12.4 years for men. The change would have been even more dramatic, but for the fact that the overall averages have been diluted by the increasing numbers each year who have left family businesses and entered employment, thereby breaking their continuous years of service. The most remarkable aspect of Figure 2.2 relates to the long servers who are in continuous employment with one company for ten or more years. In 1977, only 15.6 per cent of women employees had managed this feat, both because child-care responsibilities had intervened and also because the re-entry of middle-aged women into regular employment had only just begun to increase as could be seen on Table 2.2. But just ten years later in 1987 the women with ten or more years of service accounted for 25.7 per cent of the total, which is in complete contrast to the usual perception of Japanese women being fickle workers. These women are either those in their early thirties who have decided not to interrupt their career or re-entrants who will stay with a company for 20 or more years. Therefore there will certainly be a progressive increase in the proportion of women who have stayed with the same company for over 15 years and the wide divergence between the average figures for women and men may gradually diminish as men also pursue more flexible careers.

Moreover, a further breakdown of length of service data by Emiko Takeishi in a detailed report produced by the National Institute of Employment and Vocational Research (NIEVR, 1988) demonstrates that in small companies and in the service sector there is much less difference between women's and men's average length of service. Thus in these areas in particular Japanese women have already been indicating their willingness to pursue a career, in its widest sense, by providing longer years of service to a company in spite of the demands of child-rearing. And the trends in participation patterns, which have been outlined earlier in this chapter, will lead to another substantial increase in women's average length of service over the next ten years. Once working women are seen to be attached to their jobs, there could be a break in the vicious circle whereby relatively unpromising conditions of employment lead women to take an easygoing attitude towards their jobs, which then aggravates the prejudiced attitude of employers concerning a women's capability in learning technical skills and her attachment to the job.

Women an integral part of labour force

It should by now be evident that the position of working women in Japan reflects a strange paradox. On the one hand working women have popularly been considered to be peripheral, intermittent members of the labour force, because they have not fitted into the ideal image of permanent employment, despite the latter image being in reality restricted to only a fraction of the total labour force. But on the other hand Japanese women have generally had a relatively high participation rate except for a short period during the late 1960s and early 1970s and except for a few in the *samurai* or, later on, upper classes. Women have been working neither for pin money nor to pass the time, but because of real economic incentives: either as daughters to supplement farming family incomes before the Pacific War, or, increasingly since 1945, as middle-aged mothers to fill the gap between rising expectations of better living standards and household income.

Since to raise their families' living standards, Japanese working women are committed to economic activity, they have been an integral part of initially the agricultural and subsequently the manufacturing sector, notably on the shop floor in textile and electronics factories; and now the service sector could not function at all without them. It is true that working women, primarily because of their additional burden of homemaking, have been intermittent members of the Japanese labour force. In the 1980s, however, there has been a very clear trend towards longer years of service and an increasing proportion of married women who work. Thus the importance of work to women and of women's work to the Japanese economy is bound to intensify.

Notes

(1) OECD (1984), page 47. The weight of employment in services usually increases along with rising GNP per capita for three reasons: i. Productivity grows faster in manufacturing. ii. More is spent on health and education. iii. The income elasticity of demand for services is greater than for goods.

(2) These labour force report figures are quoted in *Fujin Rodo no Jitsujo* (1988, p.9). In fact researchers now tend to agree that the notion of company loyalty and permanent employment applies only to a fraction of the Japanese male work-force. Particularly among youths the turnover rate even in a major company is as high as in most other OECD countries. For example, see Koike (1988), pages 57 to 66.

3 | Aspects of segregation for working women

Through Western eyes one striking aspect of Japanese society is its superficial homogeneity and harmony. And many Japanese, who should be better aware of their diversity and the underlying competition among themselves, are happy to promote the notion of a homogeneous and harmonious work-force in order to explain rising productivity levels and the high quality of Japanese products in the international marketplace. Some commentators on Japan's labour market are inclined to stress the lack of class-consciousness, the relatively high and uniform educational level of the workers, 94 per cent of whom have stayed at school until at least 18 years of age, the egalitarianism in the workplace, and the co-operative commitment to company goals. While it would be foolhardy to deny any truth in these rather hackneyed comments, reality reveals considerably less homogeneity and egalitarianism, especially in respect to working women. Although egalitarian work practices do exist for some groups, the labour market is quite distinctly stratified for women. Many observers, including Robert Cole (1979, p.3) – one of the few Western scholars who has actually worked on the shop floor of Japanese companies – would argue that women are among the most disadvantaged workers in Japan. Apart from such asides, however, most commentators on the Japanese workplace have hardly considered women.

While there may be agreement on the point of being disadvantaged, there are pitfalls in trying to measure the degree of disadvantage; and so studies often rely on the subjective impressions of the working women themselves.

What is most remarkable in light of the perceived passivity of Japanese women is that they have grown more aware of discrimination in the workplace. A glance at the results of surveys carried out by the Prime Minister's Office (1979, 1984 and 1987) indicates that within the span of five years in the early 1980s the proportion of women who denied that women and men were given equal status rose from 59.3 per cent to 77.5 per cent. The more educated the respondents, the more they were aware of a lack of equality in the workplace. After the enactment of the Equal Employment Opportunity Law in May 1986 the proportion of women in the late 1980s who were still pessimistic about there being any hope of work status equality even in the future still remained at around half. And recently there has been a greater perception among most women of not only salary differences, but also of insufficient recognition of their abilities and of being given trivial assignments. A *Mainichi Shimbun* newspaper survey (29 May 1986) on the Equal Employment Opportunity Law reported that over 80 per cent of women complained of discrimination or were aware of its existence.

Such subjective impressions, while illuminating, are not sufficient. I shall be discussing in this chapter various kinds of labour market duality, in the sense that most working women are placed in what is conventionally called a secondary labour market with low wages and status, high turnover and little requirement for skills as conventionally defined. There are various ways in which the labour market is divided into stratified segments, some of which are also relevant to women elsewhere, while others are more particularly a feature of Japan. The universal forms of duality are occupational segregation and wage differentials; those more characteristic of Japan are the differing attitudes and conditions applying to the few professional women as opposed to all the other working women, and the distinction in employment conditions and associated division of the labour market between large and small companies. The secondary labour markets are more competitive with a higher degree of instability and labour turnover, while the primary labour markets are usually internal to the company and permit promotion and good employment conditions. One striking but rather generalized statistic which illustrates how even employed women are subject to unstable employment conditions concerns the proportion of employees in Japan whose contracts extend to only one year or less; while just 5.2 per cent of male employees in 1987 were not regular employees, the corresponding proportion for women was 19.3 per cent, which was, moreover, almost 5 percentage points higher than in 1975. This increase in the proportion of casual female employees does not tell the whole story, however, since the non-primary sector of the labour market also includes self-employment as well as covering a range of different kinds of jobs, which will be more fully explored in Chapter 6. When I specifically wish, therefore, to describe the kind of work in the non-primary labour market which is unstable, unskilled and poorly paid, I shall use 'casual employment' as a pejorative term, to distinguish it from the kind of job in the informal sector which should not be despised and which may be appropriate for women's employment.

Job segregation

Even though I have demonstrated in the preceding chapter that Japanese women have been relatively active and integral members of the labour force, in no way did I intend that to mean that their position is relatively strong. In fact, because of occupational segregation women are part of the secondary labour force in which their low-paying jobs are popularly considered to be inferior to those of male workers. It is important at this point to distinguish between horizontal and vertical segregation. Since Japanese women in the secondary labour force are found in a fairly wide range of unskilled occupations, horizontal segregation is less evident than in the West; but their inferior status and treatment as

53

peripheral members of the labour force reinforces vertical segregation whereby many women are denied training and promotion. It is generally agreed that the root of occupational segregation lies in the double burden which women bear; their primary responsibility in almost all cultures for running the home and caring for the children severely restricts the kinds of income-earning jobs for which they have spare time and effort. And it is hard for women to avoid the sorts of jobs in the caring, cleaning and catering professions which are an extension of their home responsibilities. Indeed much of the occupational segregation in all the OECD countries springs from the division of labour in the home and so this topic will be explored further in Chapter 5.

In Japan, where workers are expected to be completely devoted to their primary responsibility, whether they be paid employees or mothers, the potential for vertical occupational segregation is higher than in the West. In particular, women have tended to be consigned to so-called 'auxiliary' jobs, which are often only different in name and in promotion prospects from the positions of their male colleagues. Apologists for the relative paucity of female Japanese managers argue that in Japan managers have to engage not only in lengthy overtime but also in evening and weekend socializing with their subordinates and business contacts in bars and on golf courses. Such an argument mistakenly begins with the premise that men have neither the desire nor the obligation to spend time with their families and that women bear all the responsibility for homemaking.

It is difficult, if not impossible, to make an objective and accurate judgement of whether occupational segregation by sex is more severe in Japan than elsewhere, although there have been some attempts to arrive at a scale for measuring the degree of segregation. The dissimilarity index developed by the OECD (1985), under which segregation is defined as the difference between the female share of an occupational or industrial category and the female share of total employment, actually found the lowest level of occupational concentration in Japan compared to other OECD countries. Other countries with relatively low dissimilarity indices, according to the OECD's latest measures (1988, p.209), are Italy, Greece and Portugal, which contradicts the popular view that the variety of occupations for women will surely widen as a country develops. Indeed the highest indices of segregation have been found in countries with high rates of female labour participation and well-developed service sectors, because many 'new' service occupations have been taken up almost exclusively by women. But in such countries the dissimilarity index, which depends on a fairly high degree of aggregation, may not be conveying the detailed picture of a wider range of occupational opportunities for women.

Why, though, does Japan have the lowest measure of gender segregation, whether measured by occupation or by industry? Part of the reason lies in the persistence of family enterprises in the informal sector; for example, in many of the small family-run cafes, it is the man who is doing the cooking and the woman who is seeing to the accounts. Also egalitarian labour practices help to bring men into 'feminine' occupations; Japanese men are found as hair stylists, not just in the high-class hairdressers, but in most of the small, cheap establishments as well, where, though they may be the managers, they are washing women's hair. In agriculture as well, the distinction between women's and men's work is not evident. (It should be remarked, however, that in all these areas men are more usually given the chance to develop specialist skills, while women are expected to cope with a range of less-skilled jobs.) The most important cause of the lower level of measured segregation in Japan, however, is the relatively high proportion of Japanese women in the manufacturing sector, which serves to camouflage their limited opportunities for training and promotion. Superficial observation suggests that vertical segregation is particularly severe insofar as it is rare for there to be women supervisors among all the Japanese women working on the shop floor in electronics factories, though women supervisors do appear in the Japanese factories located overseas. Nor does the predominance of women even in retailing usually extend to their attaining the position of store manager in large shops.

Anyone who on even a fleeting visit to Japan sees the female bank tellers and lift attendants in their twee uniforms greet customers with excessive politeness would surely be struck by the way in which certain women's occupations – at a lower level of aggregation than that used by the OECD in its dissimilarity indices – are almost completely feminized and constricted. Indeed, since the Japanese language is clearly differentiated into distinct male and female words and expressions, a man's way of speaking could sound highly inappropriate in many feminized occupations. There do appear to be certain anomalies, such as the men who sit on the side of the street demonstrating sewing machines or the man in the bank who has to scurry after customers to help them find the right forms and operate the cash machines; but their presence is probably explained by the notion that men are better at explaining the operation of any machine and at giving even the simplest kind of advice. Unfortunately, Japanese women themselves often tend to have more trust in a man's work; mothers are often more critical of women teachers than of men teachers.

Nonetheless the apparent entrenchment of vertical occupational segregation conceals a kind of fluidity in that for a small proportion of women the distribution of their occupations has actually been shifting quite radically. (Incidentally, in the case of women who move into occupations which have mostly been the preserve of men, they are able to modify their language – merely by cutting out some of the superfluous syllables and by lowering the pitch – so that it sounds more appropriately professional.) A survey conducted by NIEVR (1988) found that in areas requiring expertise and skills, such as systems development and merchandise planning, women's employment is expanding significantly. And Table 3.1 indicates that since 1970 the proportion of women who are professional and technical workers has risen by 55 per cent and of those who are managers and officials by 100 per cent – though admittedly in the latter case from a very low base. It should be noted, however, that the level of aggregation conceals the true extent of occupational segregation. In particular, just under half of all employees in the category of professional and technical workers are women because of the inclusion of nursing and teaching, which are favoured and incidentally fairly high-status occupations for Japanese women. But there have also been some substantial increases since 1970 in the number of women in certain professions: ranging from professional sportswomen through information processing technicians to engineers.

TABLE 3.1 *Trends in ratio of Japanese female employees by occupation*

Year	Professional and technical	Managers and officials	Clerical	Sales	Process*	Other service	Other**
	A. *Percentage of females by job category:*						
1960	9.0	0.3	25.4	8.7	35.9	16.1	4.6
1970	9.1	0.5	30.7	10.2	32.7	13.7	3.0
1980	13.0	0.8	32.7	11.6	27.2	12.9	1.7
1986	13.7	0.9	33.0	12.1	27.4	11.3	1.4
1987	14.1	1.0	32.9	12.6	26.7	11.3	1.2
	B. *Females as a percentage of all employees:*						
1960	33.3	2.5	35.9	34.7	26.9	54.8	
1970	40.7	3.8	46.9	32.6	27.0	56.2	
1980	48.4	5.1	51.1	31.6	26.1	50.9	
1986	47.5	7.2	54.2	31.7	28.4	50.9	
1987	44.1	7.3	55.2	32.3	29.0	51.0	

Notes:
1. * 'Process' includes skilled production workers and labourers.
2. ** 'Other' includes employees in agriculture, transport, etc.

Source: Management and Coordination Agency, *Rodoryoku Chosa.*

Comparative ILO figures from the *Year Book of Labour Statistics* show that a much higher proportion of Japanese female employees are in production-related work than in other OECD countries and a smaller proportion are in the managerial category. Interestingly enough, however, these discrepancies with the West are even more marked in the case of South Korea where over 35 per cent of female employees are in production work and the percentage of those who are managers is rounded to zero. It is wellnigh impossible to match detailed occupational categories between Japan and Britain. The ILO has drawn up standard categories, but the aggregation is rather rough and likely to be inconsistent between countries. Nonetheless, if we were to look at the distribution of occupations in Britain, using the *New Earnings Survey* Part E, one remarkable contrast with Japan would be the differing proportions of female employees in clerical as opposed to production jobs. In Britain 42 per cent of full-time female employees – as opposed to 33 per cent in Japan – are clerical and related workers, but only 10 to 15 per cent are in the categories comparable to the processing and assembling category in which are working about 27 per cent of Japanese women employees.

A rather similar picture is apparent from the distribution by industry in Table 3.2, in which the proportion of Japanese women in the manufacturing sector actually increased in the early 1980s, while there was a radical decline in Britain, partly as a reflection of the overall decline of British manufacturing. (But, even though the proportion of German women in manufacturing is just as high as in Japan, there has been a proportionate decrease since 1979.) It is British social and community services which have primarily taken up the women who have left the manufacturing sector. There may appear to be many Japanese women in the broadly defined social and community services, but this category in the case of Japan also includes hotel employees. It is worth noting that there is a much higher proportion of British women in public administration than in Japan; the Japanese government is a relatively insignificant employer of women. One final interesting feature is the relatively high proportion of Japanese women in the construction sector: higher than in the other OECD countries. Indeed a Japanese farm woman often works on road construction and

TABLE 3.2 *Distribution of working women by industry in Japan and the United Kingdom, 1979 and 1985*

| | Japan | | United Kingdom | |
	1979	1985	1979	1985
Employment (000s)	21,170	23,040	9,680	9,517
Percentage by industry				
Total	100.00	100.00	100.0	100.0
Agriculture	13.7	10.0	0.9	0.8
Forestry	0.1	0.1	0.1	0.1
Fishing	0.5	0.6	0.1	0.1
Mining and quarrying	0.1	0.1	0.1	0.1
Manufacturing	24.0	25.0	22.3	16.4
Electricity, gas & water	0.2	0.2	0.7	0.6
Construction	3.5	3.3	1.1	1.3
Wholesale trade	4.8	5.2	3.0	3.2
Retail trade	15.7	15.8	14.1	14.7
Restaurants & hotels	6.2	6.2	6.5	7.2
Transportation, communication & storage	1.9	1.9	2.8	2.8
Finance			2.7	3.3
Insurance	6.2	7.1	1.3	1.5
Business services & real estate			4.0	5.1
Public administration	1.7	1.5	8.2	7.4
Sanitary services			1.6	1.9
Social & community services			26.0	28.7
Recreation services	21.3	23.0	2.2	2.5
Personal services			2.1	2.0
International bodies			0.1	0.1
Activity undefined	0.1	0.3	..	..

Notes:
1. The figures include self-employed and family workers.
2. In the case of Japan, hotel workers are included in social and community services.

Source: OECD, *Employment Outlook*, 1987.

59

other public-work sites during slack agricultural seasons; she is no stranger to hard physical work.

The relative strength of Japan's manufacturing sector as a general explanation of why relatively more Japanese women are in production-related work than in the West has already been considered in Chapter 2. One additional comment in respect of women's occupations in manufacturing may be revealing. The Japanese education system's relative emphases on diligence, presenting neat work, dexterity in origami (paper folding), rote learning, and physical fitness have been taken particularly to heart by women, who then transfer these skills to the shop floor. And it is probably no coincidence that Japan's internationally competitive strength lies in such areas as the manufacture of watches, electrical goods and semiconductors, where Japanese women's dexterity and perfectionism come into full play. This is one of the challenges faced by the Irish and British employees of Japanese companies and, as will be seen later (Chapter 8), it is the blue-collar women who have most successfully participated in Japanese working methods. Do we then have to accept a sexist interpretation along the lines that 'feminine qualities' are highly valued in the Japanese electronics industry? I think the answer would rather lie with the male workers who should demonstrate that they could do the work as well as any woman.

The long-term trend as working women are moving into the service sector – along with a slight decline since 1984 in the relative significance of manufacturing for women's employment – has been discussed in Chapter 2, but without considering the implications for occupational segregation. It is arguable that shifts into certain service occupations, especially those associated with the ageing of the Japanese population and with the expansion of day nurseries – notably the caring professions and cleaning – may eventually increase the degree of gender segregation. In Britain as well, Jill Rubery and Roger Tarling have demonstrated (Rubery, ed., 1988) that the growth of the service industry has been associated with a higher degree of segregation, in spite of some changes in the pattern of segregation. The tendency towards greater segregation as the tertiary sector expands may seem to be at variance with the relaxation of segregation associated with better-educated Japanese women slowly moving into male occupational strongholds; but the problem is that the reverse movement is much less likely to gain favour, because men would be considered rather foolish to take up low-paying and low-status jobs. Nonetheless, the high rate of youth unemployment in Britain means, according to *Employing School Leavers* (Incomes Data Services Study 414, 1988), that more boys leaving school are going to have to take jobs traditionally associated with women in the clerical, hairdressing, cleaning and retail sectors.

In the case of Japan I do know some men who are finding job satisfaction in working at a children's play centre and in a baby and toddlers' day-care institution. They seem not to encounter prejudice, but are instead accorded an additional bonus of the great respect given to any kind of *sensei* (teacher). Nonetheless, while the Japanese unemployment rate remains relatively low most men are not going to be tempted to compete with women by entering their occupations. Nor does the sharp role division between sexes in Japanese society help. One male kindergarten teacher commented: 'Something is wrong with society where the father is away from home for long hours and almost all teachers at nursery and primary schools are women.' (*The Japan Times*, 15 February 1987).

Social conditioning and job segregation

Under the present teenage culture in Japan not many young women are going to choose to take the kind of college courses or seek the kinds of jobs which are popularly considered to be unfeminine. This is an issue in most cultures, but in Japan the influence of the peer group under which no-one wants to be different is particularly powerful. And the femininity code is especially pervasive in Japan where the lack of privacy in tiny Japanese houses has led people to enforce rigid standards of modesty and elegance – for women. The resulting distinction between the sexes is reinforced by the way in which the language differs according to sex right from the kindergarten years. Not only are different words and expressions used by girls and boys, but, more insidiously, some of the ways in which boys address girls cannot be used in reverse. Also young Japanese women seem to be particularly susceptible to the notion of romance and usually their only ambition is to be married in a splendidly sentimental ceremony. The high cost of such a ceremony, however, does at least mean that they are in less of a hurry to get married than young British and Irish women; Japanese women are compelled to wait for marriage until their mid-twenties – their average age for marrying in 1986 was 25.6 years – when they (and their parents) have worked to save about 1 million yen (about £4,250) to cover the cost of the magnificent display. At all events there is a powerful economic motivation for young women to work.

The pervasiveness of social pressure in Japan through the family, friends and the popular media suggests that much occupational segregation is in effect imposed rather than freely chosen. Most mothers, according to a survey carried out by the Prime Minister's Office (1984), choose to bring up their sons and daughters differently, because they want their daughters to become 'happy family women' rather than to acquire the skills to enter a good profession. (In particular, usually it is only daughters who are expected to help with the housework.) Consequently more than twice as many young women opt to attend a two-year college as a four-year university with its higher cost. That may have been a rational choice until the mid-1980s since the job market was, as we have seen in Chapter 2, less favourable to four-year university female graduates, who were considered to be over-qualified. Therefore it seemed only sensible for a woman to graduate from a two-year college in a gentle or non-assertive subject, such as kindergarten education or languages, and then to work for three or four years before marrying someone, who in many cases would have been a colleague at her office.

Moreover, in both the West and Japan an overt engineering culture has been constructed by male engineers in order to exclude women from their ranks. When Japanese women do choose to enter, for example, civil engineering courses, they are exposed to a certain amount of ridicule – like on the television programme (*Nihon TV*, 15 March 1988) where they were asked whether it did not feel strange to be wearing a helmet. On the same programme male engineering students dogmatically asserted that this was a profession only suitable for men. The Japanese media is relentless in its pursuit of interesting or quaint items. Still, media exposure, which is thought to be a good thing in Japan, may ultimately have a beneficial effect in encouraging more women to enter traditional male preserves; and some Japanese women are not being deterred by such ridicule. Ministry of Education statistics indicate that in 1987 engineering jobs accounted for 14 per cent of women university graduates obtaining regular employment, whereas ten years ago the figure was only 3.6 per cent. These figures do, however, comprise a very wide definition of engineering, which includes computer-related jobs.

In Britain, despite young women engineers also being isolated by harassment and prejudice while on training courses, the picture is much brighter. Every year the percentage of engineering students who are women is increasing and has now reached over 10 per cent in Britain, compared to only about 3 per cent in Japan. Both British industry and government officials in the Equal Opportunities Commission are providing much more encouragement than in Japan through the 'Women into Science and Engineering' project. But just as in Japan it is unfortunately the mothers who, according to *The Times* (13 and 16 July 1988), are most opposed to their daughters' engineering aspirations.

It would be misleading to consider only the limited aspirations of Japanese female university graduates. There is in Japan a great respect among both men and women for training and qualifications at all stages of life. One working woman in her twenties, whom I interviewed with her small children in tow, did not go to college, but she said that her greatest ambition – coming before promotion – was to obtain skill qualifications. Her resolution may have been particularly strong because she is working for a fairly small company with just over 100 employees. Other women shop-floor workers in the large companies to whom I spoke were quite content to stay in their present positions which were secure and provided good employee benefits. The corporate image of women in Japan is that they are not interested in promotion because they are 'floating' between home and job. A highly detailed survey on how companies were utilizing women (NIEVR, 1987) found that 71.5 per cent of responding companies thought that 'women's awareness and consciousness were insufficient'. But there is conflicting evidence on whether women want to be promoted; NIEVR (1984) and Denki Roren (1985) surveys have shown that when women were long servers with a company, they did want supervisory positions, which is the career pattern provided for most long-serving Japanese men. There is a contrary pattern in the case of women, however, where long servers are often passed over in favour of promotion for mid-career female recruits, according to Emiko Takeishi's analysis (NIEVR, 1988).

Controversial impact of law on job segregation

The effect of the Equal Employment Opportunity Law on vertical occupational segregation needs to be considered; the evidence so far is rather patchy, but a few surveys have come up with results. (The reasons for the generally weak impact of the law on women's promotion prospects are discussed more fully in Chapter 9.) According to the results of a Tokyo Metropolitan Government survey (*The Japan Times*, 30 June 1988), 15 per cent of companies still hire women on different terms to those of men and pay them less, even when they begin in the same job. When Kazuko Inaba discussed the results of the NIEVR survey cited above (1988), she concluded that women were now being treated as 'key labour', since the proportion of companies intending to use women mainly for auxiliary jobs without promotion potential dropped from 33.9 per cent to 15.3 per cent in the wake of the Equal Employment Opportunity Law. The same surveys report that it is overwhelmingly the management in large companies rather than small companies which understands the provisions and spirit of the law – an example of the distinction in employment practices depending on the size of the company.

Even in large companies, however, the effect of the Equal Employment Opportunity Law on the majority of women employees is often thought to be deleterious. In many cases graduate employees now have to choose soon after entering a company between one of two tracks under the employers' concept of 'channelling management'. Those in the general or executive track are liable to be transferred quite frequently to other areas as part of the job rotation system, whereas those in the auxiliary or clerical track forego any promotion prospects in return for an assurance of not being relocated. (In a Japanese company a major part of an employee's training for promotion is embedded in the job rotation system, which requires regular re-assignments to different positions and locations.)

Although the employers argue that the two-track system is not discriminatory in the eyes of the law, most women are having to make an irreversible choice early in their careers to join the slow track because of their anxiety that transfers may upset the stability of their future family. Michiko Nakajima, a woman lawyer, found in a small survey that most women were warned by their employers that if they pursued jobs on the executive track they would risk disrupting their family life; but despite such discouragement more than half of the 31 women she surveyed were on the executive track (*The Japan Times*, 1 March 1988). Evidently her survey concentrated on the women with a higher education and longer years of service, whose increasing presence in the labour force has led to a doubling between 1977 and 1987 in the number of women with titles indicating managerial status. That doubling, however, took place from an extremely low base; by 1987 only 1.2 per cent of all employed women had achieved managerial status, (*Fujin Rodo no Jitsujo*, 1988, p.16). One researcher at the Asian Women Workers' Fellowship cites major insurance and securities companies where only around 1 per cent of those on the executive track are women. The general picture is that in many companies just a few figurehead women are entering the executive track, upon which almost all the male employees are embarking as a matter of course. Eventually this impression has been corroborated by a governmental white paper on women released by the Prime Minister's Office (1989), which reported that 63 per cent of surveyed women said that they still did not receive equal treatment at work, despite the Equal Employment Opportunity Law having been in force for almost three years.

What seems to be happening, therefore, is a more systematic application of previously informal sexual discrimination in promotion decisions. Indeed 'channelling management' seems to mean that just a few 'career women' are benefiting from the Equal Employment Opportunity Law's provisions, while all the rest will have to remain on a different stratum of low-paid monotonous jobs. Consequently some radical Japanese women commentators, such as Reiko Inoue and Etsuko Kaji (*Ampo*, 1986), believe that the law will lead to widening wage differentials; and they conclude that industry has gained a victory at the expense of women.

Discrimination contributes to wide wage differentials

The ways in which laws whose ostensible purpose is to improve the lot of working women may have some contrary effects is also illustrated by the case in Britain where occupational segregation increased in many companies as a way of justifying pay differentials in the period before the final 1975 implementation of the Equal Pay Act. There is then the convincing argument, propounded by Veronica Beechey (1987, p.182) and Jill Rubery (1988, p.121), that equal pay legislation has led to divisions within the female labour force becoming more noticeable, because it is mainly the elite women workers who have gained. In Japan as well occupational segregation has almost certainly been exacerbated by the need to comply with the original 1947 Labour Standards Law which only forbids discriminatory rates of pay for clearly identical jobs. It is not yet widely recognized in Japan that in order to prevent subtle wage discrimination what is really needed is a provision requiring equal pay for work of equal worth to the employer. Admittedly such a requirement is very difficult to make effective; in Britain the 1984 Equal Value Amendment to the Equal Pay Act has not really had any impact on the existing wage gap, presumably because not just jobs but also industries are segregated by sex.

As has been seen in Tables 1.3 and 1.4, even when overtime pay is excluded, the wage gap between women and men employees is much wider in Japan than in Britain. Data on wage differentials over different age groups (*Chingin Kozo Kihon Tokei Chosa*) show that the average wage for women aged under 20 years is over 90 per cent of the wage of men in the same age group. The gap, however, dramatically widens to reach only just over 50 per cent for those aged over 45 years. Evidently the age-wage profile for women is rather flat, in contrast to the steady rise in wages along with seniority from which Japanese men and the few women who stay the course in large companies alone benefit. Thus the average wage for women aged over 40 years is only 20 per cent higher than for women in their early twenties, but the corresponding wage differential for men reaches to over 100 per cent.

Herein surely lies the reason why average wage differentials have tended to widen recently in Japan; as more middle-aged women re-enter employment at relatively low wages, the overall average wage for working women is depressed further in comparison with the average male wage, which is being boosted yearly by seniority payments as the labour force ages. Apologists may argue that the widening wage differentials over age merely reflect the fact that women provide fewer years of service as they exit and later re-enter the labour force. But, as Figure 2.2 has shown, over a quarter of women employees have provided more than ten continuous years of service. What is bothersome then is whether, despite their attachment to their jobs, such women are still being denied the benefits of the seniority wage system, as has already been indicated by the evidence cited in the preceding section of a lack of promotion opportunites for long-serving women.

There are many pitfalls in trying to separate out the effect on wage differentials of pure discrimination from that of other causative factors: namely length of service, education, experience and occupational segregation. Indeed at the first stage it is arguable that occupational segregation and differing kinds of experience are in themselves indicative of discrimination; so where does pure discrimination begin? It would be misleading to engage in speculative figures. The most appropriate approach would require a large-scale multiple regression analysis in which the contributions of factors such as education and length of service in explaining pay rates are calculated by regressing data for those variables on wage data. Once the linear equation which shows the contributions as coefficients is established, the remaining unexplained variation between wage levels predicted by the equation and actual wage rates as a proportion of the total variation in wage rates would indicate the extent of discrimination.

One simpler, though rather rougher, way of clarifying the factors underlying wage differentials is to standardize average wages by age and education as in Table 3.3. And since the figures displayed only apply to workers who have been continuously employed by the same company since leaving school, length of service can no longer be a factor in explaining wage differentials. Therefore any remaining wage gap is wholly due to occupational segregation – including differing promotion patterns and being employed in companies with different conditions – and pure discrimination. It is important to note at the outset that even entry wages are different; other statistics for average initial wages over all companies broken down by educational level show a differential of around 95 per cent; and what is particularly disturbing is that there has only been a slight narrowing of the initial wage differentials since 1977.

The evidence in Table 3.3 is a clear rebuttal to those who would argue that wage differentials in Japan are due to women's apparent fickleness in changing jobs and thereby losing out on seniority benefits. Even where women work in the same company throughout their adult life the wage gap with men who have a similar amount of education and experience widens from around 7 percentage points to around 30 points. A fraction of the gap would be due to the fact that certain family allowances, which are often part of the wage packet in Japan, are only paid to the so-called 'household head': a practice which in itself is contentious. Another more substantial part of the wage gap in the case of the older workers is that, as we shall see later, long-serving women are usually found in small companies where wages are considerably lower; their relative absence in large companies is arguably evidence of another kind of discrimination. But, even in the case of long-serving women in large companies, their confinement in so-called auxiliary jobs has not permitted them to climb the promotion ladder and associated pay scales in the same way as their male colleagues. The inevitable conclusion is that, despite the legal provisions, pure gender-based wage discrimination, though couched in differently named jobs and positions, does exist in Japan. The extent depends on the age group but in general it would be safe to say that women over the age of 30 years have been suffering up to a 20 per cent discriminatory loss in wages, which is partly due to a denial of promotion opportunities in large companies.

TABLE 3.3 *Wage differentials in Japan by age and education, 1987*
(women's average earnings as a percentage of men's for workers who have been continuously employed in the same company)

Age (years)	under 17	18– 19	20– 24	25– 29	30– 34	35– 39	40– 44	45– 49	50– 54
Left school before 16	95.1		90.5	81.7	76.6	77.6	72.5	69.1	74.2	80.3
Left school between 16 and 18			91.8	90.2	86.5	81.0	77.4	74.4	71.0	68.8

Source: Ministry of Labour, *Fujin Rodo no Jitsujo.*

The next issue concerns the wages which are given to those women who are obliged to leave the labour force during the years when their children are small. In this case it is hard to make a direct comparison, but one can at least calculate differentials for the starting wages for mid-career recruits in different age groups, which are displayed in Table 3.4. The average wages for men and women in their thirties and forties with zero years of service reveal a gap ranging from around 37 to 47 percentage points. Again part of the wage gap is due to middle-aged women entering smaller companies where wages are in any case lower. Another part should be due to the fact that the women have often been absent from the labour force for a few years before joining a company in their thirties, while some of the men have been head-hunted and are partly being rewarded for their experience gained in another company. Nonetheless the number of head-hunted men is relatively few, because large Japanese companies have been loath – at least until recently – to hire men in mid-career. And the conventional wisdom in Japan is that, because of the system of seniority wages, male mid-career recruits must bear some wage penalties; so their average standard wages are less than 70 per cent of what their contemporaries with continuous years of service are earning. In other words women re-entrants are being particularly heavily penalized for interruptions to their participation in the labour force. Indeed the figures for average standard wages reveal that a middle-aged woman who has just re-entered the labour force is on average earning only about 70 to 80 per cent of the reward given to a 20-year-old male youth with an identical educational level who has just changed his place of employment.

TABLE 3.4 *Wage differentials for mid-career recruits in Japan by age and education, 1987*
(women's average earnings as a percentage of men's for workers with zero years of service in the company; standard monthly wages are in yen 1,000)

Age (years)	20–24	25–29	30–34	35–39	40–44	45–49
		Left school before 16				
% differential	64.9	59.0	57.4	52.4	55.2	57.3
Standard wage:						
female	103.4	109.1	109.1	112.0	112.4	116.0
male	159.4	184.8	190.1	213.8	203.5	202.3
		Left school between 16 and 18				
% differential	82.8	72.9	63.0	60.8	57.1	61.7
Standard wage:						
female	123.8	127.0	120.8	124.0	129.7	131.4
male	149.6	174.1	191.6	204.0	227.1	212.9

Source: Ministry of Labour, *Fujin Rodo no Jitsujo.*

Such severe penalties for an almost unavoidable absence from the labour force, during which housekeeping and other skills are honed, should strictly be defined as discriminatory despite arguments, which are sadly common in Japan, about older women being less willing and having a lower aptitude for learning new technical skills when they re-enter the labour force. That argument is refuted by the fact that middle-aged women have shown that they can learn assembling skills; manufacturers have been turning to them as a last resort since younger women prefer to seek office jobs and there is a shortage of male youths looking for factory work. And, incidentally, concerning a woman's aptitude for learning skills, it should not be forgotten that Japan's highly productive electronics industry depends on there being experienced women on the shop floor, where they willingly participate in the knowledge-intensive quality control circles (Chapter 8).

Do women accept discrimination in wages?

The persistence and the extent of the pure wage differentials outlined above seem to imply that Japanese women have been rather passive in accepting discrimination. While that may be true for the majority of women, a few others have taken their individual cases of discrimination to court, often with some success. Court cases have covered not only wage discrimination, but also such issues as differing retirement ages, forced transfers and contract renewals for temporary workers. The first major successes were in the 1960s, when women successfully fought the practices, referred to in Chapter 2, of compelling women to retire at marriage or childbirth.[1]

The gender discrimination may not be immediately apparent, because of a complicated wage scale upon which progress depends on being promoted and because company regulations may formally prohibit sexual discrimination in wages, as in the 1987 case against Shiba Shinyo Bank. None of the seven plaintiffs, who were all aged over 38 years and had been continuously employed by the bank throughout their working lives, had reached the position of deputy branch manager, even though over 90 per cent of their contemporary male colleagues had achieved that position or above. In this case the Tokyo District Court recognized that discrimination against women employees in promotion opportunities had led to differential wages, but its ruling was overturned when the company appealed to the High Court.

Often issues of wage and job discrimination have been linked; the December 1986 ruling against the Japan Iron and Steel Federation made invalid not only the discriminatory wage rises, but also the job classification system, which had ostensibly given the 'main' jobs to male recruits and the 'auxiliary' jobs to women, even though in practice they were doing similar work. The ruling referred to the 1947 Labour Standards Law and Civil Code in reaching its conclusion, since sexual discrimination is admitted to be against 'public order and morals'. The existence of such legislation for over 40 years has not, however, prevented there being the wide wage differentials shown in Tables 3.3 and 3.4, let alone the blatant discrimination revealed in court cases. Despite the courts having accepted that there was discrimination in many cases, companies' policies of providing family allowances to the nominal household head have been ruled acceptable as long as the woman earns less than her husband. On these grounds in January 1989 the Tokyo District Court rejected the claim of four women, who filed a lawsuit against Nissan seeking unpaid family allowances. The women's claim was supported by their husbands, who also work for Nissan, with the argument that the husband supported the first child and the wife the second child.

The attention given by the media and academics to litigation cases does not generally reflect any groundswell of activity by a lot of working women against the discriminatory systems, which have been shown in court cases to be common practice. Therefore, in order to answer the question of why women do accept such conditions, some attention must be paid to labour market discrimination theories of occupational segregation and wage differentials. It would be convenient if we could match the kinds of discrimination outlined above to accepted theories so as to understand in what aspects Japan differs from the West in the treatment accorded to working women. Unfortunately, just as is the case elsewhere, a theory is found to be relevant only to a sub-group of women; and, indeed, no single theory makes a good match with the Japanese situation. Therefore the following brief discussion reveals a mish-mash of theories, each of which provides a partial explanation.

The fact that women are often intermittent members of the labour force may suggest a buffer or substitution theory of employers treating women as a reserve labour force, which can be dispensed with during business downturns. In Japan, however, women have been an integral part of the manufacturing work-force on the shop floor and their position in family businesses in the distribution sector has been unassailable. To the extent that part-time employment is growing (Chapter 6), the position of working women in Japan may appear to be becoming more unstable, but that is really the issue of there being more scope for their terms and conditions of employment to deteriorate rather than that they may lose their jobs altogether. Similarly in Britain during the 1980s, Jane Humphries and Jill Rubery (Jenson *et al*, 1988) have shown how recessionary economic conditions have had a deleterious impact on women's employment, without any decline in their participation rate.

Both of the main institutional models – the internal labour market analysis, which stresses the primacy of a career progression through a single company in determining promotion and relative wages, and the dual labour market analysis, which suggests that women's job search is confined to a segmented, casual or secondary labour market – are particularly applicable to the Japanese case. Because a Japanese male worker over his mid-twenties usually stays with the same employer who grants him periodic seniority payments, labour markets which are internal to each firm predominate. Not only are women as intermittent members of the labour force largely excluded from these important primary labour markets, but also job segregation and wage differentials are thereby apparently justified. The sad thing is that most Japanese women as well as men, employees as well as employers, accept the existence of dual labour markets as only natural. Consequently the usual feedback effects are exacerbated insofar as women believe that there

74

is no reason to aspire to better jobs or to endeavour to be stable employees.

In this way arises the seductive argument that men are only being justly rewarded for their adherence to vocational education and investment in training, whereas women voluntarily choose to enter general education jobs where they need only limited training and can work intermittently. The human capital theory insists that, instead of imposed labour market discrimination, it is simply different levels of accumulated human capital – implying skills acquired through self-sacrifice – which explain occupational segregation and wage differentials. In the case of Japan, however, women are often as well-educated as men when entering their first job, apart from the fact that relatively more have graduated in arts subjects and from two-year colleges. Therefore the sorts of jobs 'voluntarily' chosen by Japanese women are mostly determined by the feedback effect, which in Japan is reinforced by the heavy pressure from society to conform to generally unrealistic notions of a woman's role. Women go along with the pretence; those who are working on the family farm and also taking seasonal part-time jobs outside still often describe themselves as being housewives at home all day.

It is true that young Japanese women often willingly enter jobs, such as nursery caretakers, which will also as a side-benefit train them to be better homemakers; and instead of investing in training for jobs they choose to take cookery and flower-arranging lessons in preparation for marriage. It is at this point in the discussion where the feminist theory of patriarchy may seem especially applicable to Japan. It is certainly indisputable that most Japanese women are accepting and mindful of their homemaking role when considering their career possiblities. Thus men have in some interpretations successfully kept women from competing effectively in the labour market by foisting upon them the extra burden of work at home, where there is an inequitable division of labour. Patriarchy as a power principle in the Japanese home is, however, less clear-cut than elsewhere since it is the wives who usually have complete control over financial matters to the extent that some observers, such as Takie Lebra Sugiyama (1984, p.156), argue that matriarchy governs the domestic sphere. It is also arguable that patriarchy holds sway in Japanese unions where the 'women's divisions' are more like social clubs with a correspondingly low status. Nonetheless Japanese male unionists are presumably just as keen as elsewhere to keep up the pay of women whose jobs are not completely segregated, so that their own wages are not undercut. The problem for unionists who care is that so many Japanese women workers are completely segregated into the peripheral labour markets located in small companies where union activity is almost non-existent.

Duality by company size

Thus clear distinctions depending on the size of a company are one important aspect of dual labour markets which is characteristic of Japan. The Japanese companies investing in Europe are large, successful enterprises whose workers in Japan are better paid and have better employment conditions than workers in the mass of small companies, many of which are in a subcontracting relationship with a large company. It should be mentioned that large companies are able to offer their regular male employees good and stable employment conditions precisely because the small subcontractors' workers, many of whom are women, are taking on the burden of adjustment to changing economic conditions. There are significant wage differentials between workers in large and those in small companies, even though within each company itself there is a certain measure of egalitarianism between white-collar and blue-collar employees.

One paradox of progress concerns the continued duration of this duality between large and small companies in Japan. While the economy was growing rapidly up to the mid-1970s, it was fondly imagined that the related divergence in productivity levels and labour conditions would disappear.

Statistics on wage differentials by size of enterprise, however, do not show signs of a narrowing gap, which has actually become somewhat wider since 1970. Workers in small manufacturing companies with less than 30 employees now earn less than 60 per cent on average of what large company employees receive, whereas in 1970 the differential was 61.8 per cent (*Maitsuki Kinro Tokei Chosa*). In the case of the tiniest companies – mostly restaurants and shops – with four or less employees, the workers earn only half, including bonuses, of the wages given to workers in the largest companies with 1,000 or more employees; and this substantial disparity has been tending to widen (Ministry of Labour, 1985b). Since women account for well over 50 per cent of the total employees in these tiny companies, their low wages depress the average wage for all women, which thereby contributes significantly to the wide differential with men's wages.

In addition the wage differential by company size is particularly wide for women, partly because the women working in small companies are more likely to have re-entered employment after bearing children. Furthermore, the entry-wage differentials by sex are significantly wider within smaller companies. In 1988 a Japan Recruit Research Company survey of 1,040 companies found that almost one-third of the companies with less than 99 employees gave different initial salaries to women and men hired for the same job and with the same educational levels; while just over 17 per cent of all the companies surveyed had discriminatory initial salaries (*The Japan Times*, 6 April 1988). Of course, those companies operating gender-based differential wage systems for new recruits must either be violating the Labour Standards Law and Equal Employment Opportunity Law or else evading the laws by imposing different job titles and treating women as casual employees.

These discrepancies in working conditions and wages between large and small companies are highly significant in considering the position of working women because women's long-term employment opportunities are mostly

77

found in small companies. Whereas only about one-quarter of the work-force of large manufacturing companies is female, the corresponding figure for small enterprises with less than 100 employees is over 40 per cent. Moreover, women working in the smallest companies show considerable staying power; they have given on average 8.5 years of service which is only 2.4 years less than the average for their male colleagues. The relative attachment of women employees to the largest companies is much lower; on average they give barely 7.5 years of service, whereas the average male employee of a major company has been there for over 16 years. One other remarkable feature of the data is that in the case of 'individual enterprises', or self-employment, the average number of years of continuous employment for both women and men is almost the same at around 11.3 years.[2]

Thus middle-aged women are predominantly working in the smaller companies, while the pretty young women are expected to provide a 'bright' atmosphere for a few years in the offices of the large companies. The low pay offered to employees in coffee shops and other parts of the service sector means that such jobs are almost always available for women who want to work on a casual basis. The silver lining is that small companies in the service sector permit labour mobility and provide plenty of opportunity for women to re-enter the labour force: characteristics which are almost totally lacking in the case of employment in Japan's large companies. But this kind of opportunity could also be interpreted as indicating that the small companies survive by exploiting the woman's position in the home, because she is willing to accept low wages in return for a limited amount of flexibility in hours.

Some working women whom I know well are doing assembly work in a typical small local factory, where the output of components sometimes overflows and has to be counted and packed in the adjacent public alley-way. The women are badly paid and have to work in a cramped and run-down looking building. But they feel free to move on to other jobs if conditions at their present place of employment worsen and they can usually leave work promptly at five o'clock; so they are cheerful. Their attitude is much less subservient to the management than the smart young women working in the banks and in the offices of large companies and indeed their whole appearance – being casually dressed – differs. At the same time, the replies of women working in small companies to my questionnaire indicated that their jobs are monotonous and tiring with little or no job satisfaction. Even where there is a union, they do not feel that it can improve their job conditions nor further the interests of women workers. This perception may merely reflect the fact that unions in small companies rarely have much clout; it is only large company unions which are powerful in Japan.

Partly because of the low starting salaries at small companies and their lack of prestige, women graduates put the major companies at the top of the lists of where they would like to work, even though they will have to take difficult decisions about which promotion track to join. The favourites include travel agencies and airline companies, large foreign companies like IBM and the securities companies dealing in stocks and shares, such as Nomura Securities: choices which are explained by the glamour associated with travel and the supposedly better promotion prospects for women working in foreign companies and the securities companies (*The Japan Times*, 3 September 1987). In particular the media have been giving much attention to the women who are achieving managerial positions in the securities companies. This attention seems to be part of an illusion, since the research cited earlier in this chapter indicates that proportionately such women are very few. It is true that, unlike other major Japanese companies, Daiwa and other securities companies are becoming quite enthusiastic about employing middle-aged former housewives, because many of the customers are the housewives who manage the household finances, but their position is merely that of glorified saleswomen. Nomura Securities employs 2,500 women to encourage women by telephone and at the door to buy their unit trusts, while Fuji and Sumitomo Banks are employing more middle-aged part-time women to go by bicycle and on foot on the same mission, according to a gleeful report in *The Economist* (13 June 1987).

Despite the fact that women graduates are becoming more mindful of their promotion prospects, women working for the major companies are more likely to leave on marriage or childbirth than those employed in smaller companies, under what is euphemistically known as 'early retirement' or *kata-tataki* (Chapter 2). Indeed one well-qualified woman, who had been employed by one of Japan's largest securities companies, told me that on marrying a colleague she felt compelled to leave and look for employment in a much smaller financial services company, even though there was no longer a formal system of retirement at marriage. It is ironic that the major company was willing to lose her skills to a small competitor, because presumably it was felt that home and family considerations would intrude if a husband worked with his wife, thereby upsetting the supposed 'harmony' of the workplace, upon which so much value is placed in Japan.

The existence of a dual industrial structure has important implications for our present study. One is that unless the large companies come up with better schemes for re-employing the well-educated, middle-aged women who are increasingly re-entering the labour force, their concentration in the low-paid jobs found in the smaller companies is only going to increase so that not only are wage differentials by sex likely to widen, but also valuable labour resources will have been wasted. Another implication is how the Japanese companies investing in Britain and Ireland are managing without the presence of their reliable subcontractors.

Subcontractors and Japanese overseas investment

The above discussion has indicated how important is the distinction in company size to Japanese working women's wages and conditions of employment. At present the employment conditions between large and small companies in Britain are not so distinct as in Japan, although the relaxing of minimum wage legislation is going to exacerbate any differentials. It is worth noting as well that small companies and their associated casual labour markets are becoming a feature of employment for British women. Thus the study of Japan's dual industrial structure does contain lessons for the position of women in Britain's labour markets.

And there is another important implication relevant to the direct overseas investment of Japanese companies, which concerns the subcontracting relationship of small companies to a major company. While manufacturing companies remain in Japan, they can depend upon the subcontractors to deliver parts according to an agreed and tight schedule. Once the major company is having to deal with British suppliers, however, it can no longer take up an authoritarian position. The question of whether the relationship is truly hierarchical or merely benevolent has been taken up by Ronald Dore, who argues quite convincingly that there is an important component of goodwill.[3]

Such goodwill, however, is not easily transplanted to different cultures. Those readers who saw the BBC documentaries on Komatsu in the North East (August 1987) will have had a good picture of the divergence in expectations and misunderstandings on both sides. Some of the most tense scenes occurred in the subcontractor workplace, where Komatsu was sending its engineers on quality checks and setting very tight delivery schedules. It is arguable that any reluctance on the part of Japanese companies to invest in Britain and Ireland is due much more to worries about obtaining reliable supplies of parts than about the labour force, which is more easily moulded to Japanese ways (Chapter 7).

Since the Japanese managers are accustomed to being able in Japan to lay down the law with their subcontracting companies, whose employees must bear the brunt of economic vicissitudes and lower wages, what may happen in

Britain is that the presence of major Japanese companies leads to a dualistic relationship with local suppliers, whereby the employees of the Japanese company are treated as a well-paid elite, while conditions for those working in the local supplying company are unsatisfactory. This can only be speculation for the present, but at least, unlike Japan where the majority of working women is found in small companies, the division between working conditions in large and small companies in Britain would not also be a sexual one; in Britain and Ireland it is women who are predominantly employed on the shop floor of the major Japanese companies, apart from automobile and heavy machinery firms like Nissan and Komatsu, while the supplying companies probably have a more balanced mix of female and male employees.

Alternative working structures for women

The conditions for most Japanese women employed in the formal sector today fall into one of two categories: either they work for a short time for a large company where there is little hope of them being promoted or they are bound to work on a casual basis for low wages in a small company. In both cases they in essence form part of a secondary labour market – the one exception being the few brave women who embark upon the executive track in spite of being discouraged from doing so by the threat of disruption to their future family life. All the kinds of duality that have appeared in this chapter operate both within and between companies. Many academics in Japan see such entrenched duality as merely indicative of the nature of the job market rather than evidence of discrimination against working women. Rose Carter and Lois Dilatush (Lebra *et al*, 1976, p.86) accept that there is a degree of exploitation but argue that since women want to be feminine they collude with men in their own exploitation. While both of these contentions contain some truth, they view Japanese society as a static entity where tradition is always paramount. Nor do they explain how the job market is formed and how women's perceptions of themselves are governed by the existing conditions with a resulting feedback effect. In what way could traditional values of women being in the home come into play in the agricultural sector – the major economic sector right up to the early twentieth century? Farm women have always pulled their weight in the rice fields and even more so now that the men are finding work in conveniently located factories.

It is clear, therefore, that the notion – popular even among women commentators themselves – that Japanese women have only a weak attachment to the labour force because of the persistence of traditional values is quite mistaken. As we have seen, the women working in small companies, despite being paid less than their male colleagues and being treated as casual employees, on average stay continuously with the same company for almost as long as the men; and in the informal sector they are active in looking for entrepreneurial opportunities.

Indeed the informal sector in Japan is highly receptive to women's skills; and so one solution to the issue of duality in the formal sector is for women to separate themselves off completely. Reiko Okutani, who is president of two hugely successful personnel dispatch (i.e. temp) companies which she established herself, has advocated in various interviews (*Tokyo Business Today*, November 1987 and *Tokyo Journal*, April 1987) that women should become entrepreneurs:

> Avoid the stress caused by male co-workers and form your own company . . . Women will create the new system: new values, new business know-how. Male-oriented society is changing, coming to a dead end. They get fresh air from women's ideas . . . That [human service] is what does it; not hanging expensive art objects in the guest lounge . . . We have to answer to high expectations. Women expect us to be beautiful. They see us doing men's work, while also being feminine. We have a responsibility as role models.

And, indeed, one intriguing aspect of Reiko Okutani's main temp company is that it offers complete instruction on how to serve tea, exchange business cards and bow properly. There is some irony in the persistence of the feminine ideal among successful women entrepreneurs in Japan. But that is not really surprising since such women are really just playing their best card according to society's tenets. Of the five women executives recently elected for the first time to the Doyukai – an organization of top Japanese business leaders – all but one had set up their own businesses in fashion, education and personnel dispatch. Nor need women aspire so high in order to be successful in running their own company. As has been shown earlier, there is a well-established tradition in Japan of women running their own tutoring services, whether it be in the Japanese arts of calligraphy, tea ceremony and flower arranging or in school subjects.

The information economy is also providing a number of other opportunities for women working informally from home, without necessarily setting up their own business; one woman who appears to be a full-time mother is actually juggling all her commitments so as to fit in six hours a day of transcribing tapes. She told me that she had worked at times for a variety of small companies, but her present work, though tedious, yields better pay and much more independence.

Thus the fact that women are often excluded from the main internal labour markets and have to position themselves in a separate labour market need not necessarily be a cause for despair, especially in Japan where membership of a major company as a regular employee can in any case be suffocating. Women's participation in the secondary labour markets, which extend from small companies and family businesses to temporary work and to self-employment, takes on many forms, some of which are indicative of exploitation and a casualization of work, while others enhance a woman's independence and mobility. In the next three chapters, we shall see why women as mothers take on work in these casual and informal sectors, before we return to the issue of their employment in major Japanese companies.

Notes

(1) Robins-Mowry (1983), pages 184 to 187, introduces cases which occurred in the 1960s. In addition many court cases which took place during the 1970s are usefully summarized and analysed in Cook and Hayashi (1980), pages 35 to 70. For more recent cases see *The Japan Times* 5 December 1986, 19 June 1987 and 28 January 1989.

(2) These figures have been obtained from: (i) *The White Paper on Small and Medium Enterprises in Japan, 1987*, (ii) National Tax Agency Administration data quoted in Keizai Koho Center, *Japan 1989: An International Comparison*, and iii. *Fujin Rodo no Jitsujo*, 1988, Table 13.

(3) Okimoto and Rohlen (1988), pages 90 to 99. Dore believes that 'relational contracting' between major firms and their subcontractors enables there to be risk sharing, security, dutifulness, friendliness and economic efficiency.

4 | Economic versus social pressures

We have seen in Chapter 2 how the rate at which Japanese women engaged in work, other than housework, fell during the 1960s and early 1970s; now the participation rate is on the rise again as more middle-aged women re-enter the labour force. There is a popular image of female Japanese employees as being unmarried 'office ladies' or factory girls. In fact labour force survey data show that only just over 30 per cent of women employees have never been married. Why is there then the misconception that Japanese wives do not usually do paid work? The pretence of Japanese society is that mothers wholly devote themselves to their children and Western observers have often accepted this social veneer as the reality. In fact the reasons why married women are working for pay are similar to those for British women: mostly because of economic imperatives, plus a dose of boredom at being at home with less to do once the children are at school.

Furthermore, many Japanese mothers of pre-school children are doing paid work; 34.1 per cent of women with at least one child aged under six years are economically active, one-third of whom are in family businesses or self-employment, while the remainder are in outside employment, according to an official 1987 survey of workers, *Shuugyo Kozo Kihon Chosa*, carried out by the Management and Coordination Agency. The comparable figure for British mothers of pre-school children aged under five years was just 28 per cent in 1984 (Equal Opportunities Commission, 1987). Moreover, unlike Britain where the number of children in a family is inversely related to a woman's economic activity, in Japan the rate of activity is higher for mothers with two or three children than for those with one child. Evidently the scarcity of family businesses, which are more compatible with child-rearing, is one reason for the lower percentage in Britain. Still, part-time work, which is also meant to be convenient for mothers, accounts for a much higher proportion of working British mothers with small children; a direct comparison is not possible, but the data show that part-timers account for 78.6 per cent of working British mothers compared to 31.0 per cent of employed Japanese mothers. We need to find out, therefore, why Japanese mothers are more likely to be economically active than British mothers – even among the 66 per cent of those with pre-schoolers who are not working, close to 59 per cent would like to have some kind of paid work, if the conditions were right.

Low living conditions in a wealthy country

The economic imperatives for mothers to work arise because there are no longer the improvements in living standards to match the expectations of post-war generations, who had up until the mid-1970s seen continuous growth and quite radical changes in living and working conditions. It may come as a surprise to hear that – in the parlance of economists – real discretionary disposable income is stagnating in Japan when the yen is riding so high and high-tech, made-in-Japan goods are overwhelming many world markets. Actually the per capita GNP figures in dollars are quite misleading. Most obviously, to use the declining dollar as a standard suggests that Japanese incomes are rising, when in yen terms there is much less of a change. Since 1974 the growth in disposable income has been constrained by higher taxes and social security payments. And in some years, because of rising mortgage repayments, discretionary income, which is what is left over for consumption, has actually fallen.

Then there are the consumption factors associated with rising living standards which lead to more goods being obtained from the market economy rather than from the household economy and also to luxuries becoming 'necessities' (Chapter 2). In the economic data this phenomenon appears as an increasing marginal propensity to consume out of total income. And expenditure on real necessities in Japan – in particular food and housing – takes a far larger portion of pay packets than in most other OECD countries. Therefore, scepticism is required when any comparison of living standards based simply on converting wages at prevailing exchange rates is made. One better way is to compare purchasing power, which takes account of the relatively high price of foodstuffs and energy in Japan. A simple comparison of wage levels suggests that Japanese workers are receiving 25 per cent more than British workers, but when the cost of living is considered the purchasing power of the average Japanese wage is between 15 and 20 per cent less than the the purchasing power of British wages (Economic Planning Agency, 1988).

A Westerner who stays in a hotel in central Tokyo, where the service and surroundings are impeccable, may not appreciate how low is the standard of housing for the average Japanese family. In Tokyo and Osaka most young families live in apartments which are not much bigger than a bed-sitting room with the tiny kitchen being part of the entrance-way. There may be the sort of unit-bath found in a caravan, but often the family have to troop off daily to the public bath house. One compelling motive for married women to work, therefore, would be in order to save for the hefty deposit required for obtaining a mortgage. Once Japanese workers do become home-owners, the amount paid for a tiny dwelling is usually equivalent to more than five times their annual income. The major difference in expenditure between a Japanese household where the wife works and one with only one wage-earner is that the average amount going towards saving or towards repaying a housing loan is 77 per cent higher. In striking contrast, households with only one wage-earner are paying on average relatively more in rent, which indicates that a working couple is more likely to be owning their own home.[1]

In this respect, as in most others concerning economic motivation for working, there is little difference between Japan and the West. In Britain as well, households where the wife is working are spending about 23 per cent more on housing (*Family Expenditure Survey*). But there is one important contrast. A young Irish wife working at NEC told me that her primary objective for working was to help pay off the house mortgage. She would be envied by the young Japanese wives in the major cities of Japan for whom the dream of buying a small apartment in the late 1980s is likely to remain unrealized, while land prices continue to inflate rapidly. Therefore, since for many families to save for a deposit would be a hopeless task, wives have often merely said that they are working to save for a rainy day – in case of accident or sickness – or for their children's education. But since life-insurance cover is so extensive in Japan and the public welfare safety net is now fairly wide, I do not believe that the 'rainy day' explanation for Japanese households' high savings rates any longer holds much water, although people may still feel motivated that way. It may be that the women respondents to my questionnaire did not wish to plead relative poverty as a reason for working, since in Japan around 90 per cent of people believe that they belong to the middle class.

Nonetheless, since the mid-1980s middle-aged women in particular have been tending to feel 'worse off' in each successive year. This may seem surprising since average real incomes have tended to increase with the tight labour market and the resurgence in economic growth during the late 1980s. The average, however, conceals a growing sense of inequality as just those women in one stratum are able to satisfy their more sophisticated and diversified needs, leaving the rest to wonder how they too can become up-market consumers. In urban areas, in particular, housing costs have risen sharply along with land prices. The general consequence of rising house and stock prices has been growing inequalities in asset holdings and a diminishing feeling of affluence, despite Japan's economic power.[2]

At the same time as the children are growing, not only does a two- or three-room dwelling become even more inadequate, but also education costs rise, especially at the college-age level. Almost all Japanese families feel compelled to lay out considerable sums on attendance at cram schools because of the competitive pressure for their offspring to do well in the rigorous examinations. Admiration for the high rate of attendance at non-compulsory education in Japan – 94 per cent of the relevant age group, including girls, go to senior high school and almost 40 per cent to college, as compared respectively to about 52 per cent and 22 per cent in the UK – must be tempered by concern for the strain it puts on the family budget, especially when the offspring are attending private high schools and universities. And when it comes to bringing increasing expenditure in line with stagnating incomes, it is Japanese wives who bear the burden of family budgeting.

Financial responsibility but little earning power

It is indeed true that in most cases the Japanese husband receives only an allotted amount of 'pocket money', once he has handed over his pay packet to his wife – a custom which is followed by about 80 per cent of Japanese couples, compared to about 30 per cent of British. This common practice does give the woman some financial power, but it also imposes upon her the anxiety of coping with a growing family's needs. And while the wife's financial power causes her stress, her actual power within the family is judged to be less than elsewhere. An international comparative survey (Prime Minister's Office, 1983) found that whereas in Britain about two-thirds of wives think themselves either to be the final decision maker or to hold joint power with the husband, less than one-third of Japanese wives believe that they have similar power, despite their financial control.

Japanese women are also caught in the net of devotion to their family, while trying to make ends meet. The same survey reported that over 70 per cent of Japanese women believe that a woman should centre her life on her family – implying sacrificing herself for her husband and children – while just 10 per cent of British women were so inclined. The wide disparity in the figures suggests that the translation of the question and its meaning within different cultures could have led to responses which are not really comparable; and many women reply in line with what they believe to be society's dictates. One Japanese woman scholar, Sumiko Iwao, quoted in White (1987, p.129), has suggested that women took on a strategy of self-abnegation and sacrifice as a way of coping with constant adversity and crises on the small, struggling farms. This strategy to better the long-term good of the family carried over as a conviction to the industrialized era. Indeed there is a prized cultural theme of *kuro* (hardship or worries) among women in Japan, which has been eloquently conveyed by Takie Lebra Sugiyama (1984).

But the self-sacrificing nature of Japanese women should not be seen as culturally unique. Working mothers in the USA also think 'to do for someone else is acceptable, to do for ourselves is not', according to Barbara Berg (1986, p.210) in her survey of working mothers. And indeed almost every mother anywhere makes sacrifices for her family. It is rather that Japanese society places a particularly high value on the wife bearing the burden of coping with adversity; and this role has, if anything, been intensified as men have abandoned the traditional household economy and become wedded to the company as 'salary men'. The men then seem to have neither time nor energy to concern themselves with family matters, especially the household finances. One particularly ironic result is that, though banks have been noted in the past for preferring to employ only full-time regular workers and to encourage their older women employees to quit, banks and securities companies are increasing their employment offers to women, as was mentioned in Chapter 3, so as to gear their savings accounts towards housewives.

There is then a severe and stressful anomaly. The wife controls the finances and bears the responsibility for economic adversity, but she has very little earning power herself. Because, as we have seen in the preceding chapter, middle-aged women who re-enter the labour force are generally found in small companies where they earn low wages, the housewife who is worried about the family budget knows that her potential earnings would not make much of an impact. The average amount over all households contributed to household income by working wives, though it has been rising slowly every year since 1980, is still only just 8.3 per cent of total household income (*Kakei Chosa*), whereas in Britain comparable *Family Expenditure Survey* data show that the figure is over 16 per cent. Even if we take the average only in families where both partners do actually work the Japanese wife's earnings are still fairly low – just over 20 per cent of the family income compared to an average contribution from British wives with no dependent children of 29 per cent of family income and almost 25 per cent where there are dependent children. Such averages may appear to be surprisingly low in Britain when we learn from tax returns that 13 per cent of working wives in 1985/86 earned at least as much as their husbands (Equal Opportunities Commission, 1988). Evidently those wives were the exception; most British mothers are in low-income, part-time jobs, which pulls down the overall average contribution from working wives to a figure which is not that much more than in Japan.

Other reasons for wives to work

Because the amount they can contribute to household income is so meagre, many Japanese women refuse to accept low-paid jobs, while responding to surveys that they would like to be employed. The wonder indeed is that a working wife continues to be employed in Japan when the rewards are so small and, moreover, clothing, food and child-care expenses are expected to increase somewhat with her employment. It is worth noting, however, that food, clothing, and leisure-related expenses are not, on average, dramatically higher in households where the wife works, which is contrary to the popular image of the working wife just spending her earnings on a better lifestyle. Yet when I have asked Japanese wives why they have chosen to work, one of the reasons which is often cited is to improve the family's lifestyle by providing additional money for clothes, leisure activities and the children's education, rather than actually to support the family, let alone just helping with necessary household expenses. The man is still looked upon as being the major breadwinner, because middle-aged women have very low expectations of their own earning power.

A larger survey of housewives who wanted to work (*Nihon Keizai Shimbun*, 14 June 1988), found that the two major reasons were to have their own money which they could use freely and to widen their network of acquaintances or, in a more direct translation: 'to broaden their human relationships'. (The reason concerning human relationships – along with a desire to improve one's skills – was most cited by university graduates.) Similarly, in Prime Minister's Office surveys (1982 and 1987) when housewives who wished to have a job were asked their reasons, over 30 per cent wanted to broaden their perspective on life or gain friends. In general, women believe that the major beneficial effects of a woman's employment are her broadened outlook and her life becoming more worthwhile. Lower percentages ostensibly refer to factors such as improving living standards.

Evidently for a working mother not only does economic necessity play a part, but also a desire to prove herself as being somewhat self-reliant, which goes quite beyond the popular image of the meek Japanese wife. Thus an earnest young woman engineer at NEC with a small baby preferred not to tick any of the five suggested responses – ranging from paying for necessities to being bored at home – to my question of why she was working and instead gave her own response: 'in order to enrich my life'. Indeed research work and a child were not enough to satisfy her; she explained that time was the main constraint on her wish to do more. It is hard to get a clear picture of motivation from individual responses which vary so much. Consequently, one Japanese man, Yukiro Watanabe, writing in *The Wheel Extended* (1984, No.1), has speculated that the reason more women want outside jobs is because they feel threatened by the intrusion into the home of men who are no longer so devoted to the company now that they are no longer automatically on the 'escalator' promotion system, whereby when companies were growing rapidly almost all regular workers could be assured of a steady promotion path in line with seniority.

At the same time a more comprehensive Ministry of Labour survey, *Pato Taimu Rodo Jittai Chosa* (1985a) on why married women are working, which covered neither the few elite professional women nor housewives dreaming about the social glamour associated with an occupation, but rather the mass of women already working in unskilled jobs at part-time rates, shows that about 67 per cent are working in order to supplement the household budget, while 25 per cent work for purchasing cosmetics and clothes and to have money for spending on leisure activities. Similarly Management and Coordination Agency data (1987) show that income, rather than gaining skills, killing time, or widening one's social experience, is the main motivation for the majority of middle-aged women who are re-entering employment or looking for work. These conflicting replies suggest that a woman's response all depends on how the question is phrased and what is her present situation.

Therefore, in order to judge the relative strengths of different motivations, it would be more revealing to look at changes in responses over time as in Table 4.1. The categories are rather different and the questions were asked of those actually entering part-time jobs, but the overall trend is clear. There has been a perceptible change even in a period as short as three years towards women working in order to ensure a reasonable household income and now almost 70 per cent cite that purpose rather than raising living standards or killing time.

TABLE 4.1 *Why Japanese women opt to work as part-timers (percentage of women starting in part-time work)*

	Main household income	Supplement income	Raise living standards	Use spare time	Other
1984	11.1	54.3	14.8	10.1	9.7
1987	16.4	52.3	11.0	13.4	6.9

Source: Ministry of Labour, *Koyodoko Chosa.*

Although some widows and divorced women may be entering part-time employment in order to provide the main source of household income, the prevailing wage and social systems in Japan hardly permit a mother to be financially independent all on her own. This fact is recognized in the government public welfare measures for fatherless families, which include support payments for dependent children and occupational training and subsidies to companies which employ single mothers. It is worth mentioning that there are relatively few single-mother households in Japan because of the continued stability of marriage as an institution; only about 5.5 per cent of Japanese households with children aged under 18 years of age were headed by a single parent in 1985, compared to about 14 per cent in Britain.[3]

Divorced Japanese women are noted for being resourceful and strong-minded and there are plenty of opportunities for widows to act as individual entrepreneurs in teaching or in operating small retailers. Even so, I know relatively few mothers in Japan who are working as the prime source of household finances. Those who are divorced have either set up their own businesses or are nurses, whose employment is secure; of those who are married, I have known one who is a teacher and another who works long hours at a small company while their husbands finish their postgraduate studies. In both cases the husband was then primarily responsible for taking the child to the public day nursery, so he was not taking total care of the child himself. In contrast the women I spoke to in Britain and Ireland included some who were working in major Japanese manufacturing companies while their husbands were unemployed and looking after the children or were studying. Thus these women looked upon themselves as being the main bread-winner and they tended to tick every response to my question on why they were working, including that of continuing their career and becoming more skilled. In fact these women were notable for their sense of ambition and their positive acceptance of their role as the main source of household income.

Even in the major companies of the electronics industry, (to which we shall turn in the detailed studies in Chapters 8 and 9), where most of the women are working full-time, much lower proportions of Japanese women than British are working mainly to support themselves and their families, as can be judged from Table 4.2. It is not, therefore, surprising that Japanese women seem on the surface to have a lower degree of attachment to the labour force since they do not feel that the family fortunes depend wholly upon them.

TABLE 4.2 *Why women are working in Japanese and British electronics companies*
(percentage of women respondents to 1985 survey carried out by unions)

'I work mainly to support myself and my family'

	Strongly agree	Agree	Not sure	Disagree	Strongly disagree	No response
Japan	28.4	39.5	14.1	10.9	5.0	2.1
Britain	49.6	28.9	14.3	4.4	0.3	2.5

Source: Denki Roren no Chosa Jiho, No.212.

Attitudes to working mothers

Partly because relatively few Japanese women are the main breadwinner, people tend to foster the illusion that 'jobs are for men and home is for women', in the face of the reality of working mothers. There has been, over time, a dramatic decline in the proportion agreeing with such a statement, but even now over 50 per cent of men find the notion agreeable. One can only hope that the fairly radical, but still insufficient, change in attitudes shown in Figure 4.1 continues to gather pace. It is particularly noteworthy that although the proportions of women and of men agreeing with the statement were similar in the early 1970s, there are now relatively far fewer women (36.6 per cent of those surveyed) than men (51.7 per cent) who support the notion that women should be at home. Similarly, newspaper polls show a gradual reduction in the proportion believing that women should concentrate on housekeeping and child care.[4]

FIGURE 4.1 *'Men should be at work; women should be at home' – Japan*
(percentage of respondents who agree with the statement)

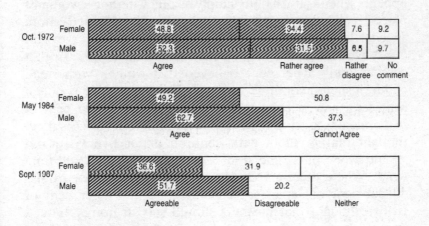

Source: Prime Minister's Office, *Public Opinion Survey on Women*

One hopeful sign may be that the older the respondent, the more likely is agreement with the asymmetric illusion of woman's place as being invariably in the home, so one might expect today's 20-year-olds to continue to be better aware of the reality of working women. On the other hand today's youths may begin to harbour the illusion themselves as they get older. Indeed it is quite disturbing that when high-school children in Japan, including those whose mothers are working, were asked whether they agree with the notion of a woman's place being in the home, only just over 30 per cent disagreed. The issue is whether those schoolchildren were perhaps just rather peeved that their own mothers were working, without understanding all the reasons or the alternatives. Indeed, the result could be put the other way to argue that, despite some possible disruption of the smooth running of a household because of a mother's work, more than 30 per cent of the schoolchildren welcomed the fact that their mothers were employed. Evidently the illusion of a mother being comfortably at home is rather attractive, but even some schoolchildren recognize that the reality is different.

Indeed a clear divergence between what Japanese society commends as an illusion and what people really think appears when, rather than simply asking whether a woman's place is in the home, the question is phrased more specifically and less dogmatically in the same surveys to query whether and when women should have jobs. In that case around 15 per cent believed that women with small children should continue to work. This percentage is only a little less than in Britain where only about 17 per cent of respondents to the *British Social Attitudes 1987* survey thought that mothers with children under five years old should work part time and 3 per cent favoured full-time work. Where there are children in their early teens, around 30 per cent of Japanese respondents and 19 per cent of British thought that mothers should stay at home. Indeed only a quarter of the women in one Japanese survey argue that 'the social concept that men work outside while women keep house has remained intact'. Again when Japanese women are specifically asked about obstacles to their careers, just over 15 per cent cite a lack of understanding on the part of family members, which suggests that the 'social concept' does not in practice prevail.

A rephrasing of the question by another major newspaper (*Mainichi Shimbun*, 29 May 1986) suggests that any resistance to wives working has fallen considerably since 1975. In agreement with the statement that wives should not work unless there are economic reasons were about 10 per cent of women respondents and 20 per cent of men. And when the question was asked by the Prime Minister's Office about when women should stop and start working, we see a fairly dramatic change between 1972 and 1987. At the beginning of the 1970s when the 'women at home' movement was at its peak only 51 per cent thought women should continue to work always or return after a period of child-rearing. Now, however, the proportion is almost 70 per cent.[5]

TABLE 4.3 *Views of when women should stay at home – international comparison*, 1982
(surveyed women aged between 20 and 60 years)

Countries	Number of surveyed persons	Better for women not to have occupations	Better to have an occupation until marriage	Better to have an occupation until birth	Better to continue working even after birth	Better to leave work on the occasion of birth and to have an occupation again after children have grown up	No comment
	persons	%	%	%	%	%	%
Japan	1,294	6.9	14.2	11.7	18.0	43.5	5.7
Philippines	1,200	3.6	23.3	9.9	37.6	21.2	4.4
USA	1,200	1.1	3.3	7.1	42.6	38.8	7.3
Sweden	1,220	0.2	0.6	4.8	55.0	35.0	4.5
West Germany	1,333	0.8	5.9	13.6	22.8	52.7	4.1
UK	1,224	0.7	1.1	9.6	19.5	61.8	7.3

Source: Prime Minister's Office. *Fujin Mondai ni kansuru Kokusai Hikaku Chosa*

Nonetheless any change in society's attitudes appears to be quite gradual and potentially reversible. Japanese attitudes in the early 1980s were still strikingly conservative compared with the West, as the sum of the first three columns of Table 4.3 testifies. The proportions of women believing that women should stay at home always after having children was only 11 per cent in Britain, but 33 per cent in Japan, which was odd since it was in Britain that child allowances are paid to all families in order to encourage mothers not to re-enter the labour force, whereas in Japan allowances are only paid to low-income families. The fact that child allowances in Britain have fallen in real terms has evidently negated their desired effect of keeping mothers at home. Meanwhile the absence of governmental child allowances in Japan is partly rectified by men's wages usually including various kinds of family and housing allowances and by fairly high tax allowances for dependents. Trade unions negotiating lay-offs follow the criteria that unmarried employees and women with employed husbands should be laid off first, because their concern is with maintaining the 'family wage' for married men.

Despite the evidence of conservatism in Japan in Table 4.3, Mariko Bando (1986, p.46) argues that a greater recognition of women's contribution in Japanese society and a corresponding change in attitudes is inevitable, because the role of women is bound to grow in importance following upon the Equal Employment Opportunity Law. But one wonders whether legislation can guide social attitudes so easily. The low percentage of British people who believe men are the breadwinners is not the result of legislation, but of the rapid increase in the number of single-parent families and of unemployed men – both of whom are relatively scarce in Japan. It is worth remarking, moreover, that partly as a result of government action there does appear from the *British Social Attitudes 1987* survey to have been a change in attitudes in Britain during the 1980s – just as there has been in the opposite direction in Japan – with the result that another large-scale international survey would almost certainly reveal a closer correspondence between Japanese and British attitudes than appears in Table 4.3. The Conservative government in Britain has, according to Jill Rubery and Roger Tarling (Rubery, ed., 1988, p.100), led the way as part of its endeavours to place strict controls on public expenditure:

> These financial objectives have been bolstered by ideological objectives to return more of the burden of income support and physical care to the family, and, by implication, to encourage women to concentrate on domestic labour.

Consequently British attitudes are highly ambivalent and appear to be becoming more conservative. Women in Britain, who had embarked on a career before having children, have told me that whichever decision they took had to be justified and they were left feeling guilty in any case – whether for temporarily abandoning their career or for leaving their children in day care. Indeed one striking result of the British attitudes survey was that even where the married respondents were actually from dual-income homes, still over 70 per cent felt that mothers of children under five years old should not go out to work. Some contrary evidence appears from a 1988 McCann-Erickson survey of Britons aged between 15 and 25 years (*The Guardian Weekly*, 21 May 1989). A more liberal attitude towards the general question of whether a woman's place is in the home is evident, since now only 15 per cent compared to a quarter in 1977 are in agreement; but over 50 per cent still think it is better to have a husband earning and a wife at home with the children. In any case the attitudes of present-day youths are not really a reliable guide to what they will be thinking when they are in their thirties. The fact that these kinds of questions keep on being asked is in itself indicative of a lack of change in society's basic attitude concerning working mothers.

But whatever are the ostensible attitudes towards mothers working, Japan is similar to Britain in that the proportion of married women in the labour force has become fairly high.

CARL A. RUDISILL LIBRARY
LENOIR-RHYNE COLLEGE

Indeed there is a remarkable correspondence between the data for Japan and Britain for mothers whose youngest child has left primary school; in both countries two-thirds of the mothers are actually working, according to the sources cited at the beginning of this chapter. Ireland may be the exception where the scarcity of jobs, church teachings and the continued role of agriculture have kept women at home or on the farms. But, just as in the rural areas of Japan, that does not mean that women are not working. Irish mothers are kept well occupied in work on the family farm or in casual work in small factories, while the grandmother looks after the children. When I have talked with mothers on farms in Ireland I am often struck by the similarities with farming women in Japan, especially because in both cases there was a sudden rise in living standards in the 1960s and 1970s, which has now tapered off and left women with aspirations which can no longer be fully satisfied.

Discouraged workers

There is a strange anomaly in what I have written above. I have suggested that financial considerations coupled with the desire of Japanese women to broaden their social contacts and kill time are increasingly leading them to want to work; just as their mothers were obliged to do so in the 1950s. Yet, as we have seen in Chapter 3, their presence in the labour force is still peripheral insofar as they are usually in unstable and badly paid jobs, as though they were standing on the fringes. Moreover, many women refrain from actively entering the labour force altogether, even though they would if they felt that they could do so. Nor does this sizeable group of discouraged workers include those who cannot work because of 'family responsibilities'. Indeed, as will be seen in the following chapter, day-care facilities for small children in Japan are relatively plentiful and of a fairly high quality.

Discouraged workers are usually defined as those who want to work but have given up looking for a job either because of personal factors, such as believing that their age or skills are inappropriate, or because of job market factors, such as an already high and persistent level of unemployment. In most OECD countries the majority of discouraged workers are women, but Japan stands out in Table 4.4 as having particularly high proportions of women who want a job, but who are not defined as unemployed. Part of the reason for discouraged workers in Japan being such a high percentage compared to the unemployment rate lies in a probable underestimate of the unemployed, for whom, as mentioned in Chapter 2, the definition is very stringent. There would also be differences in how discouraged workers are defined in different countries, but still the fact of the overwhelmingly high proportion for discouraged Japanese women must be significant.

The percentage of women in Japan who are neither working nor want a job – the real ladies of leisure and the elderly – is lower than in Britain. Moreover Japanese women who say that they want a job and are available for work are far more numerous than the women who are officially unemployed: around five times as many. Thus it is not job market factors, but a lack of appropriate jobs along with personal and social considerations which are mostly discouraging Japanese women from actively seeking work. More recent data from the Management and Coordination Agency and the *Nihon Keizai Shimbun* (14 June 1988) suggest that over 60 per cent of those who are still full-time housewives want paid employment.

Discouraged workers cover a wide spectrum of dissatisfaction from those who would be grateful for the opportunity to work at any sort of job to those who might like to work if the pay and associated glamour were sufficient. And it is hard to tell whether the women who tend to place a high value on being a wife and mother as their source of happiness are resigned to accepting the status quo or whether a bit more freedom from society's strictures would prompt them to

TABLE 4.4 *Labour force status of the population in Ireland, Japan and the UK*
(percentage distribution in 1985)

| | Population | Employed | Unemployed | Not in the labour force | | | |
| | | | | Wants a job | | | All others |
				*A	*NA	Total	
Ireland							
men	100.0	59.2	12.4	–	–	2.7	25.7
women	100.0	26.3	6.3	–	–	6.2	61.2
Japan							
men	100.0	75.6	2.2	1.6	2.5	4.1	18.1
women	100.0	45.8	1.3	6.6	8.8	15.4	37.5
UK							
men	100.0	66.9	8.9	1.9	1.7	3.6	20.6
women	100.0	44.1	5.3	3.8	3.0	6.8	43.7

Notes:
1. The population refers to persons aged 15 years and over in Japan and Ireland; and 16 years and over in the UK.
2. *A – available for work: NA – not available for work.

Source: OECD, *Employment Outlook*, 1987.

respond differently. Often Japanese women are discouraged from taking a job, because working hours in Japan are so long and inflexible that they cannot envisage how they could cope with a double burden. Certainly while the mass of women are in menial, low-status jobs, it is unlikely that they or their husbands would place much value on their work outside the home.

The couples in Japan who have achieved true dual-career status are mostly confined to the intellectual and upper classes, where it is possible to hire one or more maids. In these families both partners have careers in such professions as journalism, playwriting, law, the foreign service and as television personalities. One indication of the relative wealth and equality in such a partnership is where there are two phones with separate numbers for each partner in a fairly small apartment. Therefore when I ring the wife, I do not expect her husband to pick up the phone and thereby delay what may be an important call.

The success of such working couples does disprove the contention that the relatively stable family life in Japan would be disrupted if the partners had comparable incomes. Women teachers whose incomes are as high as their husbands are actually chastised by friends and relatives if they choose to interrupt their career for a few years of concentrating on rearing the children; the usual comment is: 'What a waste!'. Therefore women teachers often reluctantly put their children into public day nurseries and carry on. Nor need the transfer to another location of one partner be feared as being as disruptive of family life as in the West; Japanese families have already accommodated themselves to the father being posted far away for several years, while the children stay in Tokyo so that their schooling is not interrupted.

Legislation not a panacea

It may be that the Equal Employment Opportunity Law will permit the spread of such egalitarian working couples to professions beyond the intellectual. Some scepticism would come from the mass of women unaffected by the changed legislation. When I have spoken to working mothers not established in an elite career, it is evident that either the Equal Employment Opportunity Law has made little difference to their working lives or has had an adverse impact insofar as the legislation restricting overtime hours has been weakened and they are expected to be able to contribute as long working hours as men. One working mother whom I interviewed denied that the law had raised the status of women workers and instead commented that in many cases working conditions had become more severe. Her view is corroborated from larger surveys, such as the one reported in the *Nihon Keizai Shimbun* (20 May 1987). In order to explore this issue of the apparent contradiction between equality and protection, a more detailed look at the relevant legislation when equal opportunity superseded protection will have to be undertaken than occurred in Chapter 1.

At the same time as the Equal Employment Opportunity Law was implemented, so that protective legislation should no longer be used as an excuse for discrimination, the original Labour Standards Law provisions were relaxed somewhat in April 1986 by lifting overtime and night work restrictions for women in executive or supervisory positions and women in occupations requiring professional knowledge or skills, and by easing the restrictions for women in the service sector. The one exception to the lifting of protection is in cases of maternity. Employers are explicitly forbidden to make women do work that could be detrimental to pregnancy, childbirth and breastfeeding. Indeed they are advised under the Working Women's Welfare Law to arrange special commuting hours for their pregnant employees, who can thereby avoid the notorious jam-packed trains. Pregnancy and childbirth are treated with particular reverence in Japan. Mothers of older children are not so revered; and so there is a fear that without protection unreasonable demands will be made upon working mothers, which in the end will force them to give up their work. At issue is the question of whether equal opportunity can be implemented while a certain measure of protective legislation remains in force.

There is no satisfactory compromise solution to the issue of protection versus equality of opportunity, but even in the USA where equal rights are considered to be fairly uncontroversial among working women, one woman blue-collar employee, who is also a union activist and believes working women need protective legislation, told the oral archivist Jean Schroedel (1985, p.49):

> I opposed the ERA, because . . . I felt the professional women were short-sighted. They wanted to work ten and twelve and eighteen hours [a day] so they could advance and get status. They weren't thinking about health. I know. I've worked in the shipyards.

Concerning Japan's 1986 Equal Employment Opportunity Law itself, one should first note that an equal pay provision is not explicitly made because this was meant to have been enshrined in the original 1947 Labour Standards Law. The kinds of treatment which the law does explicitly forbid, such as giving women alone the condition of being unmarried or being below a certain age and of commuting to work from the home of their parents (believed to ensure a 'nicer' kind of woman), show the sorts of discrimination that working women in Japan have had to face. Indeed the Equal Employment Opportunity Law continues to view women in a rather special light by calling upon companies to enable female employees to harmonize their occupational and family lives and to respect their motherhood. Kinko Sato, a lawyer, has shown up clearly the tone of paternalistic edification and moralism in the law, which, she has argued, is excessively Japanese in its paternalism and group orientation in making employers responsible for the welfare of their female employees (*The Japan Echo*, 1984, No.4). Her argument was in response to an assertion by Michiko Hasegawa, a woman professor of philosophy, who propounded her ideas in the May and October 1984 issues of *Chuo Koron* (a prestigious monthly magazine), that the law attempts to 'thrust the values of the white race' on Japanese culture by changing the social and cultural patterns of men and women. Since the law is generally agreed, however, to reflect existing economic and social trends rather than being an instrument for change, it can hardly be imposing unwanted values on the population.

The emergence in Britain of 'neo-liberalism' under the Conservative government, whereby the state is reluctant to take on the role of ensuring equality of opportunity, has generated some debate; and the Equal Opportunities Commission has been subject to attacks couched in the guise of humour, such as when Barbara Amiel (*The Times*, 15 July 1988) ridiculed the Commission's role in ensuring that a woman tug-of-war enthusiast could train as an umpire. Nonetheless it is worth remarking that equal opportunity legislation in Britain appears to have aroused less popular interest and controversy than in Japan. The reason may be that working women in Britain have on the surface faced less discrimination, with the result that any legislation seems to be less disruptive of the established order and less epoch-making. At the same time I would not agree with the glib assessment of a US scholar (Koizara, ed., 1987, p.365) along the lines that, if Sweden is at one end of the scale on policies to further equal opportunity, then Japan and Ireland are at the other.

Despite this, there are some good reasons for criticising the Equal Employment Opportunity Law, one of which is that there are no penalties attached for failure to implement its provisions. Instead the law relies on edifying treatises on how women should be permitted to harmonize their occupational lives and their family lives. The Prefectural Women's and Young Workers' Offices of the Ministry of Labour can only act as stimulators and inspectors, not as enforcers of the spiritual guidelines. The lack of penal regulations has meant that 60 per cent of the 5,781 companies to which guidance had been offered during the first two years of the law's implementation had not yet in mid-1988 responded properly to rectify their inadequacies (*Japan Labor Bulletin*, July 1988). Similar comments concerning the lack of adequate legal machinery for enforcement could be made about Britain's Sex Discrimination Act, but the latter has worked, as noted in Chapter 1, because of its clear prohibition on differentiated rates in collective agreements and wage orders.

In Japan, though grievances may be taken to the Prefectural Women's and Young Workers' Offices for arbitration, in the case of such aspects as recruitment and promotion, where the companies themselves have merely to endeavour to give equal treatment rather than certain practices being explicitly forbidden, the arbitration committees may not be very effective. Voluntary compliance in the area of recruitment by large companies alone has been fairly widespread, although whether there has been any real change in promotion and job assignment practices is doubtful. But since the bulk of women are employed in small companies, the law's provisions are less likely to be effective. Moreover, the Equal Employment Opportunity Law's provisions do not generally apply to part-time workers. Thus the law has been criticized for its elitist quality, notably the way in which as a result of its provisions many women are irreversibly assigned to one of two tracks (Chapter 3). Indeed when I asked women on the shop floor of NEC and Matsushita plants in Japan whether they thought the Equal Employment Opportunity Law would improve the status of working women, not one could give an unequivocal 'yes'. The general response was: 'I'm not sure'. And one blue-collar working woman thought the law would probably worsen the situation of working women, because she could not see the likelihood of any improvement at all.

Despite these criticisms, ultimately the extraordinarily extensive media coverage in Japan of the Equal Employment Opportunity Law during 1985 and 1986 along with articles about and interviews with the few highly successful women, such as Ichiko Ishihara, then a director of Takashimiya Department Store, and Reiko Okutani, president of two companies, has helped to make people more enthusiastic about the potential for promoting women. The part played by the pervasive Japanese media is crucial in Japan where television and newspapers both mirror and initiate the ruthless social pressure to fit certain fixed images of how men and women should perform their roles. Consequently, not only was the law greeted favourably, but also a more sympathetic attitude towards ambitious women could be perceived. What some may consider the ultimate accolade came in 1988 when the *Nihon Keizai Shimbun* (Japan's equivalent of *The Financial Times*) established a business magazine for women.

It is interesting to note, however, that although classified job adverts in the Japanese newspapers under the category 'male' immediately disappeared, there still remains a 'female' category. One of the least-noticed acts perpetrated by the notorious Recruit company in its influence-buying schemes – the revelation of which shook the government and business world in 1988/89 – was to persuade the Ministry of Labour to change its guidelines on job adverts so as to permit Recruit to continue publishing its employment magazine *Travail*, which is directed solely towards female readers. *The Japan Times* (3 March 1989) reported that the Ministry had originally intended to ban all sex discrimination in recruiting, but ultimately, because of opposition from Recruit and other employers, gave guidelines which permitted the continued appearance of the 'female' category, despite the arguments of bar associations and women's groups that this category would help to maintain the low wages and irregular positions offered to women.

This practice may not be so blatant in Britain, although it is hard to imagine any man bothering to scan the *la crème de la crème* job adverts in *The Times*. British men could choose instead to direct their attention to the 'genuine career opportunities for rugby players', until the advertisements were found in breach of the law. Since this was reported (*The Times*, 5 August 1988) as a test case, there must be other examples of discriminatory job adverts. Thus in both countries, while many women wish to enter male preserves, occupational segregation is so lopsided that there are certain jobs, notably secretarial work, with which men would not in any case wish to be associated.

The coverage by the Japanese media of the new 1988 Labour Standards Law, on the other hand, has been much more limited and people's attitudes are more ambivalent. Trade union opponents of the law, who recognize the powerful role of the media, have gone so far as to place advertisements protesting its provisions, particularly with respect to working women, in *The Guardian*, *Le Monde* and *The New York Times* between August and October 1987. The protests concern the way in which the supposed gradual implementation of a shorter 40-hour working week for companies with more than 300 employees is coupled with the introduction of a compulsory flexitime system which permits normal working hours to be longer than eight hours during busy periods. Overtime pay is not required as long as the weekly working hours still average 40 hours or less over three months. Not only could this provision effectively be used to restrict the present fairly generous overtime payments but also women workers with family and household reponsibilities are likely to be placed in an awkward position by irregular working hours and by being required to work longer hours on certain busy days, when they had previously been exempted from excessive overtime. It appears to be paradoxical, but women are also upset by the new Labour Standards Law's attempt to ensure that workers take longer holidays. Since Japanese employees, including, as we shall see, women working on the shop floor, usually feel compelled to demonstrate their loyalty to their workplace by not using up all of their annual leave, the law now requires there to be a planned schedule for at least half of each employee's annual paid leave. This provision is not welcomed by working mothers who save most of their leave to be used at the times when they need to care for sick children or to attend school meetings.

Actually, the extent of interest in the Equal Employment Opportunity Law and the Labour Standards Law indicates, in conclusion, that the provisions are fairly intrusive, even if the balance between protection and equal opportunity is still unsatisfactory. The issue is rather one of perception and of attitudes than of legislative provisions.

Society not yet fully come to terms with working mothers

It is indeed arguable that relaxing protective legislation for women leads to less true equity for working mothers because of the extra physical and mental demands of their two roles. The only real way to alleviate the stress of working mothers in having to combine two roles is to increase the responsibility of men in the home and to shorten working hours for all workers. Neither of these aspects falls within the Japanese and British concepts of equal opportunity legislation and of providing more extensive day-care facilities. Unfortunately, in this way both Japanese society and British society, perhaps unwittingly, concur with the extreme view of Kimindo Kusaka, as put in *Economic Eye* (1989). His argument is that women who want to get ahead in society through having a career have little interest in rearing children and that, since their temperament is genetically determined, their genes will gradually disappear from the genetic pool. His expectation that in this way all women will turn out to be full-time homemakers in the next century is not likely, because, as we shall see in the next chapter, women recognize that they can have two roles to play in society – as a parent and as a worker – which many men have failed to see as their own roles as well.

Some Japanese commentators pursue another tack to the effect that there will be no real change in society's attitude, because women's consciousness is to rely upon men in the spirit of *amae* (dependency). One woman researcher, Reiko Yamaguchi, found that women wanted to marry men who had a higher status than themselves; also they should be a few years older and about 15 centimetres taller (*Nihon Keizai Shimbun*, 31 August 1987). But there is a paradox here: within the home women controlling the purse strings must eventually forego their state of dependency – so why should they have to have a dependent attitude in the workplace? More and more women themselves recognize this paradox. The figures quoted at the beginning of Chapter 3 show that women increasingly believe that sexual inequality exists in the workplace. One Japanese woman with an uninterrupted career of 26 years working for the same company told me in response to an open-ended question that the main problem for women in the workplace was that her colleagues did not honestly listen to her proposals. Her comment reflects the fact, which was discussed under the issue of promotion in Chapter 3, that even long-serving women are not being efficiently utilized in the workplace.

What is particularly needed in Japan beyond legislative provisions, therefore, is a change in the attitudes of companies and of society so that middle-aged women can enter employment with more enthusiasm. In particular, Japanese wives need to rid themselves of the commonly held notion that their employment is inconveniencing everyone else. The indefatigable Prime Minister's Office (1981) in carrying out an international survey on youths back in 1980 included some questions – directed towards parents – on whether a mother's employment caused her, for example, to give insufficient attention to household affairs or to neglect her children's discipline. Over 50 per cent of Japanese thought there was some inconvenience compared to just over 18 per cent in Britain. (It should be remarked that Britain's figure was the lowest; nearly 35 per cent of the French agreed with the Japanese perception. But it should be remembered that in such international surveys the responses to questions may not be strictly comparable, so the scale of difference in the percentage figures must be taken with a pinch of salt.)

When, however, the question was rephrased later by the Prime Minister's Office (1987) to query the effects on children of a mother's employment, 25 per cent of Japanese men and women thought that the effect was 'good'; another 18 per cent believed there could be undesirable effects and a sizeable 53 per cent felt unable to express an opinion, which suggests that Japanese society is now in a complete quandary concerning the employment of mothers. The main 'inconvenience' of a working mother which the Japanese cite is related to household affairs, to children or to tiredness; whereas in Britain, work for women appears to be more compatible with home duties, so usually their only complaint, if any, is of mental and physical fatigue when they are also having to cope with small children. In Japan there is less anxiety over child-care facilities, as will be seen in the next chapter, but household affairs and children's education are treated as serious and onerous duties. The Japanese are also worried that the wife's absence from the home because of work would trouble the neighbours – a peculiarly Japanese concern which reflects both community obligations and the excessive concern over: 'What will the neighbours think?' in Japan's rather oppressive society.

In addition, the sexual stereotyping and division of labour in the home, which will be explored in the following chapter, are probably more rigid in Japan than in the West. This factor not only limits a mother's ability to participate properly in the labour force, but also contributes to a woman feeling that she should not be assertive and that she has little to contribute in the sphere of outside work, which leaves her among the huge band of discouraged workers. But Japan is by no means unique in the way that women's lives are thought to be centred on the home. Studies of women working in factories in Britain by Veronica Beechey (1987) show that they also tend to define themselves primarily as housewives and mothers, even though financial necessity keeps them more deeply attached to the labour force than Japanese women.

Thus both women and men in both Japan and Britain tend to view working women only in the light of motherhood, which is why legislation is geared towards facilitating this role. Economic activity is seen as being merely an adjunct to motherhood: either to provide funds or to fill in time. Consequently even long-serving women without children are looked upon with little respect in the workplace. What needs to be recognized in legislation is that a child has two parents and that many men's motivation for working is quite similar to that of women. On both sides, ideally, the decision on how long to work and how to care for the children should be taken freely. But within present social mores, the family really constricts only the woman's choice, which is why the next chapter is devoted to this topic.

Notes

(1) Ministry of Labour, *Fujin Rodo no Jitsujo* (1988), pages 74 and 75. A strong indictment of Japanese housing standards has been produced by

Kazuo Hayakawa of Kobe University. His lengthy report in English is entitled 'Housing Poverty in Japan.'
(2) This information is gleaned from annual public opinion surveys and white papers on the life of the nation carried out by the Prime Minister's Office and the Economic Planning Agency.

Apart from the high population density, there are other reasons related to the tax system and speculation for the spiral in house prices. A fairly concise analysis is provided in Okimoto and Rohlen (1988), pages 66 to 68.
(3) The Japanese proportion is calculated from official data on the composition of households from the Japan Statistical Yearbook (1988). The British figure is from the Equal Opportunities Commission (1988), page 51.
(4) Prime Minister's Office, (1979), (1984), (1986) and (1987). Depending on how the questions are phrased there can be differences of about 5 percentage points in the results. By 1987 the *Asahi Shimbun* reported that 50 per cent of women and 60 per cent of men looked upon the male role as the 'breadwinner' and the female as 'housewife and mother', whereas in 1980 the respective figures were around 70 per cent and 80 per cent. Presumably the proportions are higher than in the government poll, because the statement is phrased less dogmatically. Therefore in the following discussion I have tried to summarize the overall results of official and newspaper surveys using approximate figures.
(5) A more detailed, but smaller scale survey of when women actually leave and re-enter the labour force is reported on by the Economic Planning Agency (1987), pages 16 to 24.

5 | Working women and their families

Traditionally the mission of the wife of a *samurai* in Japan was to nurture her husband and children in order to perpetuate the *ie* (the extended family system, which also incorporates the family business). Subsequently the importance of the *ie* has faded, partly because of urbanization, but wives continue to pursue their mission by furthering their children's education. Much attention has been paid by Western writers to the overwhelming and time-consuming role of the mother in rearing her children to fit the exacting norms of Japanese society. Jane Condon (1986) suggested that many Japanese women do not want any change in their status and opportunities, since they believe that their main task is to educate their children. Merry White (1987) has a more positive view of the role of Japanese mothers. She believes that the mother's devotion to the child's needs and education is not only good for society, but also gives the mother a sense of responsibility and self-expression. Even once the children are in school the mother usually feels obliged to attend Parent–Teacher Association lectures on various aspects of rearing children and to take part in numerous other events, some of which seem to be very trivial – such as jointly embroidering a cover for the classroom's piano.

Since the father's prime loyalty in Japan is to his outside work, it is thought that the mother should be fully occupied with bringing up the children and making sure that they do well in their schools. The argument goes on, therefore, to state (White, 1987, p.35) that 'the working mother of a latch-key child is . . . in Japanese eyes un-nuturant'. Such

116

arguments, however, ignore the fact that, even in pre-modern Japan, perpetuation of the *ie* involved the wife's time-consuming economic activity on the farm or in the family business. The evolution of the full-time housewife occurred even later in Japan than in other OECD countries – not really until 1960. Consequently Japanese women, as was mentioned in Chapter 2, do have a rather higher evaluation of the pleasures of being a housewife, especially as its evolution has coincided with a wealth of consumer items and housework aids. Thus the issue raised by Western feminists of domestic labour being unremunerated and unrecognized appears to be not so relevant in Japan. But, despite the transparent allure of being a housewife in Japan, the number of married women entering the labour force is increasing every year. In doing so they must usually find ways of combining their work with rearing their children and in some cases with looking after elderly relatives. The grandparent, however, is often the one who helps to solve the former problem by looking after the small children for at least part of the day, which permits, as we shall see later, more mothers to work.

Mothers who work

Nowadays Japanese mothers are again returning to the labour force. Whereas just 65 per cent of married women in 1974 were already working or wanted to work, since 1979 the proportion has always been over 71 per cent, according to survey statistics from the Management and Coordination Agency. Indeed some Japanese mothers with pre-school children may make a positive choice to work even without there being any real economic imperatives because they would suffer more fatigue in spending almost the whole day looking after a toddler on their own. I heard similar sentiments from workers in Britain. One British man at Matsushita in Cardiff thought it was 'good' that his wife worked part time in the canteen, because it helped to relieve the pressure for her of coping with their demanding five-year-old child. A University of Tokyo survey, carried out by Toshiyuki Shiomi, found that mothers who are not socially active are more susceptible to 'child-care fatigue' than working mothers whose children are in good day-care facilities (*The Japan Times*, 5 June 1988). And in Japan most of the day nurseries are set up to provide enjoyable experiences, which also serve as a prelude to social group participation, so that many working mothers opt positively to release their children from a small confined apartment into a more spacious day-care facility. In Britain, despite proposals for child-care vouchers and privately financed nurseries in school buildings, this positive view of institutional care for pre-schoolers is rarely seen among policy-makers; John Patten, Minister of State at the Home Office, in an interview in *The Independent* (12 January 1989) has stated: 'We do not want to see state or employer-provided workplace nurseries. I dread the thought of commuting children.' Contrast the early-morning scene in Japan where the roads are full of mothers and fathers taking their small children – usually strung in slings on their backs or on extra bicycle seats – to day nurseries and kindergartens. Admittedly the relatively high population density permits such facilities to be wide-spread, but even in rural areas in Japan there is usually a day nursery for the children of farmers and other workers.

But there is also physical fatigue for working mothers in both Japan and Britain, who in addition suffer a particular kind of socially sanctioned guilt at not fitting the image of the mother who is always available at home. And working hours are so long in Japan that working mothers are hard put to spend enough time with their children, which is what they usually cite as the most difficult aspect of combining work with motherhood. One Japanese mother of small children expressed her dilemma:

> Even though I am so flurried every day in trying to catch up
> with the time, it is important to me to have more contact with

my children. But I should not leave work until my subordinates have finished their assignments, so I am often late home.

This is an issue which crosses all cultures and all kinds of work for women. An Irish mother working at NEC told me that the only really difficult aspect of combining work and motherhood was that she felt that she did not have enough time with her children. This conflict between work and family, which oddly enough is almost totally unknown for fathers, causes incredible stress, whose scale I have not been fully able to assess, but which has been well documented elsewhere by, for example, Barbara Berg (1986), who supported her own questionnaire results with the comments of psychiatrists and psychologists.

Despite the attendant stress, there does not seem to be any evidence that working women in Japan are refraining from having children, since a survey on population trends has revealed that there is no appreciable difference in the number of children in families with working mothers and those with full-time housewives (*The Japan Times*, 5 May 1988). And there is almost no difference in the proportions of women with and without a job who think that child-rearing is enjoyable – in both cases about three-quarters of the women surveyed by the Ministry of Education (1987) concerning the employment of the mother and education in the home. Working mothers are, if anything, more enthusiastic about their children's education. The Japan Association for Female Executives has recruited a pool of evening baby-sitters who are university students and graduates so that they will be able to help the children with their homework. And the female executives' seminars tend to focus on topics such as 'child psychology' and 'good children's books'.

The position of women in the workplace and their attachment to the labour force cannot be discussed without knowing about what kind of facilities are available for child care and how amenable are re-employment schemes. Although the latter leave a lot to be desired in Japan, I have found that the provision of child-care facilities is much better than in Britain and Ireland. Since the Irish and British working mothers whom I met seemed to suffer greater exhaustion than was reported by working mothers in Japan, the probable major reason lies in the quality of available day-care facilities.

Day-care facilities in Japan

Let us look at one representative ward in Tokyo in order to see what kind of *hoikuen* (day nurseries) are available for small children. Meguro Ward is in a relatively prosperous part of Tokyo, but large parts of the area are characterized by small shops and tiny factories intermingled with dwellings which to Western eyes look like slums. The public *hoikuen* are provided not only for the children of those mothers who work, but also those looking after old or sick relatives, those who are giving birth to another baby and those who have a close relative sick in hospital. The family pays according to the previous year's tax payment; the maximum monthly payment for a three-year-old is about 16,000 yen (about £68), but most are paying a bit less than 11,000 yen (£47) per month. And on average just under 90 per cent of the cost of provision is subsidized, mostly from local tax revenue (*Kusei Yoran* and *Koho Meguro 1988*).

This scale of public subsidy is perhaps unexpected in Japan, but it attests to an acknowledgement that mothers of young children may need to or want to work outside the home and the state bears a responsibility to ensure that the children are not neglected. It should be remarked that not all local governments are so generous, now that the subsidy from the central government has been sharply cut back from its level of around 50 per cent ten years ago. In Funabashi City to the east of Tokyo, the increasing proportion of *hoikuen* costs borne by the parents, which has reached as high as 30,000 yen (£127) a month, has provoked strong parent protests, which were reported on television in June

1988. And in our representative ward of Meguro there are some members of the budget committee who are trying to raise the share of *hoikuen* expenditure which comes from the parents. In response parents have organized a leafleting campaign which details how a working couple with a double income are paying, because of the progressiveness of the Japanese tax system, between four and five times as much tax as a family where only the husband works. The reasoning, then, is that the hefty *hoikuen* public subsidy is partly paid by an ample contribution from the additional tax payments of working mothers.

Public facilities are not the only options for working Japanese parents; there are also *katei hoiku* (family nurseries), for those who would prefer not to send their child to institutional day care, and private *hoikuen*, most of which are licensed and subsidized by the local government. The *katei hoiku* are comparable to child-minders in Britain, but such is the pervasiveness of the Japanese bureaucracy and sense of supervision that they are under quite stringent controls, with the pay-off of receiving direct grants from the ward office for each enrolled baby. There are also some unlicensed child-minders who may belong to a club which matches up mothers who want to look after a few children with those who need occasional child care. Such child-minders also take over the care of ill infants, since public *hoikuen* insist that any child with a high temperature must stay at home.

It is interesting to note, however, that the demand for places in private *hoikuen* and for child-minders is fairly stagnant, despite their conditions of entrance and hours of operation being very flexible. This fact attests to the quality of care received at the public *hoikuen*; one mother told me that she valued highly the warm and friendly atmosphere, and so she obtained a place in a public facility for her four-year-old son on the grounds that she was looking after her invalid father-in-law. When he died not long after, the mother quickly sought some kind of paid employment, because her son would have otherwise had to forfeit his place in the public facility with its stress on home cooking and free play.

In Meguro Ward the number of day-care places, where the hours extend from 8am to 5.30pm with extensions possible at both ends, has risen since 1965 by two and a half times with nearly 2,000 children in public day nurseries, and about 400 in private day care, which in total amounts to almost 20 per cent of the total number of infants and children in the relevant age group. And in spite of the decline in the number of small children in Meguro Ward, a local government official indicated to me that there are plans to extend the scale of public day care because there are insufficient places for children aged three and under. Nonetheless the overall demand for places is fairly well satisfied, since there are vacant places for four- and five-year-olds, who need a lower ratio of staff and who may have already been found places in kindergartens.

The above scale of provision in Japan may be compared with Britain where some local authorities provide day nurseries for less than two per cent of the under-fives and other authorities make no provision at all, since it is their policy to have children looked after in ordinary homes, but without providing any back-up in the form of subsidies to child-minders. Consequently the quality, availability and reliability of child-minders in Britain is very variable. There are a few workplace day nurseries, but the employer's subsidy is counted as a taxable 'perk' on which mothers have to pay tax. (I would argue the other way completely that child-care costs should be counted as a tax-deductible expense associated with working.) Recently there has been no increase in British state provision after a period of expansion in the 1970s, with the result that day-care places of all kinds and quality are available for only about 15 per cent of the relevant age group, according to the Equal Opportunities Commission (1987, 1988). Consequently about one-half of mothers in employment with pre-school children rely for child care on their husbands, either by doing night work or because the father is unemployed.

When kindergartens – mostly two- or three-hour 'rising five' classes – are included, there are in total places for only 44 per cent of three- and four-year olds and the proportion has tended to fall in the 1980s.[1] Thus there is plenty of room in Britain for the Commons Select Committee's call in January 1989 for an expansion of kindergarten places.

In sharp contrast in Japan, where primary school does not begin until the age of six, close to 100 per cent of four- and five-year olds are in kindergartens or day nurseries. Older children aged up to ten years, with working or otherwise occupied mothers, go to the public *gakudo* (schoolchildren) clubs after school and during the holidays for games and activities, rather than to an empty house. Again in complete contrast, a letter to the *The Times* (18 July 1988) from the Working Mothers Association stated that in Britain more than three-quarters of local authorities make no provision for day care for young schoolchildren. Consequently during school holidays working British parents have to stagger their holidays and depend on friends, neighbours and relations to look after young children. Some policy-makers argue that such dependency on the home and the community is all to the good. I would rather say that the much-praised stability of family life in Japan is possible partly because the widespread state provision of day care has permitted mothers to make an independent choice on whether to work without placing a heavy burden on members of the extended family.

In any case Japanese state provision has not negated the role of the family, since grandparents do play a part in caring for small children. Curiously it is often thought that the nuclear family is more conducive to women working than a three-generation household. Certainly where a woman has to look after an invalid parent – often in Japan her husband's mother – there may be less opportunity for outside employment. However, not only casual observation, but also survey data from the Management and Coordination Agency (1987) show that where three generations are living together the mother is more likely to be working; for example in the case of mothers whose youngest child is under six, 45.5 per cent of mothers where a grandparent is present were working compared to 31.8 per cent of similar mothers living in a nuclear family household.

Thus the respect which old people have earned in Japan is partly given in return for their continuing to have to care for small children; one often sees a bent old woman or man carrying a fairly heavy child on her or his back. The care, however, need not be full time. Often the small children are in day care with a grandparent taking them there in the morning or looking after them when they are sick. Because a grandparent was living with her family, a working mother at Matsushita in Osaka told me that she could not conceive of any real problem in balancing her roles as a mother and as a worker, even though her husband played hardly any part in child care and housework. Indeed she was one of those women cited in Chapter 4 who was working not out of economic necessity but just to have more money available for clothes and leisure activities – and perhaps, one may speculate, to be out of her mother-in-law's way.

Child-care leave and maternity leave provisions

Since the social attitude – however controversial – that women are not only responsible for child-bearing, but also for child-rearing, is deeply embedded in both Japan and Britain, the immediate question becomes how best they can cope with this responsibility while maintaining their careers. Thus in most developed countries – apart from the USA which has no federal statutory provisions even for a few weeks' unpaid maternity leave – the concern is not only with the minimum paid maternity leave of 14 to 18 weeks, but also with child-care leave and re-employment, with the former being defined here as lasting for just one year.

The concept of maternity leave has actually been long established in Japan: since 1922 when the Ministry of Education instructed women teachers to take eight weeks' leave on giving birth. In Britain the concern in the past has been on encouraging women to stay at home to look after their children by paying child allowances, but this notion has been weakened with the granting of maternity leave provisions since 1977. Now statutory maternity pay is given by the British employer at 90 per cent of the existing salary for six weeks and at a lower rate for an additional 12 weeks after the birth. The provision in Ireland amounts to 14 weeks' leave during which the woman receives social security payments and, if the mother desires, an additional unpaid four weeks. Japan is rather similar to Ireland in that there is usually some form of payment for the statutory 14 weeks' leave, but not necessarily from the employer. Where the Japanese woman has been participating in the National Health Insurance scheme, she receives 60 per cent of her regular pay. In addition many companies – about 40 per cent according to official statistics – and trade unions operate their own insurance schemes, which provide a level of maternity pay not far below a woman's regular salary. It cannot be denied that paid maternity leave raises the nominal price of female labour, but there are considerable benefits to companies and to society in terms of enabling a woman to continue to use her experience and to do well at both her roles.

Fortunately many Japanese are becoming more aware – though popular views may pretend otherwise – that women usually have to play two vital roles in society: as nurturers of their children and as well-educated and diligent members of the labour force. (The same should apply to men as well, but for the moment I am following society's existing norm.) To combine both roles for the overall benefit of society, both public day nurseries and leave for child care are required. Some might sceptically query the government's interest in ensuring that working women do not neglect to bear, and then to rear, healthy children, but this is one case where the national and the individual's interest are reasonably congruent. Similarly, the family is recognized in Japan to be an important part of the social system, whose stability would be threatened if mothers were forced to be economically inactive. Therefore day nurseries have been made fairly accessible, but the notion of child-care leave is still looked at rather askance by Japanese employers, who favour total loyalty to the company.

It is not inconsistent that many mothers, who do not want completely to abandon their careers, would prefer the option of staying at home with their small children for one or two years under a child-care leave scheme, both because of the physical and mental strain of rushing babies to a day nursery and caring for them after a hard day's work, and because of their understandable concern that babies may need a mother's whole-hearted attention. This is a controversial issue. In the USA a report given to the 1988 International Conference of Infant Studies in Washington and research in Dallas, using longitudinal studies (which follow a given survey object over time), have indicated some later detrimental effects when children have been in fulltime day care from the early months of their lives (*Los Angeles Times*, January 1989). Other research, however, discussed by Tom Bower, who is a Professor of Child Psychology, in *The Observer* (10 July 1988) shows that the development and emotional needs of children in day care are not neglected.

Nonetheless there would be general agreement that for many mothers and small children there should be the option of a re-employment scheme, especially when day-care facilities are inadequate and small children are being given erratic and inconsistent care. Therefore, in addition to maternity leave for childbirth, most developed countries also encourage or require firms to grant child-care leave, which is usually unpaid, to a mother with the guarantee that she can return to her job at the same status and pay. The statutory provision in Britain is inadequate since not only are very small companies exempted, but also modifications have been made to the requirement of returning to the same job and the woman has to have been working for the same employer for at least two years, even though women are often obliged to be intermittent employees. Moreover Britain limits child-care leave to only 29 weeks after the birth of a child, whereas in some other European countries, including Italy, Sweden and Austria, the provision extends to one year. Some mothers in Britain argue that 29 weeks is an amount which places them in an awkward position. It is long enough in effect to make the mother feel that she should return to work so as not to forfeit her secure position and career expectations; but it is too short in terms of her own wish to devote at least one year to her baby. And, moreover, companies are faced with filling positions for just nine months, which has encouraged the growth of temporary work. Indeed any mother with more than one child would recognize that it is not so much the newborn baby but the older infants who require additional attention after a new member has joined the household, and – in the other camp – many employers would prefer mothers to take leave of more than a year so as stabilize the work-force. What is unfortunately true is that those mothers would then lose out on some promotion opportunities. Legislation is not enough. Society and employers – and indeed women themselves – need to acknowledge not only that leaving work for a few years to bring up small children does not neccsssarily mean that a woman is not committed to her job, but also that in doing so, she will hone some valuable managerial skills, such as resolving crises and deciding on which out of a multitude of tasks should be given priority.

On paper the situation in Japan looks a bit better. The Ministry of Labour has been promoting child-care leave (*ikuji kyugyo seido*) and re-employment of women (*joshi saikoyo seido*) since the mid-1970s with grants being given to companies for each re-employed woman and limited welfare payments made to the mother taking leave for a one-year period. Nonetheless, in 1985 the proportion of companies which permitted child-care leave was only 14.6 per cent and those with a re-employment scheme for women was just 5.6 per cent (Ministry of Labour, 1986). The Equal Employment Opportunity Law only 'advises' employers to permit mothers to leave work on giving birth and return after one or more years. Consequently the practice in Japan does not appear to conform to the principle. A private institute survey presents in Table 5.1 an even gloomier picture than the official statistics, since less than 10 per cent of companies responded that they actually operated any system and over 60 per cent argued that there was no possibility of it being begun.

TABLE 5.1 *Child-care leave provisions in Japanese companies (percentage of 511 responding companies; 1987)*

	Provision available	Soon will be available	Wish to consider	Not possible to implement
Child-care leave for men	0.8	0.2	7.4	89.6
Child-care leave for women	9.0	1.4	24.5	62.8
Re-employment of women 3 to 5 years after child's birth	11.5	4.7	39.5	42.3

Source: Yokakaihatsu Centre, *Kigyo ni okeru Rodojikan to Yokakyoju Kankyo ni kansuru Chosa.*

Even where a re-employment scheme has been put into effect, the official Ministry of Labour statistics (1988) admit that it is often not operating effectively. Either the encouragement given is not sufficient or else Japanese women seem not to wish to take the opportunity offered for child-care leave. In companies which ostensibly offer child-care leave – usually amounting to one year – less than 45 per cent of their female employees who gave birth in 1986 took advantage of the system, though that was some gain over 1982 when barely 30 per cent did so. One reason cited for the majority preferring to stay on the job or to leave altogether is because only 4.4 per cent of the 1,000 surveyed companies gave a salary to the woman during her child-care leave. Evidently new mothers feel more comfortable about taking advantage of the leave provisions when they are working for small companies, since over 80 per cent of the eligible female employees of companies with less than 30 employees took child-care leave where it was provided.

Indeed, at NEC's huge plant in Tamagawa with its 8,500 employees, I was told that cases in which women had taken child-care leave for the permitted three years were very rare. Particularly in the electronics industry women would be concerned that their skills would be outmoded by the time that they returned to work. Thus the women engineers opt to leave altogether or to take only the standard maternity leave, which is granted for 16 weeks at NEC.

Child-care leave for fathers exceedingly rare

One point to notice from both the official and the private surveys referred to above is that less than 1 per cent of companies permitted male employees to take child-care leave, (though the majority do allow a few days off at the time of a baby's birth), whereas in Scandinavian countries leave may be taken by either the father or the mother, who is also permitted flexible working hours. Even when a Japanese company does provide some such scheme, society's attitude to the idea of men taking on a fuller share of child-care responsibilities tends to lag behind. The large supermarket chain, Seiyu, which actively publicized its paternity leave system set up in 1986 to allow male and female employees to take up to two hours a day off from work without pay until the child was three years old, found that in two and a half years there were no male takers, despite an enthusiastic male response in the trade union. This failure demonstrates again that in Japan men are still viewed as being the primary breadwinner, even though their wives are economically active. Makiko Ogihara in *The Japan Economic Journal* (4 February 1989) suggests that the name of the policy should be changed to something neutral like 'flexitime' so as not to jeopardize men's promotion chances through being seen to engage in 'feminine' tasks. It is arguable, indeed, that the whole concept of maternity and child-care leave only augments the traditional mores, whereby even working women have to take all the responsibilty for child care, while the fathers may enjoy seamless careers.

But there are signs of a change in Japan. Opposition parties, with the support of the major trade union confederations, have introduced a bill in the Diet (parliament), albeit so far unsuccessfully, which would allow any worker – female or male – to take time off, with 60 per cent of the salary being paid, during a child's first year. Also some Japanese men at least are beginning to savour their fatherhood and to place less stress on loyalty to the company rather than to the family. *The Japan Times* (15 February 1987) reported that the union at an oil company had staged short strikes to press for limited child-care time so that they could take or pick up their children at the day-care centre and a citizens' action group had been set up to seek such rights. Nowadays I see many more small children being taken to *hoikuen* by their fathers, who are in jobs which permit more flexible hours than the mothers. And there are a few Japanese men who have tried to take on the whole of the housework burden: Haruki Murase gained fame in 1984 by writing a book, called *Kaiketsu Hausu Hazubando*, about his role as a 'marvellous house husband'. He described himself as a typical homemaker, but one who wore large sneakers and began the day by shaving. Just like many other homemakers in Japan his younger child went to *hoikuen* while he worked at a part-time job. It is noteworthy that even such male paragons eventually decide that, rather than taking on all the household responsibilities themselves, they would prefer to share the chores and permit both partners to have full-time jobs – but without being expected, as is usual in Japan, to stay at work for several hours after six o'clock. Thus both Haruki Maruse and his wife now work as freelance writers and share the housework.

The issue of permitting parents of small children to work fewer hours has been recognized to a limited extent in Japan by the provision for working mothers to take one or two hours off work each day for nursing during the baby's first year. Originally the idea was that there should be two half-hour breaks to enable the mother to breastfeed her child. Generally working mothers choose instead just to leave work early. In most cases for the first year one hour's leave is given, which in over 40 per cent of companies is paid, but the Seiyu supermarket chain permits an unpaid two hours per day until the child is three years old. In Japan where white-collar workers in particular are more or less expected to stay at their desks until well after the official working hours, it may be embarrassing for an ambitious woman to leave early. A confident young mother at NEC, however, said that her colleagues were rather supportive and sympathetic about her taking an hour off each day during her baby's first year, partly because such cases are quite rare in the engineering section and, more significantly, because of the reverence that Japanese men have for babies. This legislated provision for nursing leave may be dismissed in some arguments as being meaningless when only one hour, which is invariably confined to mothers rather than fathers, is at stake. Yet it is an important gesture which those who are concerned about working mothers would do well to seize upon in seeking the best way for a mother or father to combine work with bringing up small children.

The problem is that – as in the case of protective legislation – the statutory provisions and official encouragement of various systems may look very fine on paper, but can be easily evaded. While public employees and those relatively few women working for large companies are given the right to nursing leave for the baby's first year, in the numerous small companies and retail establishments working mothers are either denied this right or made to feel very uncomfortable about taking the hour off, even though it is usually unpaid. A local government official himself told me that this denial was widespread, so one wonders whether Japanese society's much vaunted respect for the family extends to a will to ensure that mothers are able to attend to their children.

The Japanese mothers themselves fall prey to the over-whelming pressure to keep harmony in the workplace. Thus the actual provision of statutory maternity leave must be treated with some scepticism. A Tokyo Metropolitan Government survey of 1000 companies found that about 37 per cent of companies, notably the smaller firms, have not been granting their women employees the minimum 14 weeks of maternity leave, even though it is a statutory provision. And in small companies with less than 30 employees, where women workers predominate, the provision for child-care leave and re-employment is reputedly almost non-existent (*The Japan Times*, 30 June 1988).

In Britain also, the spirit of the provisions for maternity leave in the Employment Protection Act is often ignored. Remedies apply only to those cases which are brought before tribunals, such as women who were dismissed merely because they were pregnant and had not been with the same employer for two years or those who were dismissed and asked to take redundancy pay rather than exercise their right to maternity leave (*The Times*, 20 August 1987).

It should also be remarked that however good are the facilities for child care, what really matters for most women is the kind of job into which they re-enter; so this issue deserves the whole of the next chapter. So much for a mother trying to cope with outside work; she must also see to the household, which in Japan is a particularly onerous responsibility.

Lack of co-operation in the home

Both the illusory stereotype under which men are still looked upon as being the breadwinner and also the reality of their long working hours suggest that Japanese working mothers in general have a greater burden than their counter-parts in the West in taking on almost all of the household and child-rearing responsibilities. Research in this area is rather hard to carry out as conclusions rest upon somewhat subjective evaluations, but Samuel Coleman (Plath, ed., 1983) verified the observation of a greater burden for Japanese wives with surveys carried out in the early 1970s, when the 'housewife boom' was at its height and wives were particularly concerned to demonstrate their diligence in their domestic service role. In the late 1980s there have been numerous surveys of the limited extent to which husbands do take on household duties, which in itself attests to the fact that the Japanese are becoming aware of the injustice of wives bearing the double burden. Nonetheless there does not seem to have been much change in practice. Nor is there much expectation of any real change. Japanese comment-ators tend to say that working mothers need more flexible and part-time work in order implicitly to continue with their double burden, rather than that there needs to be a radical change in how household roles are allotted. Thus while 69 per cent of men responding to an *Asahi Shimbun* survey in December 1988 endorsed married women working outside the home, only 20 per cent of those men would have agreed to share houehold chores on an equal basis. (Even many of those 20 per cent may have been deluding themselves about how equal would be the sharing.)

Japan is not at all unique in this respect. The *British Social Attitudes* survey discussed by Roger Jowell and Colin Airey in *Social Trends* (1985) indicated that nearly three-quarters of married women claimed to do all or most of the housework and about 70 per cent of married men agreed with their wives' claim. Similarly a large-scale survey carried out by the Education Ministry found that around 65 per cent of all Japanese men did not help at all with household chores, though the percentage was a bit lower in the case of men with working wives (*The Japan Times*, 27 September 1986). One positive point is that in the latter case fathers were more involved with their children, who thought that their working mothers were 'tired'. The following year when both women and men were asked by the Prime Minister's Office (1986) who should mainly be responsible for each of the household chores, even such a simple task as 'clearing the table' was regarded as the role of the wife by over 90 per cent of the households where both husband and wife had outside jobs.

One regrets having to admit it, but part of the reason for the sharp division of labour in the Japanese home may be due to the women's attitude. Japanese women themselves often speak ironically of how they have pampered their husbands and sons to the extent that they are 'good-for-nothing' in the home. An image, which is popular among women, of a man in the kitchen is that of a cockroach, and elsewhere in the home men are often spoken of as 'nobodies'. Thus women connive in their own exploitation. The ideal picture of a wife for many women and men is one of gentle disposition, who by her devotion to her family sacrifices her own interests. When working wives were asked by the Prime Minister's Office (1984) how housekeeping and child-care duties should be shared, only 13 per cent believed that men and women should share domestic work equally. The rest mostly thought that men should give a helping hand or undertake a job if they have more time to spare and a full 5 per cent of working wives even argued that men need not do any housework.

Since women's commuting time and overtime hours are much less than men, it is rare that the latter appear to have more time to spare than their working wives; that does not mean however that they are more tired than their wives. Who would not prefer to be relaxed at an office desk, reading on a train and entertaining business associates in a bar rather than rushing home to get the shopping done, the children fed, the laundry cleared, and the home cleaned? The amount of stress is evident in that working mothers in Japan told me that their main anxieties were that they could not give enough attention to child care and housekeeping and could not get enough rest.

The sharp division of roles within the Japanese home is often blamed on 'traditional' attitudes with the expectation that modernization will eventually provide a cure. Yet in the traditional family business – such as a small restaurant – I usually see the husband doing the cooking while the wife looks after the customers and the accounts. The fault, therefore, seems more to lie in the attitude of modern companies which expect their male employees to work long and exhausting hours. The much-touted statistics on how the annual hours worked in Japan are diminishing – though the number of hours is still well above European working hours (Chapter 10) – ignore the after-work hours which for white-collar employees are counted neither as overtime nor as regular working hours.

A change may be close, however; according to annual surveys of the young 'selfish' generation about to enter employment by the Recruit Research Company, men who said that their work will get priority over their family reached in 1988 the lowest figure ever of just over 14 per cent; and what is perhaps more surprising, almost 11 per cent of young women gave an identical response (*The Japan Times*, 13 March 1988). A mere statement of priority would not, however, convey the whole picture. The similarity in the percentages between men and women does not necessarily mean that in future men will shoulder household tasks to the same degree as their working wives. The 'traditional' role division may not change by itself, but what is perhaps changing is the 'traditional' passivity of Japanese women. As more mothers are working, so they are becoming more angered by their unequal burden within the home. An international survey carried out by the Prime Minister's Office (1983) found that 67 per cent of Japanese women felt that men received preferential treatment in family life, whereas the comparable figure for Britain was 49 per cent. 'Workaholic' husbands when they eventually return home have little to say to their wives, because of the distinct and fairly rigid division of roles which extends beyond household chores to the wife not even having to consult with her husband on how the household finances are to be used nor expecting him to be unduly concerned about the children's education. The resulting breakdown in communication, which is often cited by middle-aged Japanese women, does not seem to occur in the case of working couples who reputedly spend more time talking together. Wives say that outside work means that they have more topics to talk about, since the sharp division of household roles leaves little ground for matters of common interest when the wife is at home all day.

That is hopeful, but in other respects the lot of the working mother – though it has improved somewhat in terms of equal opportunity and quality of day-care provision – has not changed much in the home. And consequently the working mother is expected still to live up to the superwoman myth, which has been discredited elsewhere, of doing the impossible in serving husband and children without letting her outside work be diminished. In fact until the situation within the Japanese home has changed significantly, women will not have either the energy or the will to contribute to their work outside the home, as may be judged from the way their hours are used up in Table 5.2.

Unfortunately, the British aggregates do not break down essential activities, the definition of which, along with that for free time, may be different from Japan. Nor can I be sure that my calculations based on the Japanese classification of time-use exactly correspond to the British, but the overall pattern is clear. What is evident in both countries is that men have more free time than working women and, certainly in the case of Britain, more than housewives. (Housewives in Japan may include relatively more women with no dependent children.) What is also pertinent is that even on Sunday men have much more free time than their working wives, who are presumably trying to catch up on the household chores.

The responses to my questionnaire in both Japan and the British Isles indicate that working mothers are not only more efficient and accepting of lower standards in carrying out household tasks than housewives, but they would want to spend more time on child care and housework if only they could. Even when minimizing the time spent on housework, the working wives are very tired. There is an unjust asymmetry in what is expected of the women – in the case of

TABLE 5.2 *Use of time by working women, men and housewives in Britain and Japan*

	Men full time 1	Women employees full time 2	part time 3	Housewives 4
Weekly hours spent on:		*Britain (1985)*		
employment	45.0	40.8	22.2	
essential activities	33.1	45.1	61.3	76.6
sleep	56.4	57.5	57.0	59.2
free time	33.5	24.6	38.5	32.2
free time				
per weekday	2.6	2.1	3.1	4.2
on Sunday	10.2	7.2	5.9	5.6
		Japan (1986)		
employment	50.7	44.7	31.5	0.6
essential activities A.	18.4	19.9	20.2	20.7
B.	7.6	21.1	34.4	44.1
sleep	52.4	51.0	50.8	52.1
free time	36.1	28.5	30.6	45.3
free time				
per weekday	4.1	3.4		6.4
on Sunday	9.2	6.4		7.0

Notes:
1. Employment includes travel, which is generally longer for men.
2. Essential activities in Britain include both: A. eating meals, washing oneself etc., and B. cooking, shopping, child care, etc.
3. The sum of the columns for Japan are a few hours short as is the case in the original data sets.

Sources: Britain – Equal Opportunities Commission (1987). Japan – Ministry of Labour, *Fujin Rodo no Jitsujo.*

a couple without children, who are both working at the same NEC factory in Ireland, the wife is up earlier and to bed later than her husband. A Japanese working mother told me that she was getting only five and a half hours sleep a night, because her husband only sometimes helped – and then mostly with the children rather than with the laundry and cleaning.

Whether in Japan, more than elsewhere, there is a greater asymmetry in the burden of household reponsibilities could require an insidious cultural judgement, since the data cannot provide a satisfactory comparison. In my survey and others the phrasing of the questions in different languages may be interpreted differently. Even if one ignores these problems and opts for a fairly subjective judgement about what goes on in the average home, there are all sorts of exceptions. Therefore my conclusion that Japanese men are usually more inclined than their British counterparts to avoid doing cleaning and kitchen work is at best tentative. I know some Japanese men who are a dab hand at cooking and British men who can barely put together cheese on toast. In both the British Isles and Japan there are many tales of how men with wives working full time are completely remiss in taking on any household tasks, apart from repairs. Thus my interviews and other surveys have shown that the household division of labour in almost all countries has changed only a little, despite the trendy mythology of women and men sharing all household tasks equally. In Japan, however, the prevailing social ethos, against which Japanese women do not really speak out and some even tend to connive at, is less conducive to men taking on a reasonable amount of household duties. On the other hand Japanese men are probably more willing to entertain the children, though it is hard to make an overall judgement. One of the British male respondents to my questionnaire, who is a trade union shop steward at Matsushita in Cardiff, admitted that housework was easier than looking after children.

Until working hours are shortened in Japan, there is not much hope that men will contribute more to doing the household tasks, since only a minority finds that they can spend enough time with their families. Unions in Japan are now giving more attention to this issue in their demands to shorten working hours. Thus an international survey initiated by Denki Roren (Chapter 9) included questions relating to time spent at home. As is clear from Table 5.3, Japanese women working in electronics factories are a bit more satisfied than Japanese men with the amount of time they have for family life, but still the proportion is much lower than in the case of both women and men in Britain.

TABLE 5.3 *Degree of satisfaction with time available for family among women and men in Japanese and British electronics companies (percentage of respondents to 1985 survey)*

| | Women | | Men | |
	Britain	Japan	Britain	Japan
Very satisfied	20.1	2.1	21.9	1.7
Fairly satisfied	42.1	29.2	49.0	20.1
Neutral	10.2	39.8	11.1	29.1
Fairly dissatisfied	15.2	20.4	11.7	30.4
Very dissatisfied	11.6	4.2	5.4	16.7
No response	0.8	4.2	0.9	2.1

Source: Denki Roren no Chosa Jiho, No.212.

Future trends for working mothers

Whether or not there is still scope for mothers to be more economically active is a function not only of the labour market, but also of social trends. In Britain, figures from the Equal Opportunities Commission (1987, 1988) show that, despite a high level of male unemployment and the expansion of part-time work, the proportion of women with dependent children who are working has barely increased since 1973; in that year 47 per cent were working, while in the mid-1980s the proportion was around 48 per cent. There were some startling fluctuations in the intervening years – in 1980 at the peak, 54 per cent of mothers with dependent children were working – but since then the proportion has tended to decline. The only noticeable change since the early 1970s is that the proportion of part-timers among those mothers who are working has risen from around 63 per cent to almost 69 per cent.

The reaching of an apparent ceiling is partly due to a slight increase in unemployment levels for mothers and to social security arrangements for single mothers, but why else? One reason could be the levelling out in the earlier growth in provision of day-care places; but the decline in the proportion of working mothers is particularly striking for those whose youngest child is between five and ten years of age for whom day care should not be so important. Nonetheless it does appear that a lone mother, in particular, faces problems in working, even when her youngest child is at school. The proportion of such mothers who work full time has dropped significantly, along with a relative decrease in working lone mothers whose youngest child is under five years. Evidently there is a role for British fathers in being available to look after children while the mother works, though some mothers complain that that is all they do, without preparing or clearing up after meals. Indeed some British mothers who work in the evenings feel that it is incumbent on them to have the children in bed and asleep before they go out to work.

Some kind of limit has been reached in Britain. Household responsibilities are still not, except in rare cases, being fully shared. Perhaps the only way for a really radical change in the division of housework and child care to take place would be when unemployment among men leads to a reversal of roles – or at least a complete blurring of the role boundaries. But that may not be the scenario at all. In many cases unemployment, especially in the North East, is leading to a heavier burden on women whose husbands go south to seek work. (Providing employment is, indeed, the main reason why Japanese manufacturers are welcomed in both Britain and Ireland.) The woman is left alone in the North East, apart from weekends, to look after the children, which makes it hard for her to take on a job. If the employment situation for men were to improve substantially, however, the labour participation rate of middle-aged women in Britain might even decline, as working mothers, who have often taken a job because of the fear that the father will be made redundant, realize that they have let themselves in for a bad deal and their family fortunes have improved with the husband in a secure job.

In Japan, where role divisions in the home are more distinct and where the unemployment level is low, there may still be some scope for a further increase in the proportion of working mothers as long as their husbands no longer balk at taking on some of the household tasks and as long as working hours for both men and women are shortened. It is being slowly recognized that the Equal Employment Opportunity Law will not be fully effective unless there is at the same time a less unequal division of household tasks. But because male unemployment is still quite low in Japan and part-time employment is less desirable than in Britain (Chapter 6) the plateau for the rate at which mothers work outside the home may be lower than in Britain, where women have had to go to work to support their families. Although there has been a recent apparent surge in the number of employed mothers in Japan, Eiko Shinotsuka (1989) has demonstrated that those who were previously working in family businesses, rather than full-time homemakers, are tempted by the availability of low-paid employment.[2]

Unfortunately the structure of the relevant survey data in Japan has changed over time, so that the trend is not completely clear, but it does appear that between 1985 and 1987 the proportion of mothers with children aged under 15 years who were working remained stable at 49.5 per cent – a figure which is slightly higher than in Britain. Aggregate figures for all married Japanese women who are working have been provided over a longer time period, from which it appears that between 1975 and 1987 the proportion rose from 45.2 to 51.3 per cent.

But, as we shall see in the following chapter, the kind of work mothers obtain is usually precarious and of low status. Even when Japanese mothers are employed as regular employees in large companies, they are being heavily penalized for their attempt to combine a career with a family; a ranking of companies on the basis of working conditions for women carried out by the magazine *Nikkei Woman* (April 1988) found that not only were the scores for protection of motherhood and promotion to administrative positions very low, but also a relatively high ranking for the former was associated with a low score for the latter and vice versa. An ironic example of another inverse relationship is that salaried men in Japan can be penalized if they do not have a family, because if a man is not a father in a stable marriage he is thought to be irresponsible. Thus for a male employee a family is a 'good thing' in furthering his career, while for a working Japanese woman a family is a severe impediment.

Notes

(1) Figures on pre-school provision are available from *Social Trends*. In addition Shirley Dex and Lois B. Shaw provide an enlightening analysis of the percentages of working women using different kinds of day care in Britain and the USA in Hunt (ed.) (1988), pages 185 to 195.

(2) Shinotsuka, who is a woman economist, shows that the increase in the number of part-time working women has not been matched by the decline in the number of full-time homemakers. Chapter 2 of this book also discusses the movement of women out of family businesses into paid employment.

6 | Working options for mothers

The trend under which more married women in Japan are entering the labour force may one day escalate as the substantial number of discouraged workers, whom we have discussed in Chapter 4, would gladly take up employment once the labour market and social environment became more amenable. The labour market is already opening up with a higher demand for women's labour as the service sector expands and employers seek a more flexible workforce. But because of the mother's double burden and the fact that re-entrants to the labour force are rarely granted regular employment in large companies, Japanese mothers are usually found working in the secondary labour market, which, as we have seen in Chapter 3, is characterized by lower wages and worse conditions of employment. Not only in Japan, but also in Britain there are substantial wage penalties associated with being away from the labour force for a few years. One British researcher, Heather Joshi (1987), has evaluated the total cash opportunity costs of concentrating on child-rearing for eight years, then returning to work as a part-timer and being given lower pay rates because of a loss of experience as over £100,000. A severe observer might respond that the women who want a career and do not wish to forego earnings on such a scale should just remain in the labour force, but not only does that require costly child care – whether privately or publicly funded – but also there is a tremendous human cost, as well as a possible cost to society, in women having to bear the double burden. Those costs are exacerbated in Japan where a career-minded person is expected to demonstrate total loyalty to the job and to work lots of overtime.

Provisions which are intended to encourage companies to grant their female employees child-care leave do now exist in Japan, but their application is in practice limited (Chapter 5). If, instead, the woman returning to work wishes to enter regular employment in a company other than the one where she was employed before childbirth, she is hamstrung by the frequent practice in Japan of putting maximum age limits on entry to jobs, particularly clerical work. Therefore when a large-scale government survey (*Shuugyo Kozo Kihon Tokei Chosa*, 1987) asked unemployed women or women seeking to return to work what type they would like or thought to be most appropriate for them, whereas just over 14 per cent were looking for regular full-time employment, around 6 per cent wished to set up their own business or help in a family business, 17 per cent wanted to do paid work at home and the largest and rapidly growing proportion of over 57 per cent wanted part-time or free-lance work. Some women are not only thinking of the compatibility of their job and household responsibilities but also the greater likelihood of making use of their skills or qualifications than if they were to enter regular employment in a Japanese company, which usually requires its employees to become generalists. At the same time the respondents argued that, although part-time work was most appropriate for a working mother, priority should be given to a substantial improvement in working conditions for part-timers.[1]

So-called part-timers

An increasing proportion of British and Japanese mothers are likely to be part-time workers. That does not necessarily mean in Japan that their working hours are relatively few. Figures from the *New Earnings Survey, Part F* show that women working part-time in Britain average around 23 hours a week in manufacturing industries and just over 18 hours in services and others; whereas in Japan part-time women workers are on average working over 30 hours with a five-day working week, and in retailing, catering and smaller companies they are often working a six-day week (*Fujin Rodo no Jitsujo*, Table 71). It has been pointed out by Jane Humphries and Jill Rubery (Jenson, ed., 1988) that since part-timers are usually working every weekday, they have to get ready for work just as often as full-timers and spend as long commuting. But one reason why Japanese women are willing to accept long part-time working hours is because in the cities part-time work is often located relatively close to the home, whereas full-time workers have to commute for one or two hours.

There is one particularly disadvantageous kind of part-time work for Japanese women. The results from a Ministry of Labour survey on part-timers (1985) demonstrate that in manufacturing companies, in particular, over a quarter of the so-called part-time female workers are actually working about the same hours as the regular employees and another 20 per cent are working only 10 per cent fewer hours. So-called part-timers are especially prevalent in the smaller manufacturing firms. So as to distinguish between those who truly work part-time, data in Japan are given separately for those working 'short hours', which are fewer than 35 hours a week, and for so-called part-timers. Although many so-called part-timers are tantamount to full-time workers in terms of the hours they work, their employment conditions are worse than those of regular employees. Companies prefer not to take middle-aged women on as regular employees, because of the substantial allowances, regular wage increases and employment security expected. There-fore many women are offered only temporary, ostensibly 'part-time' contracts, which they accept because the immediate cash wages may be a bit higher than a newly employed regular employee could expect and in the large manufacturing companies around 80 per cent of so-called part-timers do at least receive contributions to sickness and unemployment insurance.

Expansion of part-time work for women

Since the structure of part-time work is rather different between Japan and the West, the discussion here will mostly be devoted to Japan where small manufacturers and retailers are significant employers of part-time women workers, but with some sidelong glances at the situation in Britain where part-time work for women is already highly pervasive. Even though it would be misleading to make a direct comparison of part-time working women in Japan with those in Britain, in order to get some idea of the relative scale a rough comparison of numbers of part-time workers is displayed in Tables 6.1 and 6.2, which do not include the so-called part-timers who work more than 35 hours a week.

The major reasons why there are relatively more female part-time employees in Britain than in Japan are not only the higher level of unemployment in Britain and the higher participation rate by British women, but also the way in which British employers can reduce their national insurance payments by employing part-time workers, who need not be insured if they are earning below a certain amount. One other important reason for the lower figures in Japan is because of there being more alternatives for casual employment in family businesses and self-employment than in Britain. (The reason why 'female as a proportion of all part-timers' is lower in Japan is because men over the mandatory retirement age of 55 or 60 years often work part time.) Interestingly enough, it is only in Ireland that there has been any decrease in the proportion of part-time women workers out of all working women. The reason may lie in the 1970s growth in female full-time employment opportunities in newly established electronics plants, including NEC from Japan.

The proportional figures for part-time working women shown in Table 6.1 are generally much higher in Britain, where indeed Table 6.2 shows that there would have been a sharp fall in female employment during the 1980s, but for the 7.3 percentage point contribution from part-time

TABLE 6.1 *Part-time workers as a proportion of all employees*
(percentages)

	Male and female			Female only			Female as a proportion of all part-time workers		
	1973	*1983*	*1986*	*1973*	*1983*	*1986*	*1973*	*1983*	*1986*
Ireland*	6.7	6.7	6.2	16.8	15.7	14.2	71.4	72.0	72.6
Japan	7.9	10.5	11.7	17.3	21.1	22.8	60.9	70.7	70.0
UK	16.0	19.1	21.6	39.1	42.4	45.0	90.9	89.6	88.7

TABLE 6.2 *Contribution of part-time employment to cumulative growth of female employment, 1979–1986*
(percentage growth)

	Part-time	Full-time	Total
Ireland*	1.9	3.7	5.6
Japan	6.2	5.3	11.5
UK	7.3	−4.4	2.9

Notes:
1. The figures for Ireland and the UK were originally provided by the EC.
2. * In the case of Ireland, 1973 should be read as 1975.
3. The definition of part-time workers differs between countries. In Japan it only applies to those in non-agricultural industries who actually worked less than 35 hours in the survey week, whereas in Britain and Ireland the definition encompasses all those who declare themselves to be working part time.

Sources: Ministry of Labour, *Fujin Rodo no Jitsujo.* OECD, *Employment Outlook,* 1988.

employment growth. Nonetheless in Japan as well there has recently been a rapid growth in female part-time employment. Not only are employers seeking part-time working women through legitimate channels, but also handwritten signs advertising local part-time positions are flagrantly displayed on many strategic utility poles in defiance of the relevant laws on where advertisements may be placed.

Figure 6.1 shows that by 1987 the proportion of women employees in Japan who worked part-time had reached 23.1

per cent, and their actual number was 84 per cent higher than in 1975. In Britain, meanwhile, over the same period the number of female part-timers increased by 19.4 per cent (Equal Opportunities Commission, 1987, 1988); but it is possible that since some part-time work in Britain falls within the grey economy, the Department of Employment estimates are below the actual number. The growth rate in Britain is in any case lower partly because of starting from a higher base and partly because overall employment opportunities fell in Britain during the same period.

Where part-time women workers are found

The conditions for part-time work vary so much in terms of the number of hours worked and the nature of the work that it is impossible to make a straight comparison between Japan and Britain, apart from the overall proportions and trends shown in the preceding section. Nor is it really feasible to get more than a rudimentary idea of the industries in which part-time working women are concentrated because the categories do not correspond exactly. But the *New Earnings Survey, Part E* and *Rodoryoku Chosa* (Labour Force Survey) do allow a rough comparison, when we define part-time work as being less than 35 hours a week. What is clearly different is that almost a quarter of part-time Japanese women are in the manufacturing sector working on the shop floor, whereas in Britain part-timers in manufacturing are mostly in clerical and related jobs with a paltry 2 per cent calculated to be in food, drink and tobacco manufacturing. In Britain the highest proportion, amounting to 34 per cent of all part-time women workers, is in the industrial category of professional and scientific services. A particular difference is that the public sector, which is an important employer of British women part-timers, accounts for less than 2 per cent of all Japanese women part-timers. In Japan the greatest number, reaching 38 per cent, is in the wholesale, retail and restaurant categories, while the similar

FIGURE 6.1 *Number of part-time working women in Japan (excluding those working in agriculture and forestry)*

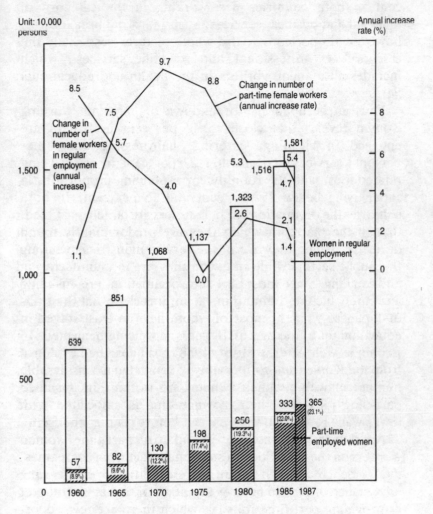

Note: In this case 'regular' employment is defined to encompass all workers who work 35 hours or more per week.

Source: Management and Coordination Agency, *Rodoryoku Chosa*.

categories in Britain account for 27 per cent of part-time women workers. Comparable proportions of around 5 per cent in both countries are working in the category of financial and business services. Such industrial breakdowns, however, do not convey the whole picture – especially the category of 'professional and scientific services', which includes all manual workers in the health and educational fields.

Thus an occupational breakdown of part-time working women reveals that close to 40 per cent in Britain are engaged in cleaning, catering, hairdressing and other personal services and another 22 per cent in clerical and related jobs, with the roughly corresponding proportions in Japan lying below 25 per cent and 15 per cent. In both countries the occupations of part-timers are largely unskilled, though the places in which they are predominantly found differ. In Britain they are in the service industries including the public sector, while in Japan they are in manufacturing and retailing. Since most part-time occupations are unskilled and rarely include training in Japan, it is clear that the skills of Japanese women, most of whom have at least stayed in education up to the age of 18 years, are being neglected. In Britain as well Audrey Hunt (1988) has unearthed evidence from the *Women and Employment Survey* that a considerable number of well-qualified women are working in unskilled part-time jobs and their downgrading is associated with lower wage rates than they earned before rearing children.

Apart from the anomaly in Japan of part-time women workers on the shop floor in small manufacturing companies, the evidence in both countries shows the overwhelming importance of certain narrow segments of the labour market in providing part-time jobs, in which there are few opportunities for gaining skills and promotion or for moving into full-time employment. Thus it appears that the expansion of part-time work has tended to exacerbate the occupational segregation of jobs between women and men, apart from the case of a few favoured professional women. If only the part-time labour market were not so thoroughly segmented from the market for full-time or skilled jobs, this trend towards part-time service sector jobs could facilitate the re-entry and mobility of women in the labour market, since in manufacturing there has been a greater loss from exiting and re-entering because of the depreciation in or redundancy of previously acquired skills.

Low-status and precarious part-time work

Part-time work is rather unattractive in Japan because the conditions of employment are much worse than for full-time, regular employees. The Ministry of Labour survey on part-time workers (1985) found that of all the companies employing part-timers, only around 45 per cent provided any kind of employment and health insurance systems, while barely 12 per cent gave a retirement allowance. So-called part-timers, who are working full-time hours, fared little better with around 60 per cent of their employers contributing to employment and health insurance schemes. These depressing figures should be compared with the fact that well over 90 per cent of Japan's paternalistic companies provide fairly generous welfare benefits to their full-time, regular employees. The hourly pay for Japanese women part-timers is between 70 and 75 per cent of that for regular female workers. In the UK the ratio of part-time pay to full-time hourly pay for female workers is over 75 per cent, but the differential would probably be just as wide as in Japan if the lowest paid part-time workers were included in the data.[2]

Since the figures above are based on all full-time workers, the calculations do not contradict my earlier assertion that Japanese women re-entering the labour force often find that part-time pay rates are more favourable than the pay offered with regular employment. The large part which length of tenure plays in determining full-time pay in Japan means that a middle-aged recruit must start way down on the wage scale. Some people in Japan like to assert that part-time working wives collude in accepting low pay, because they prefer to keep their annual incomes below the threshold for paying tax. While it is true that many Japanese seem to be quite allergic to paying taxes, because of the disrespect for a government steeped in 'money politics', the argument is basically spurious; an adequate income would more than compensate for what are admittedly fairly progressive tax rates in Japan.[3]

Furthermore part-time work has a much lower status than full-time work in Japan. Less than 20 per cent of part-timers are engaged in work requiring any kind of specialized knowledge and Japanese women working less than 35 hours a week are usually found in companies with less than 30 employees, where their hourly rates of pay are about 10 per cent less than for the few part-timers working in large companies. Even in the large companies, which are famous for the promise of permanent employment given to their elite regular employees, a part-timer has little or no job security, as the following curious story illustrates.

It was an infamous crime which demonstrated how precarious are the jobs of part-timers in Japan. When in 1984 an extortion group, which called itself the 'Man with 21 Faces' laced Morinaga food products with poison, the consequent sharp drop in sales and production led Morinaga, which is a large confectionery and biscuit maker, to lay off 450 part-time workers. It is now reported, though denied by Morinaga, that in the following year the extortion group turned to Robin Hood tactics by demanding that the laid-off workers be reinstated. In the same month Morinaga did indeed rehire about 200 of the part-time workers; and within a few weeks the extortion group wrote to the police saying that it would stop blackmailing Morinaga (*The Japan Times*, 17 February 1988).

It is worth mentioning, however, that in spite of the penalties associated with part-time work in Japan, those women who have chosen to do such work do appreciate the flexible hours in comparison to the expectation that a full-time employee should be in the workplace for a full eight-hour day plus overtime. Thus in the Ministry of Labour survey of part-time workers (1985), almost 50 per cent of women responded that they took up part-time work because they could match the working hours to their other commitments. That may be so, but another 37 per cent asserted that it was a second-best choice because either it was not feasible for them to be regular employees or they could not obtain full-time work. Consequently the demand from employers for part-time workers, most of whom would be women, is much higher than the available supply; in the late 1980s there were usually three times as many new part-time job openings as people newly seeking part-time work (*Maitsuki Kinro Tokei Chosa*).

Involuntary part-timers

The figures immediately above show that there are clearly a certain number of involuntary female part-timers in Japan who would prefer to work as regular full-time employees, but are denied the opportunity. Especially since the hours are often not much less for part-time work in Japan, some Japanese mothers would actually prefer to have all the benefits associated with full-time work, except that they are deterred by the total lack of flexibility in hours worked by regular employees. Even so, the fact that their part-time earnings are relatively low and that, in general, incomes in Japan are no longer rising does mean that there are signs of a trend towards mothers actively seeking full-time work. The *Asahi Shimbun* (26 December 1985) reported on trade union surveys which showed that the stagnation in male members' earnings was leading their wives, who presently worked part time or were homeworkers, to look for full-time jobs. And one of my respondents with two small children, who had not worked at all since graduating, took on full-time employment in her late twenties, rather than opt for part-time work.

In Britain the picture according to Veronica Beechey and Tessa Perkins (1987) is rather similar to Japan in that married women often do not have any option but to work part time in unskilled jobs with worse conditions of employment than those given to full-time employees. This issue of part-time work which is involuntary, not because of constraints placed by women themselves on their working hours, but because employers are unwilling to offer regular, full-time employment is going to become more controversial as part-time work becomes the expected norm in the female-segregated labour markets.

Overall, in both Japan and Britain part-time work for women is quite heavily penalized in terms of hourly rates, and in Japan where part-time workers are actually working close to full-time hours the total pay, welfare benefits and job security are considerably worse than those for regular employees. That is one reason why the part-time work option has not been so readily embraced by married women in Japan as it has been in Western Europe, especially Norway and Sweden, where around 45 per cent of all female employees – and the majority of mothers – are working part time, according to OECD statistics on the labour force. (Since the OECD definition of part-time work applies simply to jobs of less than 30 hours a week in Norway and less than 35 hours in Sweden, no account is taken of differences in the scope of job security and employee welfare benefits.)

The fact that part-time work is popular among Scandinavian mothers demonstrates that it is possible for part-time work to be appropriate not only for the employers but also for working women, because of its flexibility. In Europe the argument that part-time work is a rational choice for working mothers holds greater force than in Japan where part-time work may be seen as being of more benefit to the employer, who is thereby released from offering a secure job and from paying the twice-yearly bonus and various insurance payments. Meanwhile the part-time woman worker does not accumulate the on-the-job training skills and tenure benefits which are the most important determinants of power in the Japanese labour market.

Temporary workers of all kinds

The tale of Morinaga related earlier shows that the position of part-timers in Japan is often particularly insecure. The relative importance of temporary work combined with part-time status in both Japan and Ireland is much higher than in Britain. The OECD (1987, p.38) estimates that over 40 per cent of all Japanese part-timers and almost 50 per cent of Irish part-timers are on temporary contracts, but in the UK the comparable figure is only 16 per cent. Conditions for most temporary workers are in some ways similar to those for part-time workers, but this group includes such a variety of types and any data on their existence are still so rudimentary that it is hard to get a clear picture of their numbers and work conditions. In Japan a catch word, *arubaito*, which originally meant student jobs, is now often used in reference to all those jobs which are insecure or, in the modern parlance, casualized. *Arubaito* encompasses an immense and rather ambiguous range of jobs, which are being increasingly taken up by married women. Around 70 per cent of all temporary workers in Japan are women, whereas in Britain and Ireland the proportions lie between 51 and 55 per cent.

Despite the present low profile of temporary work in Britain, the number of British women in precarious employment is rapidly increasing. In just four years up to the mid-1980s, the number of temporary workers in Britain doubled (*The Guardian*, 10 June 1987); now close to 8 per cent of all employed women are temporary employees, compared to just 3.9 per cent in the case of employed men (*Social Trends*, 1988). In Britain the existence of a pool of unemployed workers, including youths and mothers who want to re-enter the labour force, with whom the female temporary worker may at any time be switched, means that women in particular are often in the poorly paid and less secure kinds of temporary work. Thus their kind of work is more likely to be casual and menial, with almost no hope of gaining skills and no employment progression (OECD, 1988, p.150).

One class of 'temporary' workers in Japan consists of those who are working regularly for the same company, but whose contracts are only for one year or less. Court cases have, however, ruled that when the contract has been renewed several times, then the worker cannot be dismissed later on at the time of renewal. Another kind of temporary worker comprises those working as subcontract or dispatch workers – much like secretaries from temp agencies in Britain. The dispatched worker is most likely to be found in the large companies, which wish to keep their regular staff to a minimum so as not to have to take on all the obligations associated with permanent employees. The usual occupations of dispatch workers range from computer programmers through clerical staff to cleaners. Some observers believe that the recent expansion of the dispatching agencies is playing an important role in forming a labour market in which women can use their skills and experience. (Certainly the usual employment pattern in Japan for regular workers, which requires long service and the acquiring of general skills, is inappropriate for many women.) A NIEVR survey (1986) – 'women in the worker dispatching industry' – found that most of the women had a high level of educational attainment and had left their regular employment because of discontent over their treatment or labour conditions. Nonetheless, despite earning higher hourly wages than regular female employees, only one-third of the surveyed women – mostly the married women and those who were making effective use of their expertise – expressed a wish to continue as dispatch workers. The rest were concerned about the level of insecurity and the irregular income. Emiko Takeishi (NIEVR, 1988) concludes that the dispatch system is appropriate for a limited group of women, but further worker protection measures than those included in the 1986 Worker Dispatching Law are needed.

In the Japanese countryside many part-time working women in green-field site factories are also working seasonally or on a temporary basis, with time off to harvest the rice. Their working conditions are, therefore, quite different to those at the green-field site plant of NEC Ireland, where the Irish women are deliberately taken on as regular permanent employees in the expectation that they will thereby have the time and motivation to become experienced and loyal employees. The fact that this expectation is largely fulfilled – as will be seen in Chapter 8 – attests to the fact that women should not be considered as only fit for the secondary labour market in which their membership is ancillary and volatile.

Future issues concerning women part-timers

Along with the expansion of the service sector, where part-time jobs are more prevalent, there will be an increasing need on both demand and supply sides for a more flexible work-force, as employers try to reduce their labour costs and working mothers to balance their roles. These trends are leading to a rapid growth in the number of both part-timers and temporary workers, who are often in unskilled work with little prospect of training and promotion. In Britain there is also the issue – which has not yet arisen in Japan – of whether married women are being taken on in part-time jobs instead of young workers who are being left unemployed. (In the Japanese labour market there is a shortage in the supply of youths – in particular those who have not graduated from university, since their wages are low and employers want to hire youths who are thought to be pliable enough to become loyal workers.)

There should be a greater sense of urgency about the plight of part-timers, since all the trends point towards their numbers increasing right through the 1990s. It should not be beyond the bureaucratic genius of the Japanese to work out, for example, practical ways of ensuring that the working women who bear the brunt of cyclical changes, while coping with bringing up a family, are properly compensated when they are made redundant. The Ministry of Labour (1985) found that almost 30 per cent of part-time workers – of whom 95 per cent were women and about 29 per cent were working more than 40 hours a week – had been in their present job for more than five years, but only 12 per cent were eligible for severance pay.

Legislation to protect part-timers in Britain is actually likely to become more limited in line with the Conservative government's policy of deregulating labour markets; the 1986 white paper, *Building Business Not Barriers*, included proposals to raise the thresholds for weekly working hours from 16 hours to 20 hours for a part-time worker to qualify for employment rights after two years. And the threshold for those with continuous service of at least five years would be raised from 8 to 12 hours. The Equal Opportunities Commission (1988) has calculated that under such policy changes a total of 20 per cent of married women employees would lose their present rights to employment protection. In Japan the situation is no better. Since part-time workers entered the Japanese scene relatively late, it was only in 1984 that a coherent set of policies was developed for their protection. The present provisions for a nominally part-time worker, who is working five days a week and has been employed for at least a year, require entitlement to paid leave in subsequent years and a certain measure of job security. The Ministry of Labour is also studying proposals for measures such as collecting a bounty percentage from employers, which would be part of retirement benefits for those part-timers with continuous work records. Even such limited measures are, however, likely to be ignored in the mass of small and struggling companies in which part-time women workers are mostly to be found.

At present part-time work in Japan has not reached the level of desirability – low as that may be – for women found in Britain, let alone the Scandinavian countries. Its fairly recent development in Japan is more the result of women being unable to enter regular employment in their middle age and of companies desiring to have a flexible and cheaper work-force. At the same time the fact that part-time hours are more flexible and that the workplace may be closer to the woman's home – though not necessarily so – does make it a rational option for mothers re-entering employment who bear the double burden of work and homemaking. And the increased concern of government and the media may ensure that some of the worst abuses in labour conditions for part-time workers are being remedied. The trouble is that part-time work for wives in both Japan and Britain is often an extension of their domestic role in catering and cleaning so that it is counted as 'unskilled', although in reality such jobs are highly skilled in depending on the woman's experience accumulated in the home.

Family businesses

The home, therefore, should not necessarily be disparaged as an extension of a worker's role. It is only in the relatively short time span since industrialization that work and home have become separate spheres with a consequent confusion over a wife's place and economic role. In Japan the persistence of family businesses, in which the wife plays an important role (often as the accountant while also tending her children), suggests that this model could also be appropriate for post-industrial society where some service and information industries can be located in the home.

Paradoxically, the strength of tradition in Japan need not impede the adaption of society; innovative forms have evolved which maintain traditional values, such as occurs when the managerial wife treats employees as family members akin to feudal retainees. Mary Lou Maxson (Lebra *et al*, 1976) vividly depicts an urban family business in which the wife controls the buying and distribution of materials for subcontractors, and is the guide in policy matters. That does not necessarily mean that a woman has always been able to play an equal part in a family business. On the farms the wife was often considered to be working under her husband and, since she did not receive a salary, she had no economic independence; but now that the men have left the farms to

159

work in nearby factories, the farm women's power has increased. And in the ideal case where the wife does have a managerial role as an extension of her role as manager of the family's finances, the structure of the family business dovetails with the family division of labour.

Often the setting up of a family business in Japan is in response to the husband becoming unemployed, in which case the business may be a small restaurant or take-away food shop requiring little capital investment. The wife resolves to ensure that the business is successful by having the children in day care and she attends to the customers while her husband carries out the cooking in the rear. Unfortunately, I have seen some of these rudimentary businesses fold up, but the couple do at least support each other in concrete ways through economic straits. Recently many couples who have managed to raise loans from friends and banks have left their regular employment and invested in the setting up of a 'pension', which is a simple, family-run hotel located in a scenic area. Again there is a lot of economic stress in running the hotel and re-paying the loans, but the parents console themselves with the thought that they can now bring their children up away from the crowded urban environment of Tokyo or Osaka. These couples had already become disillusioned with the life of a 'salary man', since a lot of the benefits of job security and industrial paternalism require a commitment to be at the company almost all one's waking hours.

At the same time there may be a tendency on the part of Western observers to be overly optimistic about the resilience and appropriateness of an enterprise household. The life of a family worker should not be idealized. The ordinary strains of married life can be exacerbated by continuous close contact between the partners and the likelihood of blaming each other when the business is less than successful. The majority of young women would still prefer to marry a 'salary man' who would be away from the home for most of the day. And they themselves want to do work which does not tie them closely into what can be a stifling family structure. Some women say that it is not only the long working hours in a household enterprise which is unattractive, but also the increased compulsion to take part in local community activities. The annual local two-day *matsuri* (festival), which requires a tremendous amount of organization, depends wholly upon the efforts of the local shop-owners and small businesses. Nor can they expect increased custom during the *matsuri*, since they have to close their shops so as to participate. People in the West may envy this expression of local community feeling, but the women who have to maintain all the never-ending obligations usually find it rather irksome. It is not perhaps so surprising, therefore, that when unemployed women have been asked what kind of work they would like to do (*Shuugyo Kozo Kihon Chosa*), only 5.4 per cent – a decline from 8.8 per cent in 1968 – wish either to be self-employed or to help in a family business, whereas a sizeable, though decreasing, 17.3 per cent want to do *naishoku* (contracted industrial home-work) despite it being tedious, poorly paid work.

Disappearing homeworkers, and emerging 'workers at home'

If you see in Japan's back alley-ways a middle-aged or elderly housewife regularly carrying a staggering pile of cardboard boxes towards the post office or a delivery service point, you may be sure that she is working long hours at home for very low piece-work rates. The woman is rarely young, because nowadays the majority of mothers prefer to seek part-time work, although as recently as the late 1960s, over 40 per cent of those wanting a paid job were looking for homework. Because of the low pay and appearance of desperation there is now a stigma attached to *naishoku* – a translator working at home, for example, would always try to avoid that appellation. Because women and their relatives are no longer likely to admit that they do homework, it is becoming more invisible, though not to the same extent as in Britain where the pervasiveness of homework is usually denied because it is not thought to be real work. While in Japan homework is becoming less visible, in Britain its public visibility is increasing, partly because of studies by the Low Pay Unit and the attention now being paid by feminist researchers, including Sheila Allen and Carol Wolkowitz (1987).

The homeworkers in Japan, who are working on average almost six hours a day and over 20 days a month, are usually engaged in making or finishing off textile products and electrical goods; the work is monotonous and the associated paraphernalia of boxes and parts fills up the scarce living space in a typical crowded apartment. What is also depressing is that the work they are doing is often so trivial – such as decorating a hand-towel with rabbit's ears, just so that it can be sold for a few more yen. Not only does the contractor not have to pay any of the lighting and other overheads associated with factory work, but also he benefits from the woman homeworker's low wages, against which collective action is impossible because she is so isolated from her fellow workers. The limited protection measures under the Industrial Homework Law merely ensure the payment of minimum wages, which are in any case very low relative to other wages. The female homeworkers' average hourly rate of pay is only about 54 per cent of that of full-time women employees doing similar jobs in firms with less than 30 employees and only 38 per cent of what male homeworkers earn, according to the Ministry of Labour's regular survey (*Kanai Rodo Gaikyo Chosa*).

Consequently Japanese women have increasingly preferred to take up part-time employment, unless there is a compelling reason to be at home; the number of homeworkers has steadily declined to not much more than half of their peak level in 1973. It is hard to get accurate figures on the number of homeworkers, because in the statistics they are usually lumped together with the self-employed, or are put in the family business category according to some abstruse classification system; but they are estimated to account for around 3.9 per cent of all working women. That level will continue to fall as the most recent survey shows that over 18 per cent of women homeworkers want to quit and instead take up outside work.

But it would in some ways be a pity if opportunities for homework were diminished. It provides paid work for women with small children who do not want them to be in day care, for those looking after aged relatives and for the handicapped too. The *Mainichi Daily News* (15 December 1986) reported on a handicapped woman who does kimono embroidery at home after taking lessons for seven years; she thereby earns more than her husband, who is also handicapped, but who has fewer working opportunities – or perhaps less initiative. The question of whether disabled people should however work in the home is controversial; ideally they should be encouraged and enabled to join able-bodied workers in workplaces where they would no longer be isolated and possibly exploited.

Even without such compelling reasons there are some independent-minded women who prefer not to be in a place of employment where they are subject to sexual stereotyping. Especially in a Japanese office, women are expected to dress conservatively and smartly. One rather unconventional Japanese woman I know has chosen to do homework, because she can wear comfortable clothes and behave more or less as she wishes. Nor does she fit the usual image of a desperate homeworker, since she lives in a relatively large house and her son is a medical doctor.

That is not to say that all Japanese homeworkers have found a carefree lifestyle, especially not when they are trying to cope with small children at the same time as they are working. In such cases the woman gets up in the early hours of the morning to work, because otherwise the toddler would be getting tangled up in the threads and boxes. The contractors' demands, the low pay for piece-work and the isolation from fellow workers often lead to a much more onerous working life than that experienced by office staff or large company shop-floor workers. It all depends on the conditions of work and the extent of protection. Even in the case of the new homeworking jobs, such as telecommuting where the work is done from a computer terminal in the home, women are likely to be confined to low-paying data entry jobs with similar disadvantages to those borne by traditional homeworkers. In any case the expected rapid growth of work in this area has been less than expected.

In its ideal form, working at home – as opposed to homeworking – belongs in some ways to the long tradition of family businesses in which there is no need for the awkward and sometimes inefficient separation of home from paid work. It could – under a different guise – become part of the post-industrial future with the installation of a computer modem and facsimile machine in the kitchen for programmers and freelance writers. One woman, who had outside employment when her sons were pre-schoolers, now prefers to work at home – transcribing interviews from tapes – because she can then participate fully in the many school activities geared towards parents and in other community activities. Such kinds of working at home should really be counted as self-employment, which covers a whole gamut of structures and occupations.

Self-employment

We have seen in Table 2.1 that there has been a relative decline since 1960 in the proportion of Japanese women who are self-employed, whereas in Britain the numbers of self-employed have risen substantially since 1979, especially in the service sector and among women (*Social Trends*, 1988). Nonetheless by 1986, still only just over 7 per cent of all working British women were self-employed compared to around 25 per cent of working Japanese women in self-employment and family businesses (excluding the agricultural sector). It is hard to believe that the figure for self-employment of 15 per cent of working British men is so much higher than that for women. In contrast the positions in Japan are reversed with just over 15 per cent of Japanese men in the same categories. Family workers are presumably lumped together in the category of self-employed in Britain, since they are not considered significant enough to be separately identified. But this is one of those treacherous cases where data sources are unreliable. Many married women in particular are concealing their work in family businesses or in self-employment because of a dread of paperwork and to evade tax payments. These categories in any case are not easy to define, let alone to make consistent for international comparisons.

In fact more opportunities for self-employment have emerged in Britain in the 1980s because of trends towards subcontracting cleaning and financial services and towards precarious employment, including temporary and some part-time jobs, in what is now dubbed, usually in a pejorative sense, a casualization of work. Leaving aside casual jobs for the moment, a more upbeat view of the growth in the informal labour market for British women could anticipate that part of the British picture is converging towards that of Japan with its vibrant informal sector for working women, which we have seen in Chapter 2. Even though the registered rate of self-employment is significantly higher among married British women than unmarried – 8 per cent of working married women compared to 4 per cent of unmarried – it is notably married Japanese women who have chosen the option of self-employment or working in family businesses, both of which accounted for 36.8 per cent of working married women in 1987 (*Shuugyo Kozo Kihon Chosa*). Evidently Japanese women have thereby been better able to shoulder their double burden of housekeeping and working roles by devoting fewer hours to the latter than required for salaried employees. In this respect the data show a striking disparity between Japan and the rest of the OECD countries. As shown in Table 6.3, self-employment usually means working longer hours than the average, except in the case of Japanese women.

TABLE 6.3 *Average hours worked per week by self-employed females in the non-agricultural sector*

	1973		1984	
Ireland*	52.0	(36.8)	46.1	(35.9)
Japan	38.4	(44.2)	34.6	(41.6)
UK	40.9	(31.2)	33.2	(29.9)

Notes:
1. *In the case of Ireland the years are 1975 and 1983.
2. Bracketed data refer to average hours worked per week by wage-earners and salaried employees.
Source: OECD, *Employment Outlook*, 1986.

Trade unions and the secondary labour market

It is particularly in Japan where unions are enterprise-based that they are guilty of not giving enough attention to issues related to part-time and other kinds of work in the secondary labour market. This attitude is, however, becoming subject to criticism among union employees themselves. Denki Roren officials told me that they are now campaigning to gain employee welfare benefits, including redundancy payments, for so-called part-timers who have been working at least seven hours a day for more than a year. At the same time they are encouraging part-time and seasonal workers to become unionized by offering lower membership dues.

It is possible that the energetic woman official of Denki Roren whom I met may be able to organize the women in the secondary labour market at the same time as dispelling the rather fusty atmosphere of unions. Her image of vitality and originality stood in marked contrast to the lounge at the union headquarters with its vases, plaques and furnishings dating from the heyday of male-dominated Japanese unions in the late 1940s. It is significant that though my original appointment was with a male assistant director of research, he invited the woman official and let her take over much of the initiative in the discussion. Indeed women are becoming among the first to break away from enterprise unions, by forming women's unions which are not based on any one industry, let alone a single company. Their argument is that the existing unions are male-oriented and will not take up women's demands.

In trying to organize women workers Denki Roren faces a wider variety of conditions and needs than in the case of male workers. Women are dispersed in the secondary or informal labour markets; their backgrounds in terms of qualifications and experience cover a wide span; the ages of their children and the presence of grandparents affect their capacity to work certain hours; and their life-stage – from young and single to elderly and widowed – is also a determining factor. And as a result of all this variety in conditions women themselves have widely different expect-ations and desires – especially over the issue of protection versus complete equality of opportunity. Thus the women's section of Denki Roren has a very hard time putting together a coherent set of policies. In the context of the importance Japanese society places on the family, a lot of their discussion is devoted to how to extend systems for granting child-care leave and for re-employment. Yet they are not rewarded with much interest in union activities from working women. Denki Roren's 1985 survey of over 7,000 women working in electrical companies found that almost 60 per cent were uninterested in union activities.

The lack of union interest even on the part of those women who are union members indicates that the present union structure and atmosphere is not conducive to their active participation. Union officials suggest that there should be training especially geared towards women who are not accustomed to speaking out in Japanese society. And women need child-care facilities or reimbursement for baby-sitter fees when they take part in weekend or evening union activities.

In any case the gradual decrease in unionization rates – now standing at just over 30 per cent of all male employees and only 20 per cent of female employees – is impelling the major trade union confederations, Rengo (Private Sector Trade Union Confederation) and Sohyo (General Council of Trade Unions), to step up campaigns for organizing part-time and temporary workers so as to recoup some of their reduced power. Unionization rates continue to be high – approaching 70 per cent – in large companies. But a 1988 Rengo survey found that the unionization rate of part-time labour was just 6.2 per cent and even in unionized firms stood at only around 15 per cent. Yasuo Suwa writing in the *Japan Labor Bulletin* (1 February 1989) believes that many enterprise unions in large companies have been negligent in their attitude towards part-time workers. The situation is even worse for part-time workers in the small companies where wages are much lower and non-union labour is quiescent. Sohyo has, therefore, established regional unions which include part-time workers in small companies (*The Japan Times*, 23 November 1987 and 26 January 1988). The unions are aware that unless they attend to the working conditions of part-timers, whose numbers will keep expanding, ultimately the conditions for full-time workers will be adversely affected. Yasuo Suwa argues that it will be difficult to unionize women part-time workers, who dislike being fettered and paying union dues. If unions, however, were to demonstrate their commitment to fighting dis-advantageous conditions for part-time workers and to gear mutual aid activities towards them, there would be scope for a rise in the unionization rate among women.

Alternatives to casual employment

While the involvement of the unions may lead to improvements in the working conditions for married women in the secondary labour market, what is ultimately required is greater freedom for such women to enter regular employment in the primary labour market if they so wish. Union surveys of women have found that most women are interested in their work, which is quite contrary to the usual perception of Japanese women being only concerned about home affairs. Indeed the Denki Roren survey (1985) mentioned above found that only 68 per cent of the working women were interested in love and marriage, while 84 per cent were concerned about their work and 82 per cent wanted to improve their level of skills and training.

Evidently there is a great need for Japanese industry to be more adaptive to career breaks – especially those now being promoted under the child-care leave scheme – and for more career development and training courses designed for older women, so that they can re-enter the labour market with confidence and the appropriate skills. Vocational training in Britain where women can take courses in computer-related skills appears to provide a better and more accessible range of courses than is available in Japan where the job-training and Women's Employment Assistance centres mostly offer training in skills such as sewing and word processing, along with counselling.

There will still, however, be a place for the informal labour market – as distinct from the casual market – because of the benefits of flexible hours and proximity to their homes for women with significant family obligations. The opening up of the primary labour market may be seized upon by only a minority of married women, but it will be those who want to accumulate skills and experience, which can only be a good thing for their employers. Most of those women who do re-enter the labour market experience downward mobility in terms of skills, salary and conditions of employment, which is a loss not only for themselves but also for society, especially since Japanese women are relatively highly educated.

The casual labour market is usually seen in Britain as a symptom of economic recession where males and youths are facing unemployment while middle-aged women are given low-paid work with little job security. In Japan, however, there has been a resurgence of economic growth in the late 1980s, so the reasons why older women are entering and being welcomed in the peripheral labour market are rather different. Ideally through a mixture of economic forces and government encouragement the informal labour market should, in time, take better advantage of women's abilities. It would be a real and radical breakthrough in Japan if the secondary labour market in its ideal form of a flexible vibrant labour force, part of which is self-employed, were to replace the primary market as the main source of skilled labour. But that will only be possible once women are no longer treated on the basis of their gender as casual workers to whom employers owe no legal or other obligations and for whom they believe low pay is justified.

Notes

(1) Ministry of Labour *Fujin Rodo no Jitsujo*, 1988, appendix, page 77. Also see data from the Prime Minister's Office (1984) in which 16 per cent favoured self-employment for married women and 13 per cent work in a family business or homework.

(2) Since regular workers in Japan are paid at monthly rates, calculations of their average hourly pay have to be an approximation, for which I have relied upon data from *Chingin Kozo Kihon Tokei Chosa*. In the case of Britain, the calculations come from the *New Earnings Survey, Parts A and F*. It should be noted, however, that the *New Earnings Survey* does not cover the significant number of employees who are not members of PAYE schemes, usually because their earnings are below £35.50 per week, which means that about one-third of all part-time employees are not included in the survey's figures. Since the bulk of those excluded are women, their exclusion would have depressed the earnings differential for Britain further. Another point to note is that whereas part-time females on average tend to earn a little more per hour than manual full-time female workers, their earnings are considerably less than those of non-manual female workers, as is clear from Table B39 in the *New Earnings Survey*.

(3) The tax threshold for part-timers and informal workers is based on annual income, whereas for full-time employees it is monthly income which is the determining factor. The monthly income threshold multiplied by twelve is only a little higher than that for part-timers. But since many regular employees receive a twice-yearly bonus ranging from one to three months' salary, an employee's monthly salary could be below the threshold so that she does not have to pay tax, but her annual income may be a lot higher than that of a part-timer who has to pay tax.

7 | Japanese companies in Britain and Ireland

The picture that has been presented so far about Japanese women in the workplace has been quite dispiriting. The same sad story does not necessarily apply, however, to those women employed by Japanese companies overseas. And so the next stage is to consider the situation of British and Irish women working in Japanese companies. My choice of Japanese companies to observe in Britain and Ireland was dictated by certain factors. I have only looked at manufacturing companies – not at any of the numerous Japanese commercial and financial companies located in London. The latter are not such significant employers of Britons as the manufacturers and, in particular, only a fraction of their employees are women without formal qualifications. The position of white-collar women employees is not without significance – indeed in the USA Honda and Nissan have faced formal sex-discrimination complaints over hiring and promotion practices for their white-collar employees – but in this study I wanted to see how a woman working on the shop floor was affected by Japanese work practices.

In particular I am interested in the Japanese plants located in regional development areas – notably South Wales and Ireland. (Japanese manufacturers in the North East are receiving a lot of media attention, because of their concentration in an area of high unemployment; but those firms, such as Komatsu and Nissan, are mostly employing men on the shop floor.) The regional development areas are where the authorities have been the most welcoming and where the work-force before the 1970s had been least exposed to any notion of Japan, let alone of its management methods. I

171

chose plants which had been established for a reasonable length of time and where Japanese expatriate management was still playing an important part, since Michael White and Malcolm Trevor (1983, p.84), who carried out extensive interviews with employees of Japanese companies, have found out that where British managers have taken over the plant has lost much of its Japanese character. My final criterion was that I should be able to survey the same companies' plants in Japan so as to be able to make a direct comparison of the conditions under which women work when employed by a given company in Japan and in Europe.

A rural area and an industrial estate

NEC Semiconductors Ireland Ltd is quite a revelation: a sleek plant of one of Japan's technological leaders located deep among the hedges and fields of rural Ireland. I travelled along narrow winding roads, mostly through farmland, with some delay caused by a herd of cows blocking the whole road. I had made detours to the old towns of Trim and Navan, which are exceptionally sleepy-looking places, where employment opportunities are rare and married women who take jobs while men are unemployed are viewed with some disapproval. In the case of those Irish women who work in a Japanese plant, their relative isolation from the social pressures which might be found in an Irish-owned workplace and their presumed good fortune mean that they are less likely to have to cope with cultural and social deterrents to their employment. That may explain why they had a remarkably positive view of working in a Japanese company – as we shall see in Chapter 8.

The women on the small farms in the counties of Meath and Cavan around NEC Ireland would like to have part-time employment, since the partial modernization of Irish agriculture has left them with little farmwork to do. Yet, as we have seen in Chapter 1, their participation in the labour force is particularly low. Any manufacturing industries are mostly confined to dairy plants and carpet factories, although a US electronics firm, Zenith, does have a plant near Kells. The man in Navan's youth employment office, which also doubles up as the tourist office, said that high youth unemployment in the area showed no sign of diminishing. Evidently one reason is that foreign electronics companies are employing more women than men on the shop floor and, therefore, more women than before are registered as seeking work. The incentives granted by the Industrial Development Authority (IDA) in Ireland to foreign manufacturing firms are deliberately geared towards attracting electronics and other high-tech industries, which provide employment for Ireland's relatively well-educated young people and which are better suited to isolated green-field sites than are heavy industries and automobile plants.

Eventually I arrived at a small town in County Meath called Ballivor, whose insignificance may be gauged from the sum of its entry in the road gazetteer: 'near the extensive Bog of Clonycavan'. The NEC plant with its spacious lawns seems almost as large as the town and certainly more imposing, even though the building itself is a low-lying structure. The peace of the place came in complete contrast to the large NEC plant in Tamagawa, which is hemmed in between other factories and railway lines. (Perhaps that is why NEC chose such a remote place as Ballivor – a choice which somewhat baffles other foreign investors and the IDA.) But the high technology processes for the production of integrated circuits (ICs) are similar in both Ballivor and Tamagawa, except that NEC Ireland imports the silicon wafers for dicing and the subsequent processes. I was assured that the output and quality levels of the semi-conductor devices from NEC Ireland were comparable to those from NEC's plants in Japan. Nor, incidentally, do the tractors and cows on the narrow roads seem to have unduly impeded the transportation of goods and materials between Ballivor and Dublin airport, which is about an hour's drive away.

There is no need to advertise for shop-floor recruits. Almost every day in this area of high youth unemployment,

173

people turn up requesting a job. They are usually dis-
appointed since NEC Ireland employees are exhibiting signs
of being permanently employed. (This judgement is perhaps
premature since the plant has only been in operation since
1976, but the workers to whom I spoke evidently had no
intention of leaving.) NEC Ireland deliberately located its
plant in a rural area where it could recruit farmers' children
straight from school. A 'fresh' work-force is preferred to
skilled labour, since all training takes place within the firm.
Recruits only have to pass an aptitude test and an interview.

The dramatic appearance of NEC Ireland is a special case.
In contrast, the Matsushita plant established in 1974 near
Cardiff is just one among many rather similar-looking
factories located on an industrial estate, which is indisputably
much more spacious and well-planned than the industrial
areas in Kawasaki and Osaka. The commonplace location
seems to convey to the workers a more nonchalant attitude
towards their employment in a Japanese plant than I was
aware of in Ireland. Whereas the woman receptionist at
NEC Ireland had been joyously proud to welcome me to the
plant – which admittedly may not have many visitors being
so out of the way and relatively small – in Cardiff my visit
was treated in a more relaxed way. In addition, Matsushita's
product line of colour televisions, monitors and tuners are
less mysterious than the ICs produced at Ballivor. Nor is the
technology as awesome.

The nonchalance of employees at Matsushita in Cardiff is
also perhaps a way of coping with the more overt company
philosophy of Matsushita. Whereas NEC publicity brochures
emphasize the technology embedded in the company's
products, Matsushita's begin with its 'corporate creed'
of 'serving society'. Framed and hung up on the wall is
Matsushita's corporate slogan, 'Act with Courage' and basic
business principles (national service, harmony, courtesy,
gratitude, etc); but it is doubtful that its employees in
Cardiff are impressionable enough to accept the whole
philosophy without any cynicism. I was told that Matsushita
is mostly recruiting school-leavers or middle-aged women,

though there are some honourable exceptions. All entrants are given a three-month probationary period. Thereafter the workers are assured that the job is virtually secure; one woman employee herself stated firmly that if there were sales problems, then there would be product diversification so as to keep the work-force employed. In Ireland as well, both the IDA and the work-force have a strongly perceptible sense that a Japanese plant offers virtually complete job security. I was told by the IDA that even when a venture may not appear to be running profitably in the short run, the Japanese will keep on the work-force with the long-term view that business will turn up again.

Rush of Japanese investment into Britain

The plants introduced above are but two examples of many cases. It would be as well, therefore, to consider the overall trend of Japanese overseas direct investment in Britain and Ireland so as to illuminate some of the issues involved. What I write may soon be out of date, because one feature is how recent and rapid is the growth of Japanese manufacturing in the British Isles. It was only in the 1970s that Japanese plants – initially quite small – began to be established in Britain, but in the late 1980s there has been such a tremendous upsurge that, compared to just 50 established projects in 1987, there were over 95 in 1989. In 1987 to 1989 the share of the UK in the total amount of new Japanese direct overseas investment, including financial and commercial subsidiaries, was higher than any other country apart from the USA, according to figures from the Japanese Ministry of Finance's annual report on direct overseas investment. (The figures are subject to some qualifications, because some investments may be approved or registered, but then not actually carried out.)

It is the large Japanese companies which are entering Britain. In some Asian and South American countries, the actual number of cases of overseas investment each year is higher than in the UK, but the latter entertains much larger amounts by value of overseas investment. The cumulative amount of Japanese investment in the UK is relatively low, however, since it was just in 1984 that new Japanese overseas investment in manufacturing in Europe began to surpass that in Asia. Nor is the existing level of Japanese investment particularly high compared to that from other countries. In Wales the number of Japanese plants is only just over half of those from the USA.

There is likely, however, to be a further rush of Japanese investment into the European Community (EC) prior to the creation of a unified market in 1992, because there is some anxiety that after that date there will be new kinds of regulations, which may cramp the style of the Japanese manufacturers. For example, some EC officials are demanding 'reciprocity' in external trade and investment – a rather ill-defined notion which seems to imply at its extreme that the number of Japanese televisions sold in Europe should be matched by an equivalent number of European-made models sold in Japan. There is also the serious accusation that the Japanese are building 'screw-driver' plants, in which almost all the components are made in Japan and then merely assembled in European plants. For that reason various local content requirements have been established amid some controversy. In particular the IC production which I saw at NEC Ireland is subject to the charge of being mere assembly. NEC, however, was the first Japanese semiconductor maker in Europe to set up an integrated facility for fabricating silicon wafers (on which the individual semiconductors are etched in NEC Ireland) and for producing the powerful one-megabit DRAM (dynamic random-access memory) devices, when its Livingstone, Scotland, plant began production in 1987. Now that Fujitsu has announced plans in early 1989 for a similar integrated wafer-fabrication plant in the North East of England, the other major Japanese makers can be expected to follow suit, despite the large-scale investment required, especially as the EC has ruled that semiconductor manufacturers must have integrated European factories to benefit from duty-free access to the EC market.

Already the Japanese electronics industry, of which Matsushita and NEC are good representatives, has had a particularly high profile in Japan's direct investment in the British Isles. The emphasis has previously been on electrical consumer goods, but this is changing as the semiconductor makers sharply increase their investment outlays. All of the major Japanese consumer electronics companies have at least one plant in Britain, which is usually located in a regional development area or in a new town. The sector accounting for the highest proportion of British employees working for Japanese manufacturers is the electronics industry; and most of those on the shop floor are women. Both Matsushita and NEC are continuing to expand, with the latter diversifying its British product line in a massive new investment in Telford, Shropshire. In South Wales, where there are two Matsushita plants, Japanese companies in the electronics industry are expected by 1990 to provide 6,000 jobs (*Mainichi Shimbun*, 17 July 1988); and the vast majority of those jobs are being filled by young women. The fact that these new employment opportunities are mostly confined to women has aroused some controversy in South Wales, where skilled men are losing their jobs in the coal and heavy industries; many households are now characterized by there being an unemployed father whose daughter is employed in a Japanese company.

Some of the reasons for the popularity of Britain as a location for Japanese investment are obvious. All Japanese study English at school, so there are fewer language problems than in non-English speaking countries, and to invest in Britain gains a fairly friction-free foothold in the important EC market. Even before facsimile machines could become a trade issue, as in the case of automobiles, NEC decided to start their production at Telford for sale in Europe, along with video cassette recorders and cellular mobile telephones. (The last-mentioned had already been subject to an anti-dumping enquiry because of allegations that the export price did not cover all the costs of production.) Ultimately the NEC Telford plant will be producing a full computer system including peripherals.

In addition to language and market benefits, there have been fairly generous financial incentives granted by the government through the Invest in Britain Bureau and its agency for investment in Wales, Winvest. The regional selective assistance scheme includes initial grants of around 20 per cent of the capital costs and sites to encourage manufacturers to enter areas of high unemployment, which are supplemented with tax concessions (by offsetting capital expenditure against tax for a certain period) and freedom from some regulations. (These incentives may have to be reined in to quieten EC criticism of excessive British generosity.) An additional incentive, which is not courtesy of the taxpayer, is the yen appreciation, which has further lowered relative production costs, including labour costs, in the British Isles.

One more reason why Japanese manufacturers are happy to be in Britain has only fairly recently emerged: the high quality of the labour force. And most of those workers who so impress the Japanese are women in the electronics factories. Originally there were some doubts among the Japanese about the incidence of industrial disputes and the supposed British predilection for tea breaks. Now a major survey of Japanese companies in Britain carried out by the *Nihon Keizai Shimbun* (4 and 5 January 1988) has revealed that the image of the British worker has changed and that the employees work hard and diligently. Fifty Japanese subsidiaries in Britain were surveyed, of which only one-third had had any prior expectation that the quality of labour would be satisfactory. The rest had only chosen to invest in Britain as a simple way of reaching markets in the EC. Once manufacturing had begun, however, the most important reason why Britain was a favoured location became: 'the high quality of the labour force', and many companies also assented to the response: 'the labour unions are not as belligerent as we had believed.'

A research project, which was carried out by Kanagawa University, Japan, and Michigan University, USA, has also shown that in spite of the longer presence and closer links between the USA and Japanese companies, labour turnover in British subsidiaries is much lower than in the US subsidiaries and the 'information sharing system' between labour and management, which includes aspects such as the extent of consultation, quality control circles and on-the-job training, is evaluated more highly in the British plants (*Nihon Keizai Shimbun*, 15 July 1988). One of the reasons cited for the higher evaluation of the latter is the way in which the Japanese companies have successfully forged agreements, many of which include a no-strike clause, with the plant union so as to engender open communication and co-operation; so this aspect deserves a section on its own later on.

Slower investment in Ireland

It should be mentioned at this point that Japanese investment in Ireland has not seen such dramatic growth nor are the plants as large as in Britain – in 1987 the work-force numbered under 300 in each of the largest Japanese employers, which include NEC and Asahi Synthetic Fibres. There are advantages for Japanese investors in Ireland similar to those in Britain, with the additional incentives of being a particularly low cost beachhead into the EC and having a low corporate tax rate of only 10 per cent. Moreover the communications infrastructure has received huge investment during the 1980s to become one of the most developed in Europe. The IDA offers a generous incentive package to foreign manufacturers, which includes a grant to cover 20 to 30 per cent of the initial capital investment and a training grant, both of which need not usually be repaid. The latter, which is also intended to cover the costs of induction training courses for Irish employees sent to Japan, is one of the main planks of the package, because of the importance which the Irish government attaches to the acquisition of skills, as a long-lasting 'investment in human resources'. Subsequently the main form of financial aid for NEC Ireland is tax relief on profits from exports until 1990. Since the whole output of semiconductors from NEC Ireland is exported to the NEC sales office in West Germany, the company has in effect been paying no corporate taxes.

It has been suggested by Taro Matsuo (Sasaki, ed., 1987), who has conducted research in Japanese firms located in Ireland, that the employee in Ireland has less loyalty to the company than in Japan. He cites the case of a few employees who moved to another company soon after their return from training in Japan. In another case, because the whole work-force at one electronic parts factory went on strike in 1979 when one woman with a 'bad attitude to employment' was laid off, Matsuo concluded that the workers were more concerned about ties to relatives and friends in the closely knit local community than about their jobs.

But I heard conflicting evidence to the effect that the Irish who gain employment in a Japanese factory consider themselves to be so lucky that they would not dream of leaving. And the strength of local ties enabled a local community in County Mayo to get together to ostracize some workers whom they believed were trouble-makers at the Japanese Hollister plant. Even though only around 20 of the almost 1,000 foreign firms in Ireland are Japanese, their fame has spread widely. In rural areas a long way from Ballivor and any other Japanese factories, people spoke admiringly to me of Japanese methods. Indeed Matsuo admits that Japanese management methods are appreciated by the Irish workers at NEC and Sord in Ireland. It was pointed out to me that whereas in the USA and the UK, there was some residue of anti-Japanese feeling left over from the Pacific War, in Ireland Japanese firms are particularly welcome because they bring both a strong commitment to the work-force and sophisticated levels of technology.

NEC chose in 1976 to locate its first overseas facility for IC production in Ireland, which was also the first Japanese IC plant in Europe. And the Japanese manager and engineer at NEC Ireland whom I met had a very positive view of the Irish employees. They mentioned such factors as good communication, their willingness to work overtime, and the low rate of turnover. What is particularly pertinent to this book is that the Japanese engineer's unreserved opinion was that the Irish women worked better than the men. In spite of the praise of the Japanese management at NEC Ireland for their female work-force, however, the prize for really large-scale, high-tech production went to the larger and more vertically integrated NEC plant mentioned earlier, which was set up ten years later in Scotland. This decision by NEC came as a disappointment to the IDA, whose officials believe that the reason lay not at all in the quality of the work-force and the advantages of investing in Ireland, but in an extraneous matter: NEC not gaining the contract to supply telephone exchanges to the Irish government.

Even though Ireland's share of Japanese overseas investment is still quite small – though larger than, say, Italy's – I have included NEC Ireland in this study because of the interest in seeing the impact of a Japanese company in a country where both the agricultural sector and the position of men are still of considerable weight. Moreover, since 1987 the IDA has embarked on a four-year plan to attract more Japanese investment, with stress on its abundance of electronics engineers and computer specialists, so that by the 1990s NEC Ireland is unlikely to remain as a rather unusual case. In any case the NEC Ireland plant is interesting in that it is a perhaps extreme example of a green-field site, which is where the Japanese electronics companies prefer to locate their plants. More than half of the projects announced by Japanese firms for investing in Britain in the late 1980s are on green-field sites, where the whole plant is built from scratch such as Star Micronics Company's electronic printer plant at Tredegar in Wales. Often such sites arouse particular concern among those who are suspicious about the relative absence of industrial disputes at Japanese plants.

Turnover and absenteeism rates

Japanese newspapers have taken to reporting anything good about investment in Britain. The *Nihon Keizai Shimbun* survey mentioned above asserted that the rate for unjustified absenteeism in more than half of the surveyed 50 Japanese companies in Britain was less than 1 per cent and labour turnover was low and decreasing, and since 1980 nine out of ten Japanese companies located in Wales had not lost one single day of production because of industrial action. Such slightly hyperbolic views on the quality of British labour do need to be qualified. Part of the reason for the relative absence of industrial disputes in South Wales is undoubtedly the high unemployment rate. Turnover rates in Japanese factories are still fairly high for women, because of unavoidable family commitments. At NEC Ireland about 12 per cent of female employees quit each year, compared to only about 2 per cent of men, which suggests that women are not taking full advantage of maternity leave provisions. The turnover rate at Matsushita in Cardiff is higher – on average about 18 per cent – partly because of the school-leaver recruits tending to change jobs easily. Consequently the average age of the work-force is in the mid-twenties, which prompted the personnel manager to describe himself as feeling quite antiquated.

Still, in spite of the high proportion of female employees, the turnover rates at NEC Ireland and Matsushita in Cardiff are relatively low compared to the situation ten years ago. A comparative study carried out at the end of the 1970s by Faith Jenner and Malcolm Trevor (Takamiya and Thurley, eds., 1985) found that not only British, but also Japanese and US manufacturing companies producing similar products located in Britain had higher, though erratic, turnover rates than those which were quoted to me by personnel managers in 1987.

Measurements of rates of absenteeism are strangely unsatisfactory, with it not always being clear if the rate includes explained and justified absences for sickness. The

Japanese survey referred to above would have been taking the narrowest definition of unexplained absences, since even in Matsushita's plants in Japan the absenteeism rate as conventionally defined is around 2 per cent for male employees and 3 per cent for female. I was given figures in Ireland of absenteeism rates, defined to include all those off sick, of around 5 per cent for women and 3 per cent for men. In Matsushita in Cardiff the absenteeism rate is about 3.5 per cent, whereas the average in Britain is over 5 per cent. Therefore it does seem that – without any hyperbole – absenteeism at Japanese plants in the British Isles is less than the average, but more than at similar plants in Japan.

Unions at Japanese plants

Usual union activities at Japanese plants in Britain may appear to be limited because of the absence of strikes, but in fact most manufacturing plants are unionized, apart from, say, Mitsubishi Electric; and the union is engaged in negotiations over not only pay and conditions, but also attendance and productivity bonuses. There does appear to have been some change in attitudes since the 1970s when the newly arrived Japanese managers were more willing to make compromises, but any such change may be just part of the generally changing picture of industrial relations in Britain. Nick Oliver and Barry Wilkinson (1988, p.154) have pointed out that without the 'new realist deals' with unions, workers in a Japanese plant would be in a stronger bargaining position than elsewhere because production methods depend upon a flexible work-force and tight delivery schedules with inventories kept to a minimum level – in other words, the 'just-in-time' system. Usually there is a single union agreement, which is reminiscent of the enterprise union back in Japan. Partly in response to agreements on single status (common terms and conditions of employment) and training provisions, many union officials in the Japanese subsidiaries appear to have adopted the Japanese practice of *roshi kyocho* (co-operation between management and labour) by agreeing to flexible work practices and a no-strike clause. The latter clause, which strictly means 'no industrial action while an issue is in procedure with automatic reference to arbitration' (Wickens, 1987, p.144), is often combined with pendulum arbitration. The pendulum indicates that there can be no compromise solution, which has the effect of compelling both sides to adopt reasonable demands at the beginning so that the decision should not go against them. 'Bargaining' then becomes a whole different game of striking reasonable positions in the early stages, which reflects the important difference between consensual industrial relations and the 'traditional' practice where both sides would start out in a tough way and eventually have to agree to a weak compromise.

Nor is it perhaps a coincidence that the single union at the Japanese electronics plants is often the buccaneering electricians union, the EETPU (Electrical, Electronic, Telecommunication and Plumbing Union). When Matsushita opened its new plant at Newport near Cardiff, it came to an agreement with the EETPU instead of the union recognized in the Cardiff plant, which is the GMBATU (General, Municipal, Boilermakers and Allied Trades Union). Much of the dissension about Japanese plants and unions springs from problems over which union gets the right to be the single one; and the Japanese companies appear to have a deliberate policy of choosing different unions so as to ensure that the enterprise-union structure remains and that disputes are contained within a plant. The EETPU has conducted enthusiastic campaigns in Japan to attract companies to Britain; but its policy of accommodation with the Japanese manufacturers has now been rewarded with expulsion from the Trades Union Congress (TUC) in September 1988, though the ostensible justification for expulsion was that the EETPU had violated the provisions agreed on by the TUC for single-union agreements.

It is important to recognize that at some Japanese plants the unionization rate is very low, though Oliver and

Wilkinson (1988, p.128) estimated from their sample of 16 Japanese companies an average rate of 59 per cent. Young women on the shop floor of electronics plants are often not very interested in union activities – as we shall see below. The unionization rate at the NEC plant in Livingstone is reportedly as low as one-third because the management is pursuing a non-union strategy (Trevor, 1988, p.27), in which presumably the women employees are acquiescing. At Nissan as well there is evidence, according to Sunderland Poly-technic researchers, that the union's activities are restricted, since union membership is below 10 per cent and the principal negotiating body is the company council. Such councils – known at some plants as company advisory boards, on which both management and worker represent-atives serve – have received a mixed press. Malcolm Trevor (1988, p.10), who is director of the Japan Industrial Studies Programme at the Policy Studies Institute, quoted a woman shop steward at Toshiba as saying that the company advisory board system was honest and worked. Is the system more appropriate for a female work-force, who may prefer a less confrontational form of industrial relations? This is one of those sexist questions which I have not been able to avoid and have attempted to answer after evaluating the responses to my questionnaire in Chapter 9.

At Matsushita in Cardiff, where the Japanese attitude towards the union was set in the more conciliatory period before the 1980s (Oliver and Wilkinson, 1988, p.149), the shop stewards are given time off of about an hour a week for meetings. The larger meetings attended by rank and file members are outside working hours except for the one held towards the end of the pay negotiations when the manage-ment has reached its final offer. A shop steward remarked that the work atmosphere was more strict than at his previous place of employment, but it was not too extreme and certainly he felt that the division of work was fairer. The process of negotiation seems a little unwieldy with the union negotiating with the British personnel manager – a Japanese may be present but rather inscrutable – and then the personnel manager negotiating with the Japanese managers. Evidently it is, as I was told, 'a battle of wits' rather than a case of violent arguments for the shop stewards engaged in negotiations. They feel that even though the Japanese managers stay rather aloof from union negotiations, it is their opinions, though consensual and to some extent accommodating, that determine the outcome on wages and the sizes of production and attendance bonuses.

All operators at NEC Ireland belong to the ITGWU (Irish Transport and General Workers Union), about one-third of whose total membership are women, most of whom are blue-collar employees. Deborah Schuster King (Cook *et al*, 1984) has found that while women in Ireland have a fairly high rate of organization into unions, relatively few occupy leadership positions. Their low profile in the union reflects the way in which married working women in Ireland have to face the accusation of taking scarce jobs from youths.

In evaluating the union presence in Japanese plants, I was particularly concerned with women's activities; and so I asked the women employees whether they felt that their union was geared towards the concerns of women.

> They [the union] seem to look at you as though to say . . . 'if you have children, that's your business'. You're supposed to be able to work on a parallel with a man.

The mother who spoke thus at NEC Ireland was in fact working, according to the managers, better than most of the men. The women there generally felt that there was a rather unsympathetic union attitude towards working women. It is then hardly surprising that only a few become involved in union activities as was bemoaned by the union official at Matsushita in Cardiff, where just one shop steward was a woman. I was told that the union had often tried to get women to be shop stewards because of the need of giving more attention to work problems faced by women, but:

Nobody seems to want to do it, which is a pity because a lot of the girls will not query any problem they've got. If there's no woman around they wouldn't come to us. We can go through a lot of procedures, but women have different problems.

It is worth mentioning at this point that the picture in Japan is rather similar. At NEC's Tamagawa plant all the operators are union members, but none of the union officials are women. The NEC women whom I asked were unhesitating in their denial of the union being sympathetic towards women employees. There were, however, different responses from Matsushita employees who were happy to give a positive response to their union's attitude. Evidently in Japan the enterprise-based union at Matsushita has been more successful in convincing women that the union is there to serve all the workers, which reflects the whole company ethos of employee involvement and ostensible harmony.

This rather more positive attitude towards unions, though still with a sizeable body of dissenters, among Japanese women employed in large electronics companies has been corroborated by the Denki Roren survey (1986) on employee attitudes in the electronics industry in different countries. The survey, which was not confined to Japanese companies, found that only around 10 per cent of both British men and women employees reported fairly frequent participation in local union activities, but the figure for Japanese women was about 40 per cent and for Japanese men about 50 per cent. Over 35 per cent of the Japanese women, which was only 4 percentage points less than the proportion of Japanese men, said that they were satisfied with labour union activities, whereas only just over 10 per cent of British women and 12 per cent of British men were similarly satisfied. The fact that the proportions for men and women were so similar – though there were substantial inter-country differences – suggests that working women have not yet really become aware of how the union can assist or impede them in issues such as equal opportunities and re-employment after rearing children.

Will duality in Japanese industry be duplicated in Britain?

The Japanese companies which have established plants in Britain and Ireland are generally the large, successful companies. Recently there has been an acceleration in the trend whereby the small subcontracting companies or *kokaisha* ('child companies') are following their parent overseas; component makers accounted for 70 to 80 per cent of the annual rise in the number of Japanese manufacturing investors in Britain during the late 1980s (*The Japan Times*, 7 April 1989). Both parent and child have such a symbiotic relationship that the parent who has to depend on local sourcing, because of local content agreements and the EC's anti-dumping duties on parts (intended to deter companies from setting up 'screwdriver' assembly plants), expects to have a hard time. Unfortunately such expectations sometimes bear fruit insofar as the only real complaint of the Japanese electronics companies with factories in Britain, according to Takao Sasaki (1987, p.186), is that the quality and supply of parts is not up to standard.

Some of the major Japanese companies are now encouraging their parts manufacturers in Japan to locate production in Europe. Nissan has resold part of the land it bought in Sunderland to its subcontractors who are following Nissan from Japan. Not only does the Japanese plant want its suppliers to be physically nearby so as to facilitate 'just-in-time' production, but also Nissan aims to have at least 20 per cent shareholding in its suppliers (Oliver and Wilkinson, 1988, p.60). Consequently many of the companies which have recently announced plans for producing electrical goods components and electronics components in Britain are no longer household names – such as Tenma Ltd and Tsuda Plastic Industry Company, which manufacture injection-moulded components for the electronics industry, and Mitsubishi Plastics, whose product is the cabinets for television sets and video cassette recorders. One particularly significant investment in Scotland has been a raw-silicon facility, which was set up in 1989 by the major supplier to semiconductor makers, Shin-Etsu Handotai. These moves indicate that the Japanese semiconductor industry, in which a substantial proportion of the employees on the shop floor is female, is going to be a considerable presence in Britain.

One question may then be whether British women will eventually find themselves consigned to work in the smaller supplying companies and whether the pay and conditions of employment will be worse than in the major contracting company as is the situation in Japan (Chapter 3). So far there is no evidence that such a trend will occur. Since the British and Irish women on the shop floor of Japanese electronics plants are proving themselves to be able and diligent workers with a reasonable degree of attachment to the company as shown in their years of service, they are the equivalent of the privileged regular, usually male, work-force found in the large companies within Japan. If a dual labour market comparable to that in Japan were to arise in Britain, with the secondary sector located in smaller Japanese companies or British suppliers, then it would be highly unlikely to follow the gender lines discussed in Chapter 3.

Another way in which duality in employment for Japanese companies could appear, however, is through the use of temporary employees. In Japan regular employees are assured of not only job security, but also generally better employment conditions than temporary workers, who have traditionally come from rural areas. At present British and Irish women working in Japanese plants usually have the status of regular employees, but several Japanese companies in Britain, including Nissan, are now employing temporary workers when demand for their output is high and others, including Matsushita in Cardiff, are considering this option. This development of a casual sector for labour in Japanese plants should not necessarily be deplored. At present the only opportunities for part-time work are in the canteens of Matsushita and NEC Ireland, so women with more than one small child usually find that they cannot continue their employment with a Japanese company at all. Temporary part-time work may be one route by which mothers who used to work at a Japanese company could find a way of gradually getting back to work. Temporary labour at Nissan, Peter Wickens (1988, p.59) contends, is one step towards becoming permanently employed.

Blue-collar and white-collar workers

Although any local hostility towards Japanese investment in Britain has not reached the levels apparent in the USA, the argument over whether or not the Japanese presence is beneficial still arouses considerable controversy. Interestingly enough the debate is not so much conducted by the workers themselves as by other peripheral parties. It was reported on the front page of *The Times* (18 July 1987) that Lord Weinstock, the head of GEC (General Electric Company), expressed anger over the way Japanese companies with subsidies from the British government could get round import barriers and he railed against Prince Charles, who had welcomed the creation of jobs and the introduction of Japanese management methods.

The issue of import barriers is illusory. If barriers are in place, the main rationale can only be to protect jobs and the trade balance; the nationality of the company producing behind the barrier should not matter since world financial and stock markets are now so integrated. British companies may not be happy that their Japanese competitors located in Britain are defusing protectionist sentiment, but it is consumers and workers who are the beneficiaries of Japanese investment in manufacturing. There is, however, the legitimate concern that the European electronics industry will be extinguished by the success of the Japanese manufacturers, although a higher level of competition could engender greater efficiency and innovation. British companies may lose some profits in competition with Japanese manufacturers and there is also the issue of how profits can be moved on paper between the subsidiaries of multinational companies through accounting techniques, though much of the Japanese profit made overseas is in any case being ploughed back into further local and more vertically integrated investment. These are all important issues, but my focus is on how women who are employed by Japanese manufacturers in Britain and Ireland are affected at the plant level. I do not intend here to measure the costs of tax relief and grants against the benefits of the number of jobs created, which is the real basis of the controversy.

Nor will the question of indigenization of management be taken up. At many of the Japanese plants in Britain and Ireland, although there are some exceptions where most of the executive postions are held by Britons, the top-level management is usually Japanese, apart from personnel managers. This may create problems for the white-collar workers, who sometimes resent the way that the Japanese managers can effectively exclude them by engaging in telephone conversations and facsimile messages conducted in Japanese with the head office in Japan. The local staff then feel a measure of discomfort and, more significantly, as though they are shut out from some decision making. While white-collar workers may not on the surface object to the common terms and conditions of employment, they may believe that they are not sufficiently compensated for the long hours that they sometimes work. Such dissatisfaction does not, however, extend to the female shop-floor workers with whom I am concerned. Their image of the Japanese managers is mostly of smiling faces, whose owners are always very fair.

The story is not quite so simple as all that. White-collar workers are in much closer proximity to their Japanese colleagues than workers on the shop floor. The attention to detail and the perfectionism, which on the shop floor permit zero defect production, in the office can seem very tedious and even irritating when the object to be fussed over is merely an internal memo. British managers also feel under more pressure than blue-collar employees because of the apparent expectation that work should take precedence over time spent with the family. This is a contentious point which some Japanese subsidiaries in Britain are trying to relieve through holding 'family days' at the plant. And there does seem to be an awkward desire on the part of the Japanese managers to bring their companies into the local community, which has not been one of the original characteristics of the Japanese company in its own country. Becoming part of the local community is maybe not so difficult in such outlying areas as Ballivor where there is little option for the NEC managers but to send their children to local schools, where they also study Gaelic.

The divergence between blue-collar and white-collar workers in their impression of the Japanese managers has been one of the most striking results to transpire from earlier large-scale surveys of employment in Japanese companies, which were initiated by the Suntory-Toyota, International Centre for Economics and Related Disciplines, based at the London School of Economics. British and Irish employees in Japanese plants and commercial establishments were surveyed by Keith Thurley (1980, 1981), Malcolm Trevor (1983, 1986) and others, who found that the blue-collar workers were much more content with Japanese management methods than were the white-collar workers. The British white-collar employees are expected by the Japanese to be generalists rather than specialists and their own individualism leads to mutual incomprehension. In the few cases where the management is wholly indigenized, the blue-collar employees then become dissatisfied with what they view as the hypocrisy of British managers, whom they think have not fully embraced Japanese notions of single-status employment conditions. (I have not specifically studied white-collar employees, apart from those to whom I spoke in general terms while preparing for interviewing shop-floor employees. Therefore the preceding observations depend a great deal on the work of the cited studies.)

The awkwardness of the Japanese managers, while provoking a sympathetic response on the shop floor, does lead to the British white-collar employees being unsure about their responsibilities. Evidently this is one of the reasons why Matsushita plans to set up a European training facility for local middle-level management. However, in fairly small plants with a full complement of Japanese managers, white-collar workers would have fewer opportunities for advancement than shop-floor workers who can set their sights on becoming first a group leader, then a supervisor and then possibly an assistant manager. Nonetheless there is the potential for blue-collar employees also to be discontented with the level of discipline and the expectation that they should become multi-skilled. There is the argument that the requirement for a flexible work-force is equivalent to an attack on job conditions and security as well as undermining traditional trade union organization. Therefore in the questionnaire I sought responses, which are detailed in the next chapter, concerning job satisfaction, job rotation and the increasing level of automation.

Training opportunities are limited

Apart from the progression towards being a supervisor for those with the potential, there seemed to be less possibility for advancement and training in the Japanese subsidiaries than I had expected. One reason is that the level of general education of school-leaver recruits is felt to be too low. School-leavers in Japan have a reasonably good grounding in mathematics and physics on which training can be based. Maybe once a substantial number of British and Irish employees have demonstrated that they are willing to make a lifelong commitment to their job in a Japanese company there may be more justification for establishing training courses which include a measure of general education.

After the initial probationary period of three to six months, training appeared, at the time of my visits in 1987, to be confined to the occasions on which the company needed to rotate jobs or introduce new machinery. Internal company qualifications, apart from simple grading schemes, were non-existent. The absence of internal qualifications at

NEC Ireland was explained away to me by stating that since each operator was monitored regularly by the training section and the results filed – with awards being made for the 'employees of the year' – this was a de facto qualification system which was quite similar to the practice in Japan. At Matsushita in Cardiff with its much larger work-force the appraisal appeared to be rather more systematic than in NEC Ireland. The employees were assessed every six months and any of those with potential supervisory skills were singled out for training. There was also a rudimentary grading scheme in effect. A lack of internal qualifications should not, however, be taken to indicate that there is no acquisition of skills. The fact that workers are expected to become skilled in using a variety of machines is a form of training.

Another way in which a few women at NEC Ireland are being trained is by moving operators into maintenance jobs, which, it was suggested, could have the side benefit of imparting a more diligent work attitude among the men working in maintenance. Quality control (QC) circle activities, which are audited and certified by the Irish Quality Control Association, are also a kind of training. (When the 25 per cent drop in sales of ICs in 1985, following upon friction in semiconductor trade with the EC, resulted in reduced production activity, employees were engaged during working hours in QC training rather than being laid off.) Aside from the issue of promoting quality, such activities require preparatory tuition and training in statistical techniques and, in addition, enable the production staff to respond more positively and flexibly to technical changes. It is perhaps significant that the women employees seem to be more enthusiastic about drawing the charts for the presentations displayed in the corridors than are the men. It may be a sexist observation but in this way aspects of Japanese working methods, which appear to some to be too pernickety and detailed, are approached with enthusiasm by many women.

Those production workers at NEC Ireland and Matsushita in Cardiff who are judged to have the potential and the wish to become supervisors and group leaders do receive more formal training; and one of the carrots for becoming a supervisor is being sent to Japan. One highly motivated woman supervisor in Cardiff had twice been to Japan for training as well as attending a course in supervisory studies at the local college of education, which included evening classes and one half-day a week spent on in-service training. From Matsushita in Cardiff between ten and 15 employees go every year to Japan for limited training and to learn about the parent company's methods. But these trips seem more to be just a reward for good work or an opportunity to impart the head office's philosophy rather than a practical exercise in acquiring new skills. In any case to the extent that special training courses are confined to potential supervisors and group leaders, most of whom are men, women are losing out on training opportunities.

The lack of research and design facilities within Japanese plants in the British Isles offers one partial explanation for training opportunities being rather limited. Japanese electronics firms, apart from the less risk-adverse NEC and Fujitsu, have tended to prefer to keep the production which depends upon higher technologies and their research facilities within Japan and let the investment diaspora of Japanese plants in convenient locations around the world receive only the mature technologies (*The Economist*, 12 March 1988). In such cases the female work-force is not required to acquire many skills. Indeed, I found that in general the British and Irish women in Japanese companies did not feel that they could join a real career path on which qualifications and extra skills could be obtained. This situation may, however, change as the Japanese companies begin in the 1990s to establish research and development institutes in the British Isles (Chapter 10).

Even though there may be little formal training beyond the initial probationary period, the subsequent limited rotation between jobs and the QC activities, the British and Irish employees of Japanese firms do seem to take some pride in their work and their ability to handle the machinery,

195

which is a reflection of the way in which the Japanese employer treats labour as a resource potential rather than just as a cost of production. The encouragement to participate in QC circles, without additional financial incentives, does seem to make employees feel involved and proud. The British car industry is attempting (Marsden *et al*, 1985) to emulate the notion of employee involvement especially through self-inspection – but so far with only mixed success. Is it that women working in electronics plants are more amenable – or gullible – to the notions associated with employee involvement? Still, whether the basis is sexist or not, a wholly integrated approach towards man and woman management, in which workers as a team become multi-skilled and flexible in their job allocation is evidently a large part of the reason for the Japanese success in management.

The Electronic Industries Association of Japan seems to be confident in its glossy and upbeat publications that Japanese electronics plants in Britain have trouble-free industrial relations with low labour turnover and low rates of absenteeism. It is part of my purpose to study how this was achieved and what are the implications for women employees. It is not enough just to refer to the fact that the Japanese plants have an agreement with a single union. What is more interesting is how loyalty is maintained – beyond the free trips to Japan for group leaders and managerial staff. The responses of women on the shop floor in the following chapter may provide some clues.

8 | On the shop floor in Ireland, Britain and Japan

Japanese companies have been accustomed to recruiting their work-force from rural areas, because at least up until the 1950s and 1960s young workers – the most favoured kind of recruit – were often from the still sizeable farming population. Even now at the NEC plant in Tamagawa many of the young women in the dormitories are from far-away areas like Tohoku. Rural recruits were expected to be more compliant; but in fact Rodney Clark (1979) noted that they were the most vociferous in complaining. Also Japanese companies have tended to rely on personal connections to attract new school-leaver employees. And, as has been discussed in Chapter 7, this pattern of recruitment has been duplicated at NEC Ireland where the majority of shop-floor employees is from local villages and there is no need to advertise operators' positions, since people just turn up looking for work on the recommendations of their friends. In Cardiff most of the women are from the city but, again like their counterparts in Japan, they have usually been recruited as school-leavers.

Thus, at first sight, there appear to be a lot of similarities between the female employees of a major Japanese corporation, whether it is located in Japan or in the West. It is the purpose of this chapter to see how far any similarities do extend and what are the important differences. In doing so, I am not concerned with such issues as the effectiveness of company advisory boards or the use of clocking, which do not concern women alone. There are some issues, however, which may not seem to be related to gender – such as responses to automation – which I shall discuss, because of their importance for the future of women's employment in electronics factories.

Job satisfaction

Whether or not women on the shop floor feel a sense of job satisfaction is highly important, because of the way that they have so often been consigned to doing meaningless repetitive tasks with no hope of advancement. It would then not be surprising that they would become uncommitted members of the labour force. The women employees in Britain and Ireland whom I interviewed and observed on the shop floor, however, had high levels of job satisfaction, despite having to work fairly hard. One woman who had been working at NEC Ireland for 11 years said feelingly:

> I love the job I'm doing now . . . I wouldn't like to change [to another firm] . . . I like work and to be kept going. I don't mind how hard it is . . . I'd rather work a machine any day [than clerical work].

And another Irish woman, who had previously been employed as a civil servant asserted that the production side was much more interesting than working in an office. (Having achieved the position of group leader she was particularly satisfied with her measure of responsibility and the freedom to talk with managers.) Similarly in South Wales a woman, who had changed jobs several times in her early twenties, but had now been with Matsushita for ten years, remarked:

> If it wasn't satisfying, I wouldn't have stayed this long. I would have left a long time ago. It was only going to be a stop gap . . . You wouldn't have time to be bored . . . I prefer to stay in the production department [where work] . . . is not really easy, but once you've had the training you could accomplish it with more ease.

Oddly enough it was a young Japanese blue-collar woman in NEC's Tamagawa plant who showed the least satisfaction with her job, because she said that it was too simple and everyday she was just doing 'the same thing over and over again'. In many respects the plant where the Japanese woman works follows the practices which presumably engender job satisfaction such as good communication within work groups, workers keeping records of their own output and at times their being involved in the final inspection of the ICs. Why she is dissatisfied would be because job rotation is not all it is cracked up to be on paper. (Job rotation, however, is deservedly famous in certain other industries, such as iron and steel, where labour is a heavy fixed cost at a time of declining demand.) It would seem that some Japanese women, who have usually stayed at school until the age of 18 years, are less passive in accepting routine, repetitive tasks on the shop floor of the major companies than are the British and Irish women who are just grateful to have a reasonable and secure job with Matsushita or NEC.

Part of the Japanese success in production has often been attributed to the way in which the workers are happy to engage in team-work. And in this respect Matsushita seems to have been more sucessful at motivating its women employees overseas than in Japan itself. When women employees of Matsushita in five different countries were asked what out of eight aspects of their work caused them the most happiness, it was over 30 per cent of the British women who gave the most points to 'when we co-operate together as a team' – a feature which attracted only 6 per cent of the Japanese women. The in-house magazine *Matsukaze* (September 1986) when reporting these results requested its Japanese employees to consider once more their attitude to work.

Why then are the Irish and British women so satisfied with their work? It is not that they are just easy to please, since Malcolm Trevor (1988, p.203) found in his study of Toshiba employees in Plymouth that women were less satisfied than men with factors such as 'have interesting work' and 'get credit for a good job'. Partly the women employees in

Ireland and South Wales are just glad to have a reasonable job at all and, as will be explored later in this chapter, they can participate in QC circles and job rotation. But also the work itself is looked upon as intrinsically interesting because they learn as part of a team to operate several machines:

> It's very interesting [to work on a new machine]. Definitely at the beginning I was a bit wary, but I was trained and the training was very good. I found it no problem.

Responses to automated processes

Thus women not only have the aptitude for operating high-technology machinery, but also they enjoy the work. At first the highly automated machines at NEC Ireland – an impressive array which includes monitors with constantly moving images – do inspire them with some awe, but they find that they can learn quickly and end up preferring operating the machinery to clerical work. One woman I met was proud to have been one of the first workers to operate the recently introduced dicing machine – after being trained for six weeks by a process engineer. The superficial operations may not be too difficult but the ensuring of quality and high levels of output are not easily attained. A Japanese engineer, who had been posted at NEC Ireland for four years, volunteered that in some senses the Irish were more receptive to new technology than the Japanese. Nor did the women in the Matsushita plant in Cardiff fear new technology; they recognized that it would do away with menial jobs.

In Japan the reason why a lot of women on the shop floor accept increasing levels of automation without reservations is rather illuminating – as one woman put it: 'because it is necessary for the company.' Thus their loyalty to the company – its success and profits – takes precedence over any worries about job security or learning new skills. In this respect Japanese women are possibly more loyal than men who might question the effect of automation on jobs. One

Japanese male respondent at the same plant suggested conditions such as that there should be discussions with the workers beforehand to obtain their agreement to the installation of more highly automated machinery. And it should be remarked that Japanese women in the small subcontracting companies, where employment is not so secure, are more wary of increased levels of automation. One employee of a small company said, 'It is only acceptable if it reduces the heavy work and if it leads to no reduction in employment opportunities.'

The processes at NEC Ireland are so automated that in some cases one woman is operating five machines. There are some arguments that this level of automation thereby puts an unacceptable strain on operators in electronics plants. Indeed in Japan there has been criticism of the work that women are expected to do in semiconductor factories. Keiko Nakajima writing in the radical journal *Ampo* (1986) charges that the work requires the handling of dangerous chemicals during which there have been accidents leading to death; and she suggests that the long exposure to a dust-free atmosphere means less resistance to disease. Many semi-conductor factories are in rural areas of Japan where farm wives are employed along with young women living in dormitories. They often quit their jobs after two or three years because it is said that they cannot stand the work. Nonetheless the women at NEC Ireland are showing considerable staying power. Their average length of service of six years is quite remarkable considering that the plant significantly expanded its work-force only after 1979. In complete contrast the average for women production workers at all NEC plants in Japan is only 4.3 years.

Women's reluctance to become supervisors

Some indication of why the average length of service for Japanese women in NEC is so short came from the responses of Japanese shop-floor workers to the questionnaire. Most of the young women operators at NEC in Tamagawa and at Matsushita in Osaka only expect to work in their present large company for a few years. Nor do they have any job-related ambitions to obtain qualifications or promotion, whereas the representative men I interviewed unfailingly put down that they sought both. Even one of the liveliest production workers I met in Japan confined her ambition to moving to another company, although she was a rarity in saying that she would at least accept promotion if it was offered to her. But the fact that women generally spend only a few years on the shop floor of a major company does not mean they will give up work altogether; the secondary sector of so-called part-timers working in small companies, such as we saw in Chapters 3 and 6, is where they will spend most of their working life.

One consequence of this pattern of employment is that women supervisors on the shop floor of the large electronics plants in Japan are extremely rare, which can only be considered a great wastage of ability and experience. The British woman supervisor at Matsushita in Cardiff, who had been to Japan twice for month-long training periods, commented that the Japanese women on the shop floor seemed not to care about none of their number being a supervisor, since they did not look on their jobs as a career. One woman, who had worked at Matsushita in Osaka for 12 years, told me that she did not want to become a supervisor; nor did she want to gain any qualifications; she merely wanted her present situation to continue.

That is an attitude which is not, however, confined to Japanese women. One Irish woman, who had been at NEC Ireland for almost 11 years, had no wish to be promoted beyond the position of group leader, although her husband, who had been working at the same plant for the same period was already a group leader and was hoping for further promotion. Nor, despite her expressed wish, had she taken any steps to apply to be a group leader.

202

I wouldn't like to be a supervisor . . . You have to take a lot. You're inclined to be the workers' enemy more than a friend. But I wouldn't mind being a group leader . . . at least then you can deal with something that's wrong. [But] I've never tried for one, even though there are a lot [advertised internally].

The personnel manager at Matsushita in Cardiff spoke of the hassle in trying to encourage women to train for supervisory positions: 'They've got the ability. It's the psychological problem – "I don't want that responsibility" - they believe they can't do it.' But I was assured that women were given every encouragement to be promoted; and the woman supervisor herself said:

Personally, I didn't set out to go on the supervisory ladder, but your superiors see that your ability is there, I suppose, and you just tended to be promoted from that approach. It wasn't intentional. But now I want to reach the next step of assistant manager.

Maybe the argument would be that women shop-floor workers are not assertive enough and have a less positive attitude to their work: hence the lack of promotion. But the women I met in Britain and Ireland seemed to have a more positive attitude to their work than their male colleagues; and indeed at NEC Ireland over 80 per cent of group leaders were women. When Faith Jenner and Malcolm Trevor (Takamiya and Thurley, eds., 1985, p.126) carried out a survey of British and US consumer electronics companies operating in Britain where women are the overwhelming majority on the shop floor, they found that between one-third and one-half of the supervisors were women. Yet when I visited NEC Ireland in 1987 only 20 per cent of supervisors were women, despite 60 per cent of the production workers being female. At the Matsushita plant in Cardiff, where the proportion of female production workers was also around 60 per cent, the figures were even more depressing; only about 17 per cent of supervisors and 40 per cent of group leaders were women. Such figures imply that at Japanese plants the likelihood of a woman becoming a supervisor is less than in

British and American plants – though a more complete set of data would be required to confirm this point.

Therefore it is not just an issue of the attitudes of the women themselves. The Japanese plants' preference for recruiting school-leavers for the shop floor means that the turnover rate is higher than if they looked towards older women who have already finished bearing children. It is notable that the women supervisors whom I met in Britain and Ireland had worked at other companies before joining NEC and Matsushita; they were not only older, therefore, but also more experienced in other kinds of work than the other women on the shop floor.

One must also query the attitude of the Japanese management themselves who have arrived from plants in Japan where there are usually no women supervisors, because even the low percentages for women supervisors at NEC Ireland and Matsushita in Cardiff seem somewhat impressive when compared with the Matsushita plant in Osaka where, despite over 50 per cent of operators being women, there were absolutely no female group leaders or supervisors in 1987. Similarly at the huge NEC plant in Tamagawa there were no women supervisors or group leaders on the shop floor, though there was at least one woman group leader in the design engineering section. In general, employees acted with surprise that I should even ask such an unlikely question as to the percentage of women supervisors.

The reason that the woman supervisor whom I met at Matsushita in Cardiff had reached her position would have partly been because she had no children and was supporting her student husband, but then that was not the whole story. It was her positive interest in her work and her evident diligence and energy – she only slept six hours a night – rather than any distinct assertiveness which would have earned her the position; and now she was aiming to become an assistant manager. She identified the closeness between some supervisors and shop-floor workers as emanating from the internal promotion system in that they had 'all grown together' in the company. (Up to half of the supervisors, however, have been recruited from outside the company.) And her own promotion had not soured her relationship with her co-workers, though her open and sensitive personality was obviously an important contributory factor.

Nor does there seem to be any problem for men working under a women. It was pointed out to me that on the shop floor of an electronics plant in Britain most of the men are just 'boys': 'We've never had any problems that it's a woman telling them what to do.' And the supervisor herself considered that female supervisors were able to do a better job than male where the shop-floor workers were mostly women:

> They [the workers] tend to accept women supervisors more than the men, because we're predominantly female workers in the production area. Usually the female workers with a male foreman will try and pull the wool over his eyes in the allocation of work; female supervisors can see through them. So actually it's an asset [being a woman supervisor].

But it is important to note that she went on to say that the Japanese management would think that a male supervisor would be better at keeping up productivity levels.

Some British and Irish women do have the ability and the drive to reach a certain level; after all women in NEC Ireland were a higher proportion of group leaders than of production workers. But the truly supervisory positions are usually beyond their grasp – or beyond their desire. One reason may be that younger women depart for child-rearing, yet on average their length of service at NEC Ireland was only six months less than that of men. It is, then, more a problem of there being a higher expectation of women departing, rather than that they actually do so. Another factor may be the amount of overtime that supervisors are expected to do in a Japanese plant. Supervisors at Matsushita in Cardiff generally had to work two hours overtime every day.

Incidentally it is an interesting point that women at NEC Ireland and Matsushita in Cardiff were generally doing more

205

overtime than the women employees in Japan. One young woman at NEC in Tamagawa said she did none at all, which may have merely reflected the particular characteristics of the Tamagawa plant itself and of trade friction in semi-conductors. But even at Matsushita in Osaka most women were doing only about ten hours overtime a month and without having to work on any Saturdays. One Japanese woman, however, who was a group leader in the design engineering department of NEC in Tamagawa, was doing up to 49 hours a month, which was leading her department manager to fret: an odd response one might think in a country where anyone in a position of responsibility is expected to stay on the job until everyone else has left. Then his reasoning became clearer. This group leader was married and the manager could not but believe that long hours of overtime would have adverse consequences for her marriage.

Women's aptitude for electronics work

Thus women in the electronics plants in the British Isles do not shirk overtime work, which often poses more problems for them than for men, though I was told that men are rather more willing to do overtime than women, especially when it is at short notice. Still, despite also an unwillingness among some women to be promoted, they were quite clear in their assessment of how well a woman could do the work. One woman group leader at NEC Ireland declared that women definitely worked as well as men; and another woman on the shop floor, where the men are mostly employed in the packing and despatch section, asserted:

> The fellas are given all the easy jobs, while we do the hard ones. We seem to have a lot more attached to our jobs than they would . . . To us it looks like they're just sitting around . . . like you'd be going an awful lot.

It was a man shop steward at Matsushita in Cardiff who observed: 'We've got some very good women workers and we've got some very poor men workers.' He added that it was only in jobs like lifting or cabinet assembly that women were at a disadvantage. The supervisor whom I met at Matsushita in assessing the relative ability on the shop floor of women and men remarked:

> The female workers are more flexible, so we can put them on a number of jobs. But with males – they tend to be only skilled at only one type of job and they're not easy to adapt. It may be because it's the type of work we do perhaps, but you find that the males tend to like to stay on one job and that's it. But females – they like to change. It helps us and it helps them to develop their skills of course. And they're definitely more concerned about quality, and also about the cleanliness and tidiness of the production area [than the men].

The fact that the women operators are considered to be more flexible than the men and more willing to develop a range of skills is highly important in a Japanese company where workers are expected to be multi-skilled. Similarly the emphasis on each individual worker's responsibility for quality and cleaniness – rather than such tasks being allocated to line inspectors and the cleaning staff – seems to be more agreeable to the female employees of Japanese companies. It could be that women are less impatient than men with the attention given to detail and quality in a Japanese electronics plant. Managers at NEC Ireland were unanimous in asserting that in jobs such as the final inspection of chips, women were far better than men and their aptitude was considered to be higher. (In recent years there had been almost no complaints about the quality of the dispatched chips; there were only cases of a few 'rogue' chips which had inadvertently been packed.)

One clear indication of a sense of equality among women themselves is that the British and Irish women do not feel at all handicapped in comparing themselves to men – over 90 per cent of Matsushita's British women employees in the internal company survey, which was cited earlier, responded 'no' to the idea that they might have a handicap, whereas only a minority of the Japanese women working in similar plants felt a similar sense of equality. However, the Japanese women whom I interviewed almost all said that women had an ability equal to that of men for the work. Evidently the response of women concerning their ability partly depends on who is asking the question. The Matsushita survey was carried out by the company, to whom Japanese women wanted to give the 'correct' answer. Thus the lack of confidence among Japanese women is not simply the result of an internalized assessment, but also of how their abilities are viewed by their male colleagues and supervisors. In corroboration of this point one of the male respondents in Japan, who works on the shop floor at NEC in Tamagawa, categorically denied that women might have a working ability equal to that of men, which would not bode well for any woman who did ever have the chance to be his supervisor – unlikely though that possibility remains.

A younger man, however, at Matsushita in Osaka agreed with the statement that women could work just as well as men, which perhaps signals a change in generational attitudes in Japan. And a particularly thoughtful and intelligent Japanese woman gave an interesting response to the effect that: 'A woman's ability is more individualistic than that of a man.' Therefore some Japanese women do not fit so well into the frame of team-work, which as we saw in an earlier section does not give them much job satisfaction either, even though the ability to work as a member of a team is much prized on the Japanese shop floor. At the same time all of my respondents in Japan denied that women faced any particular problems or difficulties in their work on the shop floor, which suggests that their output and quality levels are as good as those of the men workers.

Another Japanese man – a manager – defined the gender difference, therefore, as being that Japanese women possessed less 'sense of endeavour' than men. One major problem seems to be then that many women themselves still seem to lack the will to prove themselves as diligent workers. In response to my question about how long they wished to work, Japanese women working at NEC and Matsushita usually said that they wanted to leave before reaching retirement age at an 'appropriate time'. Japanese women themselves – perhaps because they are more individualistic than many Japanese men – do not wish to become part of the permanent employment pattern.

Productivity, QC circles and job rotation

In order to confirm the equivalence of output levels, I posed questions to the management in all the plants on whether overall productivity levels were comparable – both between women and men and also between plants in Japan and those in Britain and Ireland. On the first point there were generally no unfavourable comparisons made of women employees. Indeed at NEC Ireland, in particular, the general consensus seemed to be that the female employees, who were earning, on average, merit payments which were equal to or a bit higher than those earned by men, had a better working attitude. In Japan my explicit questions concerning women's productivity levels and leadership qualities tended to be ignored in favour of such revealing comments as: 'Women use the available time more efficiently'; but they 'lack perseverance'. If that is so, it is most likely to be a function of employing very young women who have no expectation of being able to make a career in a major electronics plant and so are justifiably unwilling to persevere.

The answers I obtained to the question of whether the women working in NEC Ireland and in Matsushita's Cardiff plant achieved productivity levels comparable to those in Japan were cautious, but positive. At NEC Ireland the output and quality levels are reportedly almost the same as those in Japan. Another study by John Dunning (1986, p.98) has estimated that productivity in Japanese plants in Britain is 90 to 95 per cent of levels in Japan. It is suggested that the remaining gap is due to work attitudes and inappropriate institutions rather than some sort of cultural gap or differences in innate ability. Women at Matsushita in Cardiff, according to one (British) personnel manager, 'certainly have the right commitment and the aptitude, though probably not as good as in Japan'.

In speaking with the British and Irish women employees, their attitudes indicated that they were very aware of the need for perfect quality in their output of televisions and semiconductors. Thus the work of checking the ICs for faults in the final inspection area was acknowledged to be the most demanding at NEC Ireland. And the women's attitude is more encompassing of all the aspects of work than that of the men. One woman at Matsushita in Cardiff volunteered: 'Keeping your own work area clean and tidy helps in the attitude towards quality'.

Although the suggestion system has not often been successfully transplanted to the overseas subsidiary companies – at Matsushita in Cardiff there would be only occasional campaigns to initiate suggestions – almost all Japanese companies do at some point introduce QC circles. The small groups of blue-collar employees which meet to find out ways of improving productivity and improve quality were still not fully established at the plants I visited in Britain and Ireland in 1987. One woman at Matsushita in Cardiff admitted that their QC circles were rather weak compared to what she had been told went on in Japan, but then the groups were still at the pilot project stage.

At NEC Ireland workers were being trained in how to participate in QC circles, but subsequently attendance was to be optional. The six circles in progress while I was there ranged from designing stickers to be placed on urgent jobs to a more challenging effort concerning how to reduce the number of discarded metal lead frames, on which are mounted the diced silicon wafers. Unlike many places in Japan the small group activities are being held during working hours. Thus QC circles may be seen as a form of on-the-job training, including acquiring statistical techniques, coupled with a practical engendering of team-work. And some women seem to have a particular aptitude for the kind of work required in a QC circle – identifying problems, finding a solution and checking the outcome. I was told without rancour that a woman engineer at NEC Ireland had become the key person in QC circle activities. And another woman took considerable pride in detailing the reasons why her QC circle had won a prize.

The QC circle not only helps to make assembly work less boring, but can also be an important medium in which a woman develops confidence and assertiveness, since the circle leader at some point has to make a presentation to the management. This is of particular significance in Japan where women are not accustomed to speaking up. (Even at local community and school meetings where women are in the clear majority I have been depressed to see mostly men offer opinions or suggestions.) A manager at the NEC plant in Tamagawa made a particular point of showing me the displays of the QC circles which had been led by women. Indeed all the women shop-floor workers at NEC and Matsushita in Japan say that they are participating in QC circles, which are evidently very much a normal part of their working duties.

Just as with QC circles, job rotation appears to be less well established in the British and Irish plants than in Japan. At NEC Ireland there is a general aim of acquainting operators with at least five of the identified 36 processes. Thus, even though there is no fixed job rotation system, jobs tend to be switched every two to three years so as to encourage multi-operation. But it would seem that there could be more scope for changing jobs, since women at both NEC Ireland and Matsushita in Cardiff have proved themselves to be flexible and capable of handling new machinery. Even in Japan, however, job rotation is not necessarily – as has been mentioned in the section on job satisfaction – carried out on a formal basis, although workers are expected to be flexible in accepting different allocations depending on demand and supply conditions.

While on the subject of Japan, it should be remembered that, until the implementation of the Equal Employment

Opportunity Law in 1986, women were often given much briefer initial training courses and less on-the-job training than men. I was assured at NEC and Matsushita in Japan that women were receiving equivalent training to men, but since job rotation is not necessarily practised systematically and since there are almost no women supervisors, for whom special training is provided, it is doubtful that women on the shop floor in the major Japanese companies are receiving the full range of training. One Japanese woman employee in an electronics plant told me that she had never had any on-the-job training after the initial six months training period – or at least not that she was aware of – nor was there a formal job rotation system.

Variety in discipline, uniform and leave

I was generally surprised at how relaxed was the attitude at the electronics plants in Japan. In one plant's design engineering department, where the desks were crowded together, not only were photographs affixed to the back of the desks, but also on one desk was a map of a ski resort – presumably so that during slack periods the worker could daydream about which pistes he would soon be skiing down. The image of discipline and total devotion to work, therefore, which is often associated with a Japanese manufacturing plant, may be an illusion even on the home ground.

Similarly there has been altogether too much emphasis on the formal uniform supposedly worn by all employees of a Japanese company, although it is true that the Matsushita philosophy embraces a standard uniform for all employees. However in a lot of Japanese factories, whether in Japan or the West, the shop-floor uniform usually amounts to no more than a simple jacket with a small badge – as long as the latter has not been mislaid. What is perhaps significant is that the managers usually wear the same sort of jacket – rather than a suit – though with a tie underneath. Although in the reception area of NEC in Tamagawa the office staff wear a complete uniform of blouse, skirt and waistcoat, on the shop floor the simple standard jacket is often worn over jeans. The exception is in the IC production areas in Japan and Ireland where the women wear head-to-toe coveralls. (Interestingly, the baggy, comfortable trousers are in the style worn traditionally by Japanese farm women.) The coveralls are not intended to be a uniform, but are required in order to maintain a dust-free atmosphere. Managerial staff and visitors to the plants in Tamagawa and Ballivor change their shoes or put on shoe covers for functional reasons even when just walking in the corridors.

There has been a lot of interest in the British media over whether employees of a Japanese company are subject to an unnecessary amount of discipline. The employees to whom I spoke did perceive the Japanese managers to be particularly strict about absenteeism and time keeping. Absenteeism is treated with interviews followed by warnings and disciplinary action, with the result that at Matsushita in Cardiff absenteeism rates were similar to those in Osaka at 2 per cent for men and 3 per cent for women. There is also the carrot of a weekly attendance bonus at Matsushita in Cardiff; being one minute late on one day would mean the bonus would be lost for the week. Interestingly enough it was a British manager who felt that there should not be a bonus for what workers should be doing anyway.

One woman at Matsushita in Cardiff stated that the discipline did not amount to a strong fear of losing one's job, but the salient points concerned regular attendance and maintaining quality standards:

> It's more discipline as far as attending work regularly – they can't emphasize that enough – and wearing company uniform at all times. This type of thing. And because of the high quality of the product demanded there does tend to be more pressure on the production line [than at British plants].

Evidently many of the British and Irish employees at the Japanese plants I visited have internalized the company's

213

goals sufficiently to accept that a certain amount of discipline is necessary to ensure that high levels of productivity and quality are maintained. Are they then in danger of becoming excessively dedicated to their work to the extent of becoming workaholics – just as the Japanese are reputed to be?

Because of the reputation of the Japanese as workaholics, I had expected before visiting the Matsushita and NEC plants that I would find that the shop-floor workers in Japan had far fewer holidays than their counterparts in the West. Indeed, although at NEC in Tamagawa and Matsushita in Osaka the amount of leave entitlement may be similar to the plants in Ireland and Britain, in practice the operators often find that they can only take about half of their entitlement, amounting to about ten days a year. In contrast workers at NEC Ireland are entitled to, and do take, 20 days a year, which includes two plant shut downs and a few floating days depending on years of service, in addition to public holidays. At Matsushita in Cardiff the leave allowance is rather similar: two plant shut downs of 18 days plus five to eight floating days. There seems to be little danger of the British and Irish employees whom I met ever accepting infringements on their holiday allowances or allowing work to take over their lives.

The lack of holidays in the plants in Japan makes it all the more difficult for working mothers to commit themselves to regular employment in large companies. This is one of the major reasons why Japanese women do not, as we saw in Chapter 5, take advantage of the child-care leave which NEC and other major companies now offer. Unless they live in a three-generation household with grandparents able to take care of a sick child or able to attend the numerous school meetings, mothers tend to return to work by joining a small company where leave can be taken with more flexibility, even though the entitlement on paper is less than in the major companies.

As in Japan leave entitlements at NEC Ireland and Matsushita in Cardiff are similar for managerial and shop-floor workers. I queried whether the management applied rigid rules to the taking of leave without pay, since the issue had been raised on a BBC television documentary in August 1987 when a British manager at Komatsu in the North East wished to take leave for a honeymoon. It was pointed out to me that workers were expected to get married during the plant shut downs – an unwritten requirement which white-collar workers at Matsushita in Cardiff do follow. But operators apparently tend to be more spontaneous in their marriage plans and then they are permitted to take leave without pay, since the number at any one time is very few. In Japan taking leave for a funeral is looked upon more kindly than taking special leave for a honeymoon. Indeed since most marriages are elaborately planned months in advance, a sudden demand for honeymoon leave, which in any case would only be for a few days, is not an issue which is likely to arise.

Family and work

In spite of the absence of day nurseries in Ballivor a lot of women at NEC Ireland do take their maternity leave and go back to work after the birth of at least one child, with the result that the average age of the women employees is about 25 years. Since it is easier to find a trustworthy child-minder for one than for two children, the birth of a second child does usually lead to their withdrawal from employment. One of the women employees I met did have two small children, but she could depend on her recently unemployed husband to be at home with them; and previously her mother had been available. She found that alternating each week between the two shifts – from 7am to 3pm and from 3am to 7pm – gave her more time with the children than if she had been working regular hours. It is noteworthy that this woman, despite being the mother of small children, was the one who was particularly praised by the management for her work and her attitude; and she had already reached the position of group leader after seven years with NEC.

215

Her success in combining the roles of mother and group leader should not blind one to the difficulties and simple hard work that women who are also homemakers must face. Another woman at NEC Ireland who was married, but did not have a child, said:

> Well it is tough going. I'm always on the go right from when I get up at six o'clock in the morning until it's time to go to bed [at midnight]. Like I find I can never sit down. I always stand; I never sit down even when we have a visitor. Like when you've finished here and you go home you have to start into another's day's work. But I get through somehow.

At Matsushita in Cardiff with its large young female work-force, there were 'quite a few' women who would have liked to return to work after childbirth, if there had been a creche. A shop steward said that the company would have benefited from keeping on the skilled women who were leaving after giving birth, because:

> [such departures] cause a lot of problems in the long run because everybody has got to be retrained again. And so it's not just about the women themselves, it's everybody in the factory then has got to tend do a bit more; and so it works out a bit harder all around. So I think it [a creche] would be an ideal sort of thing – but it's never come up before because 50 per cent of the women are young girls.

He went on to suggest that even though the company would have preferred the older experienced worker to a new recruit, it could always find another school-leaver to replace a departing mother, since there was a lot of unemployment in Cardiff. Evidently there is a spirit of just carrying on with the present practice of taking on a school-leaver to replace an experienced departing mother, rather than trying to find a better solution. The shop steward himself was aware of the inadequacies of an immature work-force. He volunteered: 'If there's any problem the young girls will just tend to leave whereas the older ones will sit down and argue through it because they need the money.'

216

While women have to bear the double burden, there are many who would prefer to leave work in any case and concentrate on child-rearing. In South Wales, in particular, a substantial proportion of women at the Matsushita plant want to stop work once they have a child. The internal Matsushita survey, cited earlier, of women employees in five different countries – including the USA and Thailand – found that it was only in Japan and Britain that high proportions, amounting to around 60 per cent in Japan and 47 per cent in Britain, of its women employees wanted to stop work on getting married or having a child. The notable difference between the Japanese and the British women was that over a quarter of the former said they would leave the company once they got married, whereas in Britain the comparable figure was only 1 per cent, with the remaining 46 per cent preferring to leave just before childbirth.

Thus the young Japanese women on the shop floor of major companies like NEC and Matsushita expect their present work to last only a few years, just as was the case about one hundred years ago for their predecessors in the textile factories of the Meiji era (Chapter 2). They live in dormitories and they dream of becoming 'just a housewife'. The young women working at Matsushita in Osaka who were not yet married told me that they intended to work only until marriage. But there are exceptions. The response of a particularly vivacious woman at NEC was that she expected to change her place of employment, but she would continue to work while bearing children.

One reason why the Japanese women are ready to quit work earlier is that they have a vision of housework as being time-consuming and their responsibility alone, as was evident from the general survey results quoted in Chapter 5. Indeed the Matsushita survey referred to above reported that almost 75 per cent of the Japanese women employees of Matsushita would only expect occasional help from their husbands with housework and child-rearing. It is striking that an equivalent percentage of the British women, over half of whom were not yet married, said that the housework and child-rearing tasks should be shared with the husbands. Whether that will happen in practice is, of course, another matter. Whereas the proportions of unmarried respondents to a *British Social Attitudes Survey* (1983) who asserted that household tasks extending from washing and ironing to washing dishes should be shared equally ranged from 32 to 73 per cent, among married couples the actual percentages sharing these tasks ranged from 10 per cent to 40 per cent.

In fact the fairly widespread provision of state-aided child-care facilities in Japan (Chapter 5), means that it is quite feasible for Japanese mothers to work. A woman engineer at NEC Tamagawa preferred to return to work while her child who was less than one year old attended a day nursery, even though NEC has implemented a child-care leave system of up to three years and there were no pressing financial reasons for her to be at work. A shop-floor worker at Matsushita in Osaka depended on the child's grandparents, with whom they lived, for child care. Even though her husband helped hardly at all with household tasks, she felt that there were no particular problems in combining paid employment with being a mother. Nor did the responses to my specific questions indicate that the husbands of the employed Japanese mothers whom I interviewed object to their being employed.

Therefore since there are not severe obstacles to Japanese women staying in a large company's employment for many years, the reasons why many of them intend to leave are more subtle. The previous sections have demonstrated that Japanese women are less keen on team-work and more individualistic than men in their approach to work. Nor do they develop – or are not inculcated with – the kind of loyalty that inspires a long term commitment to one company. Most significantly, there is the traditional expectation, which is hard for young women to resist, that they will only stay with a major company for a few years.

What is particularly interesting in the context of this study is that in the British Isles a reverse pattern seems to be emerging where the women employed in Japanese plants are more committed to their work than the men. The plants have not been established long enough in the British Isles to enable me to back up this observation with empirical evidence; and younger women – especially in South Wales – tend to leave the company on childbirth. Nonetheless the observations made in earlier sections of this chapter about how women employees were enthusiastic about quality and about becoming multi-skilled and their attitudes compared to the representative male employees whom I also interviewed indicated a high level of commitment.

What is different about working for a Japanese company?

Naturally enough, this was a question which I posed only to the shop-floor workers in Britain and Ireland. The responses at Matsushita in Cardiff tended to focus on the hard work involved, whereas at NEC Ireland there was a stronger perception that the conditions of employment and the facilities were better than elsewhere. Several of the respondents said that they were now so accustomed to working in a Japanese plant that differences were no longer so obvious to them:

> The longer you're here, the more you think of it as the norm and you forget what other places are like. So it's difficult to draw a comparison unless you're new here.

The women's responses, therefore, were usually based on what their friends outside the plant would say. Those in Cardiff reportedly ask: 'How can you stick the discipline?', while apparently thinking of the Matsushita employees not only having to work hard and regularly, but also having to wear a uniform. In contrast, the women at NEC Ireland said that their friends were envious of their employment.

It is true that the Matsushita philosophy, which boils down to job security in return for hard work and a measure of conformity to certain principles, comes over more strongly than the more muted NEC line, but evidently the environment also determines the response. At Ballivor there are few alternatives to paid employment with NEC, whereas in Cardiff the conditions at Matsushita can be easily compared with other local factories. It was a shop-floor worker at Matsushita, however, who suggested that the security of employment could lead to workers becoming slack; so workers generally accept that job security requires an acceptance of discipline since disciplinary dismissals are more or less ruled out. Therefore my earlier rhetorical sexist question (Chapter 7) about whether women were more amenable to apparently authoritarian forms of Japanese management is answered by the fact that women in Japanese plants acknowledged the link between discipline and job security and also that discipline was necessary to ensure the high quality of their output.

Despite the 'stricter' atmosphere compared to previous places of employment which were 'easy-going', therefore, women who had previously changed employment every three to five years, now stayed with Matsushita in Cardiff. Nor did I detect any signs of a rebellion or a wish to move to another company – though the explanation may lie simply in a lack of alternatives. The women I met seemed to feel at home in the Japanese company, perhaps because there has been no real attempt by the Japanese management to break with traditional British practices such as workers having tea breaks both morning and afternoon. The fact of continuing tea breaks may help to explain why the women employees chose to give their friends' attitudes as a response to my question on differences between Japanese companies and local employers; the women themselves no longer noticed any significant differences in their employment with a Japanese company – it had become commonplace. This suggests that the women are very adaptable to different working conditions. I was also struck by their lack of prejudice towards managers and engineers from faraway, whose English is usually not fluent.

Consequently the women at NEC Ireland felt that they could speak fairly freely with the managers and their supervisors: thereby fitting the image of the Japanese company as a family or community. That may have been a function of the fairly small size of the plant – about 300 employees – and the nature of Ballivor, but even at the much larger Matsushita plant in Cardiff – with close to 900 employees – a friendly atmosphere was evident and production staff were on first name terms with the British managers. (One should not be surprised that the Japanese are still addressed by their family names; even fairly close friends in Japan, including school children, invariably use only family names.)

But the degree of friendliness may be no more than in any plant where there are no major disputes nor fear of redundancies. Observers of Japanese companies have tended to stress the apparently egalitarian work practices without noticing that the basic structure of worker, supervisor, manager is still intact. Indeed the woman who did not want to become a supervisor, because she would then be looked upon as an 'enemy', demonstrated that the feeling of 'them and us' has not been erased, even on a green-field site where the employees feel particularly fortunate in finding secure work. At NEC Ireland the managerial staff have on occasion worked on the shop floor, but only for a short time when there is a temporary high demand for their semiconductors. The managers do make the effort to wear a uniform rather than a suit, but that does not really impress the operators. It is good to see just one canteen for the whole plant, but naturally enough the Japanese managers and engineers tend to sit together, partly for language reasons, but also one may speculate because they see no need for unnecessary fraternizing.

Nevertheless the attempt of the management, whether cosmetic or not, to involve the employees in the company as a community does seem to arouse less cynicism among the women employees at Matsushita in Cardiff and NEC Ireland than the men. And the way in which the Japanese company is perceived as a community makes high standards of discipline more acceptable. The Japanese company may be a mutually supportive 'family', but at home in Japan companies are subject to the criticism of not caring enough about the wider community outside their own employees and their families. Since arriving overseas, however, Japanese companies seem to have made more of an effort to be a welcome addition to local community life; and to a great extent they seem to have succeeded. The Japanese in Ballivor were fully accepted in the local community and their children were happy in the local schools. And the welcome is reciprocated; the NEC tennis courts are mostly used by the village children.

Why don't women seek promotion?

In general the women whom I met at the plants in Britain and Ireland seem to have been more adaptable than the men to the discipline and emphasis on quality required in the electronics factories. I have deliberately written 'electronics' rather than 'Japanese' since such requirements are a function of the machinery and the output rather than of the culture or a certain kind of management method. The fact that the women set themselves high standards at NEC Ireland to ensure that the ICs they produced were perfect specimens was indicated by their willing participation in QC circles. Also the women evidently enjoyed the challenge and the training involved in operating a new machine.

It is unfortunate then that most of the women on the shop floor in Britain and Ireland, but even more so in Japan, are reluctant to take on supervisory responsibilities. One of the reasons – apart from family concerns – would be their lack of confidence because of the absence of real career planning and opportunities for gaining qualifications, which is an issue already raised in Chapter 7. The Japanese plants in Britain and Ireland are no longer so new or so small that this excuse can be used. In 1987 the only formal training courses after the initial probationary period – apart from the analytical training geared to QC circle activities and attendance at

government-run evening classes for potential supervisors –
seemed to be periodic trips to Japan for long-serving workers
and those in the higher grades.

The odd thing is that on-the-job training is usually
considered to be an integral part of Japanese management
methods, because for that reason seniority advancement and
permanent employment are justified. But, as we have seen,
Japanese women on the shop floor, even in the major
companies, receive relatively little real training, partly
because they are only expected to stay for a few years. The
circle is then compounded because bright and diligent
women neither see any future in staying in the major
company, despite the general preference of Japanese for
employment in large companies, nor do they have the
confidence to seek promotion.

Most of the women whom I met in both Japan and the
British Isles did regret the lack of tests and the rather
restricted promotion path; those who had been longest in
the department and worked reasonably well would be
promoted before anyone else, which one worker suggested
could lead to some dissatisfaction among more recent
recruits and less of a drive among those already in line for
promotion. This issue of internal promotion, therefore, will
be considered in more depth in the following chapter,
because its requirements for continuous service conflict with
the anticipated career pattern for most women. Consequently
the expectations of women on the shop floor of Japanese
companies are restricted by a system which is ostensibly
'gender-blind' but serves to discriminate against them.

9 | Implications of Japanese employment for women

In order to obtain a better overview of what is going on in a Japanese company more consideration needs to be given to employment practices affecting Japanese women who are regular employees of large companies. This group, which includes white-collar female workers, has been rather neglected in earlier chapters, while our focus has primarily been on women working in small companies or on the shop floor. It would also be as well to reconsider briefly the legislation relevant to the employment of women in Japan and in Britain. The mass of working women may appear to be unaffected by the granting of equal opportunities, since their actual opportunities are in any case so confined because of their dual responsibilities at work and in the home. Nonetheless a filtering-down effect is evident insofar as, for example, the British women employed by Matsushita, who have benefited from the outlawing of sex discrimination since 1975, are both more ambitious and more determined to make their husbands or partners share the household chores than are the women on the shop floor at a Matsushita plant in Japan. It is only since 1986 that women in Japan have enjoyed equal opportunity legislation, whereas legislation which was excessively protective of motherhood had been in effect since 1947.

Egalitarianism does not extend to Japanese women

The situation for Japanese women working in the secondary sector of small companies leaves a lot to be desired in terms of wage differentials and conditions of employment (Chapters 3 and 6). In large companies their position is on the surface better, but at least until the spirit of the Equal Employment Opportunity Law is fully implemented they lack promotion prospects and their length of service is generally expected to be too short to permit better prospects. Thus, even though in terms of the technology and the conditions of employment the situation for the regular women employees of Japanese electronics firms is rather similar whether in Kawasaki and Osaka or in Cardiff and Ballivor, we have seen in Chapter 8 certain striking differences in their prospects and in their attitudes, because the Japanese women are in effect considered in a different light to their male colleagues.

The way in which each shop-floor worker in a Japanese factory feels a sense of progression through jobs and grades was given particular attention by Ronald Dore (1973, pp.60 to 68). Later, the egalitarian work practices and benefits, including the progression ladder of succeeding grades, extended to male blue-collar employees of large Japanese companies was dubbed 'white-collarization' by Kazuo Koike (1988). He demonstrates that 'white-collarization', rather than cultural or social aspects, is the main factor explaining not only the relatively peaceful industrial relations within a Japanese company, but also the high productivity and the constant improvements in mass-production methods. There is no reason why 'white-collarization' should be unique to a Japanese work-force, since certain elements are found in other countries' manufacturing companies. But within Japan at least it does seem that the benefits of continual on-the-job training, equality in status and a sense of progression are confined to the male work-force of large companies.

Apologists would argue that since women are intermittent members of the labour force their situation is like that of the temporary or subcontract male employees which the large companies employ to tide them over at times of heavy production schedules; and the benefits of 'white-collarization' are intended only for the regular employees who are expected to be with the company long enough to make an investment in their training and comfort worthwhile. Such an argument misses the point that not all women would be truly intermittent employees if their conditions of work, including child-care leave, were appropriate. And the overall data, which cover all sizes of company, have shown that many younger women are already giving almost as many years of service as their male colleagues (Figure 2.2).

In order to know why the position of Japanese women in large companies is so abysmal we need to understand the nature of the internal labour market, which is one special and exclusive case of primary labour markets, from which women are in general excluded. It is characteristic of Japanese firms – and indeed of large companies in the USA and West Germany – that the work-force is largely recruited on leaving school or university. Subsequently any vacancies for supervisory positions are filled by employees within the firm through internal promotion instead of being advertised in the external labour market, where (as neoclassical theory would have it) skills are transferable between firms and wages are determined by the supply and demand for certain universal kinds of skills. One disadvantage of the internal labour market is that skills, which are acquired in the long term through a rotation of jobs, become specific to the firm and it is hard for the firm to expand its skilled labour force quickly. Each employee's skills, however, are broad enough to allow a flexible re-allocation of production staff in response to changing product demand conditions. And Japanese companies also have no qualms about temporarily expanding their work-force through the use of contract and seasonal labour.

Japanese employers have presumed that the intermittent nature of women's participation in the labour force and their apparent peripherality means that they are unsuited for the internal labour market. Thus they have not been given the same opportunities for on-the-job training and rotation between jobs even when they have been employed in firms where an internal labour market functions. In the USA as well, despite the existence of affirmative action policies, the segmentation of labour markets has meant that women are often excluded from the primary internal labour market, according to Jane Bayes (Kelly and Bayes, eds., 1988). Although the internal labour market is not unique to Japanese firms, it is less common in British firms (David Marsden *et al*, 1985, p.78).

The implementation of the Equal Employment Opportunity Law has permitted some better-educated women to participate in the internal labour market, but on the shop floor in Japan little has changed, because young women themselves – living in dormitories as if they were at a temporary boarding school – only expect to stay with the company for a few years. Thus women supervisors on the shop floor are much rarer in the Japanese plants of NEC and Matsushita than at their plants in Britain and Ireland. One reason which some may cite is that their length of service is so much shorter than the male Japanese operators: only about six years on average compared to about 18 years for men at the Matsushita plant in Osaka. The figures averaged over all the NEC plants and offices are lower: four and a half years for women and just over 13 years for men, presumably because semiconductor plants located in rural areas see shorter years of service.

Nevertheless apart from expectations and social pressures there is no real reason why there should be such a wide divergence between the length of service for Japanese men and women at Matsushita and NEC. In fact Japanese women's short service is the result of an expectation on all sides that women cannot progress and will not stay long. In contrast we have seen in the preceding chapter that the British and Irish women working at Japanese plants have no intention of leaving and their average length of service is almost equal to that of the male employees. The internal labour market can, therefore, be appropriate for women in NEC Ireland where the practice of rotating employees between jobs does operate to a limited extent, most group leaders and supervisors are promoted from within and most of the women employees do stay on the job after the birth of their first child.

The second child, however, does usually lead to the withdrawal of Irish women from employment with NEC Ireland, even though there are few opportunities for part-time work in Ballivor. This withdrawal does indicate some of the limits on women fully participating in the labour market, because of the home division of labour. Thus a woman employee will almost inevitably have at least one break in her years of employment. As long as the employer, however, operates a sensible child-care leave scheme, the expected break need not be a deterrent to a woman employee also being given the opportunity to acquire a flexible and wide range of skills, which will make it worth her while – and worth the employer's while – to return to the company and offer longer years of service. Even when Japanese companies are located in Britain, the management appears not fully to realize this simple point. Matsushita in Cardiff still emphasizes the recruitment of school-leavers to replace departing soon-to-be mothers. And even though all supervisory vacancies at Matsushita in Cardiff are advertised internally, almost half of the supervisors come from outside as supposedly useful 'new blood'.

Underemployed 'office ladies'

It is especially Japanese women in clerical positions in large companies who, despite being regular employees, have in effect been excluded from the primary internal labour market because of their limited opportunities for advancement. Therefore the position of relatively skilled Japanese women on the shop floor should not be confused with that of the 'office ladies'. Often the only view that foreigners have of female employees in Japan is of the smiling receptionist and office women in uniform who bring them tea. Office

228

women's work, which includes a lot of time serving tea and at the copy machine, seems to be quite superficial and indeed wholly non-productive, though it may be conceded that their presence in the office does serve a decorative function and perhaps engenders the much-prized harmony in the workplace.

Evidently Japanese companies in Japan do not know how to use some women employees efficiently, although there are some gains from using intelligent women in unskilled positions such as the receptionist who can handle visitors with tact and intelligence. Unfortunately, there has been a popular view in Japan that, since women are less wedded to the company than their male colleagues, they are slack in their work. But at least such women can feel free to criticise authority. Nor would the women employees of the company where Rodney Clark (1979) worked often accept the order to transfer to another location, which is very much part of the usual career path for a 'salary man'. Thus, just as we have seen in the case of Japanese women on the shop floor (Chapter 8), office women who do not receive the benefits of the internal labour market in a Japanese company can afford to be more individualistic. Indeed they rather value their freedom; so most of them are not envious of their male colleagues who are tied to long work hours, including tedious after-work hours in bars, and who face competitive pressures in the scramble for promotion. Former 'office ladies', one now the mother of three children and the other of five (an unusual number in present-day Japan) told me that they had no nostalgia for their former work and were happier just to be coping with their broods of small children.

At the same time the fact that the qualities most prized in receptionists, bank tellers and other women employees in direct contact with the customer are those of politeness, modesty and obedience does immediately put the female clerical or sales employee in a subservient and non-critical position. The short, sad and superficial career of these white-collar women employees, among whom he worked for two years, has been graphically and sympathetically

229

described by James McLendon (Plath, ed., 1983). Their only role is to please their colleagues, so their career amounts to either a one-way station on the way to marriage – the *koshikake* ('temporary bench') – and early retirement, or else a blind alley for those who fail to get married and become outcasts at their workplace, partly because their seniority status with respect to the younger male employees then becomes ambiguous.

Significantly in the late 1980s, however, the terms *koshikake* and its sequel, *kata-tataki* (the 'tap on the shoulder' to advise early retirement) can no longer be applied to all women working in office jobs. In the 1970s young intelligent women working in large companies were very aware of the pressures to work for only a few years, but now – perhaps because of the Equal Employment Opportunity Law which has permitted at least a few women to receive the same training as men – many women seem to have a longer time perspective to their careers. This has already been translated into a dramatic lengthening of the average years of service. Some at least of the wastage of the potential of better-educated women is now under scrutiny.

Nonetheless the impact of both schemes to encourage some women in their careers and also the Equal Employment Opportunity Law has been thrown in doubt by the results of a survey carried out by the Ministry of Labour (1987) on how women's promotion prospects had changed not long after the implementation of the new law. The fact that 53.8 per cent of the responding companies stated that they had not discriminated against women before the passage of the Equal Employment Opportunity Law left scope for only 16.3 per cent to profess that they were actually now taking or just considering any measures to improve their job assignment systems. (The reason why the majority of companies could confidently assert that they had not previously pursued discriminatory promotion policies was largely because many of their women employees had been confined to so-called auxiliary jobs, as was seen in Chapter 3). The remaining 30 per cent responded that they were not yet even examining the issue of improving promotion opportunities for women. Indeed, when queried on why women failed to be promoted, almost 30 per cent of the companies stated that there was a problem in employing women because of their 'inadequate ability and will to work' and around 35 per cent argued that they had to take into consideration women's domestic duties. Such responses reveal that equal opportunity is a sham while companies take such factors into account when making decisions on promotion; and so the internal promotion system continues to be discriminatory in spite of the 1986 Equal Employment Opportunity Law.

Blue-collar women in the British Isles

Such company attitudes coupled with the sorts of social conditioning we have seen in Chapters 3 and 4 have the paradoxical effect of imparting a feeling of acute inferiority to the better-educated Japanese women. I have known a woman systems analyst who could not work effectively, because her shyness and lack of assertiveness was exacerbated by being surrounded by male colleagues. The usual comment in Britain is that women white-collar employees are more confident and articulate than blue-collar employees. In Japan the reverse seems to hold where white-collar women employees are usually thought to be in the 'office lady' category and are unskilled, intermittent members of the labour force, whereas blue-collar employees who are in regular employment have contributed longer years of service, since they did not go to college, and have probably acquired skills on the way. Thus the blue-collar Japanese women speak more confidently of their work and some at least have a little sense of ambition.

I would also venture one step further and say that the British and Irish blue-collar employees of Japanese companies – at least the ones whom I have met – are especially articulate and assertive. They have a particular pride in their job and a notable confidence about their future employment, which is not so evident among their blue-collar counterparts in Japan and appears least of all among female Japanese white-collar employees. The personnel manager at NEC Ireland commented how the local doctor had told him that the women employees of the Japanese plant exuded a brightness, but he found that the male shop-floor employees were a bit surly. His comment confirmed the impression conveyed in Chapter 8 of the women on the shop floor in the British Isles being more diligent and taking more pride in their work than their male colleagues.

The present favourable image of British and Irish working women in Japanese eyes may be subject to revision once plants become larger and the Japanese become less inclined to praise. In the USA where Japanese manufacturing has been established for longer and where there appear to have been more overt attempts to import the whole Japanese way of management, there has been a measure of disillusion with the employees, especially because they are apparently unwilling to engage in team-work. Ironically, one Japanese manager after returning to Japan complained to a *Los Angeles Times* reporter that Americans go too far with egalitarianism, including trying to open all jobs to women (*The Japan Times*, 17 August 1988). The returning managers may be speaking more frankly than when they are located in the host country; they feel freer to express their *honne* (real feeling), instead of *tatemae* (correct priniciples). Yet I did not feel that the Japanese managers and engineers to whom I spoke were only engaging in *tatemae*. Unlike in the USA, the Japanese manufacturers in the British Isles have preferred to pursue a middle way in working methods, which takes into consideration local working practices, and thereby they appear to have kept latent hostility among employees at bay.

An international comparison of employee attitudes

In order to explore some of these points further – beyond

considering the responses of the individual employees whom I met – an overall picture may be obtained from the trade union survey briefly cited earlier (Chapters 4 and 7), which was initiated by Denki Roren (1986). The survey encompassed 11,000 employees in the electronics industries of ten countries, among which were Japan and the UK, but not, unfortunately, Ireland. It should be noted that the survey was not confined to Japanese companies, nor to shop-floor employees.

Incidentally, before considering the results from the assorted parts of Table 9.1, one interesting psychological point should be made: the Japanese respondents tended to favour the less extreme responses. The results would possibly be more meaningful, therefore, if the category 1 figure were added to 2 and category 4 to 5. And when a sizeable percentage falls into category 3, one is left with some doubt as to what the Japanese would have responded had they been speaking more frankly or at least less cautiously. Even when the employees simply assessed whether they could use their abilities, almost 40 per cent of Japanese women – compared to just 13 per cent of British women – were not sure either way.

TABLE 9.1 *Worker attitudes in British and in Japanese electronics companies*
(percentage of respondents to 1985 survey)

	Women		Men	
	Britain	Japan	Britain	Japan
I can use my abilities at work:				
1. Absolutely true	21.8	2.7	34.8	10.1
2. Fairly true	22.9	30.0	42.7	43.4
3. Not sure	12.9	38.5	5.4	30.5
4. Only slightly	14.9	18.8	6.8	12.5
5. Not at all true	22.9	8.0	9.4	2.2
No response	4.7	2.1	0.9	1.5

continued over

233

	Women		Men	
	Britain	*Japan*	*Britain*	*Japan*
I can learn new things in my work:				
1. Absolutely true	24.5	14.6	40.7	22.4
2. Fairly true	28.1	25.2	30.2	39.2
3. Not sure	5.8	26.5	3.7	20.9
4. Only slightly	18.2	25.7	12.5	13.4
5. Not at all true	21.2	6.6	11.7	2.7
No response	2.2	1.3	1.1	1.4
Degree of satisfaction with promotion opportunities:				
1. Very satisfied	3.3	0.8	4.8	0.7
2. Fairly satisfied	17.9	8.5	27.6	14.7
3. Indifferent	22.0	54.9	17.1	45.5
4. Fairly dissatisfied	20.7	22.3	24.8	26.8
5. Very dissatisfied	34.2	9.5	24.8	10.6
No response	1.9	4.0	0.9	1.7
Degree of satisfaction with training and re-training:				
1. Very satisfied	6.1	1.1	7.1	1.7
2. Fairly satisfied	30.6	17.0	29.9	21.1
3. Indifferent	19.8	39.0	18.5	35.4
4. Fairly dissatisfied	19.6	28.1	27.1	29.1
5. Very dissatisfied	21.2	11.9	16.8	11.3
No response	2.8	2.9	0.6	1.6
Degree of satisfaction with relationship with your boss:				
1. Very satisfied	17.4	2.1	21.7	3.3
2. Fairly satisfied	39.9	32.1	48.4	34.1
3. Indifferent	20.7	34.0	16.0	36.4
4. Fairly dissatisfied	10.2	22.8	7.4	18.4
5. Very dissatisfied	11.3	6.6	6.0	6.3
No response	0.6	2.4	0.6	1.5
Degree of satisfaction with equal opportunities for women and men:				
1. Very satisfied	11.0	1.1	15.7	1.9
2. Fairly satisfied	37.5	18.3	38.5	26.3
3. Indifferent	23.4	34.5	31.6	53.3
4. Fairly dissatisfied	13.2	28.1	9.1	12.9
5. Very dissatisfied	14.0	15.1	4.6	3.6
No response	0.8	2.9	0.6	1.9

Source: Denki Roren no Chosa Jiho, No. 212.

It is particularly interesting that only one-third of the Japanese women employees who were surveyed considered that they could give full play to their abilities, whereas the figure was 45 per cent for British women. But even in the British case a much higher proportion of men – almost 80 per cent – felt they could use their abilities at work. A similar ranking of percentages is evident over the question of learning new things; the order British men, Japanese men, British women, Japanese women reflects a perception of access to training and skill acquisition which is least for the Japanese women. This perception corroborates the point made above that in Japan women are in effect excluded from the internal promotion system, despite all its egalitarian trappings.

One remarkable result of the Denki Roren survey, as can partly be deduced from Table 9.1, was that the Japanese employees were found to be less satisfied than their British counterparts with not only wages and the length of working hours, but also with their promotion opportunities, the amount of training and the level of confidence between management and employees. For example, only 34 per cent of Japanese women were satisfied with their relationship with their supervisors, whereas the comparable figure for British women was 57 per cent. Incidentally it is worth noting that in the case of both Japan and the UK, a higher proportion of men than women had a satisfactory relationship with their boss. This does not reflect a general disharmony; women and men had more or less equal responses in terms of relationships with co-workers with well over 90 per cent of British workers being satisfied, but only around 63 per cent of Japanese: so much for the much vaunted harmony in the Japanese workplace.

The low Japanese responses may simply, however, reflect a higher expectation of satisfaction on their part, whereas the British employees are happy to have a job at all, especially a relatively well-paid one in an electronics plant. And the divergence in results may also have arisen because the samples of workers were not strictly comparable; in particular the Japanese sample included relatively more engineers as well as research and development staff, who would probably have higher expectations.

Even though the responses on a national basis may not be entirely reliable, the distinction between women and men within each culture is still very revealing. Thus less than 10 per cent of Japanese women, compared to over 15 per cent of Japanese men, were satisfied with promotion opportunities, with a similar discrepancy arising in terms of training and re-training. But we would be blind to ignore the rather similar pattern pertaining to British women and men in respect of promotion; 32 per cent of British men, but only 21 per cent of women, were satisfied with promotion opportunities. In the case of training, however, there is a remarkable symmetry between British women and men in the degree of satisfaction; and, as we might have expected, only 19 per cent of Japanese women employees, but 28 per cent of men, were satisfied with equal opportunities. The evidence of Japanese women not being satisfied with promotion and training could suggest a greater level of ambition than I came across, except for the fact that 55 per cent of the same survey were indifferent concerning promotion.

Since it has become clear that the situation for women working in Japan is so different, both in terms of opportunities and the corresponding attitudes towards such aspects as promotion, the discussion that follows will be strictly limited to the impact of Japanese plants only in Britain and Ireland on women employees. Any resulting judgements cannot be applied to Japanese women working in the same companies in Japan.

Are Japanese methods transferable to Britain and Ireland?

So much has been written about the Japanese company as a special creature that one could be forgiven for being sceptical about the possibility of British and Irish women being able to participate successfully in their mass-production methods. Lawrence G. Franko (1983, p.43) goes so far as to suggest that the excellence of Japan's large-scale process production is the result of the Japanese people being ethnically, linguistically and educationally homogeneous. Similarly many Japanese, such as Masaaki Imai (1986, p.172), argue that high and growing productivity and the level of quality depend upon not only education and training but also the way in which management communicates with and understands labour.

Nor does the level of technology in an electronics plant mean that the role of the worker has been minimized. Indeed the need for constant checking of each component in order to insure that there are no defects requires the workers to be particularly highly motivated and diligent. And the Japanese stress on keeping minimum stock inventories means that operators have to be flexible in being deployed in response to market conditions. Finally the constant innovation in the electronics industry would not be possible unless the operators were able to adapt their skills to new machinery and products.

Nonetheless any scepticism about the transferability of Japanese production methods appears to have been disproved – and not only by my study which has confined itself to women. One of the most complete, though dated, appraisals is given by Michael White and Malcolm Trevor (1983), who suggest that the Japanese have been able to rekindle the British work ethic – at least among blue-collar workers. More important than supposed national characteristics in obtaining a flexible and motivated work-force is the promise of secure employment and investment in training. On the first point the British and Irish employees of Japanese companies whom I met were unanimous in their perception of job security. The second point concerning training provided less positive answers, but the absence of formal training need not be a deterrent to nurturing a highly motivated work-force. Moreover it would seem that Japanese companies have been more adaptable than some would give them credit for, in that they make schedules more flexible to individual workers than would be the case in Japan. This view of adaptation to 'local customs' comes across most strongly in the observations of Japanese who visit plants in Britain, such as those reported in *The Japan Economic Journal* (18 March 1989). A British visitor with a different perspective may have a contrary impression of an oppressed work-force.

But there is an initially unsuspected problem here. The places where Japanese methods have proved to be most successful are mostly where women predominate on the shop floor. Far more problems have appeared between workers and management at those large Japanese plants with a predominantly male work-force, such as Komatsu and Nissan in the North East. It has been reported in the *The Daily Telegraph* (29 May 1987) that Japanese scholars who had visited Nissan's Sunderland car plant found that the blue-collar employees resented the intensity of work and had a poor rapport with managers. The picture from Komatsu is just as tense and muddled – undue stress seems to be laid upon the success of its quintessentially Japanese morning exercises – a feature which I did not actually unearth at other Japanese plants in Britain. It is thought that the success of Japanese management methods depends upon a paternalistic, and when required authoritarian, relationship between manager and submissive workers. Does that mean then that it is only because women are more submissive than men that management of the Japanese electronics plants in Britain and Ireland can be successful?

Submissive women employees?

Having raised this tricky question, I would be foolish to answer it with a simple 'yes' or 'no'; but I am going to attempt an overall appraisal insofar as I can perceive the impact of Japanese managerial practices on women employees outside Japan by drawing on some of the topics discussed in Chapter 8. One important point to make at the outset is that the personnel managers and officers in Japanese plants located in Britain and Ireland are invariably not Japanese. They have usually been sent on study trips to Japan and they try to some extent to follow the head office's ideas on personnel management; but I detected some cynicism in their views of what Japanese personnel management could possibly entail.

There have been many general studies of Japanese management, mostly hagiographic, but a few debunking essays. The personnel practices and organizational systems of Matsushita have in particular attracted admiration, such as that rendered by Richard Pascale and Anthony Athos (1981). Their conclusion is that the organization has 'astonishing resilience and vitality' (p.57). Yet the Matsushita plant in South Wales did not strike me as being particularly Japanese in tone, in spite of its rather ostentatious display of the company philosophy displayed on the walls of the meeting room. And at most Japanese subsidiaries in Britain and Ireland, apart from notable exceptions like Komatsu, there are no group morning exercises nor a company song, although there are frequent, practical workplace meetings to keep supervisors and operators in close contact, which the women whom I met seemed to value.

In the electronics industry, where quality is all important, it is arguable that the focus of the Japanese managers is on tasks and results rather than being unduly orientated towards human relations (Trevor, 1986, p.25). But the two are by no means mutually exclusive and can in fact be complementary, especially in respect of working women. They appreciate the commitment to employee welfare – even though it does not extend to child-care facilities – and the way that managers have chains of communication to all levels. Nor does the level of strictness irritate them in the way that it affects some male employees. Consequently the women I met in Japanese factories in the British Isles are largely content with their work, which in turn encourages their good performance in maintaining quality.

It does also appear that the notion of egalitarianism, which in Japan extends only so far as male blue-collar employees, does succeed in Britain and Ireland by permitting the women employees to feel a particular pride in their work, even though, as will be discussed later, the egalitarian notion has not changed the overall hierarchical structure in the workplace. In any case the willingness of managers to join production staff on the shop floor at times of high demand reduces the feeling of being overworked. At NEC Ireland when semiconductor sales suddenly doubled in 1984 the presence of managers – both Japanese and Irish – working on the shop floor, as mentioned earlier, meant that it was not necessary to hire extra workers and a good level of morale was maintained. Stability of employment can only be achieved by tight staffing with a consequent need for frequent overtime work. And even though overtime causes more problems for most women, the women at Matsushita's plant did take it on without undue complaints, once it had been made clear to them that there was a good reason for the extra output. The woman supervisor whom I met herself led the way by doing almost 60 hours overtime a month. Thus, as has been seen earlier, Japanese companies in the British Isles have successfully inculcated upon their female employees the company goals which link hard work with good employment conditions.

Other ways in which women respond to employment in a Japanese plant are perhaps open to sexist interpretations – but for the moment that risk has to be taken. It is not that the women are more submissive to discipline, since Table 9.1 showed that British women are not so satisfied with their relationship with their superiors as are British men. It is rather that women working in electronics plants imbibe the goals of high quality and productivity, which they also link to how clean and tidy is the production area. The women I met did not appear to be subservient; what rather impressed me was that they empathized with the company goals, because they saw the connection with their own job security. This empathy left them with a positive attitude towards the work and a recognition of the need for fairly disciplined team-work and flexibility. Consequently the work, though still basically repetitive, seemed to be satisfying. Another study by Paul Worm (Thurley *et al*, 1981) also reported that, despite there being little career planning, the female operators in a Japanese plant in Belgium showed particularly high levels of job satisfaction. It may also be that women respond better to the notion of the company as a family and they seem to be less bothered by language and cultural difficulties that may sometimes be encountered in their work. And now this is going into even more tricky realms; the women to whom I spoke often seemed to view their Japanese managers with a wry affection, perhaps because of their shyness in speaking English and absence of an overtly domineering nature.

Japanese management methods

Maybe harmonious working relationships are more agreeable to women? A similar rather sexist question about less confrontational industrial relations was rhetorically asked in the section on unions (Chapter 7). But the response to both questions is that it is in any case debatable whether harmony and contentment are special features of the Japanese shop floor. The view of more harmonious workplaces in Japan certainly received no support from Table 9.1. Japanese employees seem to be just as likely as those in the West to be dissatisfied and to disagree with their supervisors; it is just that their disagreements are more quickly channelled through the suggestion system and meetings rather than being smouldered over and being built up into a large amount of aggression. Thus a disciplined work environment need not necessarily imply an authoritarian structure; there can be room for dissent.

Nor should superficial egalitarianism be unduly played up. As was noted in Chapter 8 the egalitarian atmosphere is due to little more than the gratuitous signs of inequality concerning parking and dining facilities being left out. The implementation of common terms and conditions of employment for production and managerial staff is important, but that measure – which certainly should not be seen as a privilege for production staff, but as a natural right – is not at all confined to Japanese companies. Neither are the employee welfare provisions concerning sick pay and so forth especially generous, but tend merely to be in line with the relevant legislation in Britain and Ireland, though rates of pay do seem to be relatively good. It is really these factors of pay and conditions rather than cosmetic egalitarianism which determine the employees' loyalty. It was suggested by a British personnel manager that commitment to the job in a Japanese plant arises because:

> We are more paternalistic than a British company; we try to treat people equally. The system that we have here in terms of conditions of employment is good; salaries are very competitive [compared to other jobs in the area.]

The opening of new Japanese plants in Britain and Ireland leads to quite a lot of hullabaloo about what management methods the Japanese are using, but after several years' operation the plant's organization settles down into a less radical pattern. Before the end of the 1970s, YKK's zip fastener factory in Runcorn – the first Japanese manufacturing plant in Britain, where production began in 1972 – had already lost some of its family atmosphere or what is known as industrial familism. But that loss seems not to matter, being only the decorative packaging to the initial success of Japanese manufacturing in Britain. 'Familism' may in any case have ultimately been a cause of dissatisfaction; one Japanese company, according to Wolf Reitsperger (Takamiya and Thurley, eds.,1985) abandoned the practice of sick visits and other 'people-oriented' measures, because they were judged as being too intrusive of people's privacy.

A more convoluted – or, to speak more kindly, sophisticated – approach to Japanese success taken by Tadashi Mito (*The Wheel Extended*, 1984, No.1) is to consider that the secret is that management is based on 'heteronomy' as opposed to autonomy. The explanation is that actions are based on social relations and adapting behaviour to the social positions of others, whereas autonomous behaviour is based on own volition and personal responsibility. It might, therefore, be suggested that heteronomous behaviour or groupism is more agreeable to women than to men on the shop floor in the British Isles. In the case of Japan itself, however, women on the shop floor have been seen to be somewhat more individualistic than the men (Chapter 8). The trouble is that in Japan, where groupism is meant to govern relationships in all spheres of life, women have been allotted the rule of acting with consideration to social relations with regard to the family but not to the company; consequently they lose out in what is actually a highly competitive society. Meanwhile on the shop floor Japanese men pursue the company's goals in accordance with their own competitive spirit, while not paying enough attention to the family. All of that may be so, but such explanations concerning social relations ignore the point that Japanese efficiency is more a function of organization and production methods than social and cultural practices.

Indeed, despite all I have said concerning Japanese managerial methods in Britain and Ireland, I would be very wary of giving any culturalist interpretation to the success of Japanese management methods, which does not mean that non-pecuniary factors play no part; the will to work shown by women in Japanese plants is a function of many different aspects in addition to the relatively good pay scales compared to other factories in South Wales and in Ireland. The Japanese managers are merely doing what is most appropriate for the achievement of high productivity levels, while the response of the women employees shows that there is no need for them either to be inclined to groupism or to know anything about the precision and control of the tea ceremony in order to be diligent on the shop floor. Indeed the success of such 'Japanese' features as QC circles, which were originally promoted by an American statistician in the

1950s, simply reflects the best use of automated production processes, without which it would be meaningless to engage in statistical analyses of output. In other words modern manufacturing techniques combined with good organization and initiation into simple statistical and other skills are the factors which largely determine Japanese success.

Japanese subsidiaries in Europe are not managed in a dramatically different way to other European firms. Therefore the relatively good industrial relations and productivity are more a function of both good organization and being on green-field sites than because of different practices. The emphasis on Japanese personnel practices has been misplaced; it is the system of production manangement and supervision that determines productivity levels. In other words what really distinguishes the Japanese approach is one of organization, flexibility and the opportunity for employees to feel in control of their work. At NEC Ireland the workers finish the day by feeding their own output and quality results into a computer. Making records on control charts and frequently checking quality and machinery, all of which are a normal part of the day's work in a Japanese factory, give blue-collar employees a sense of pride and intellectual achievement, which are of more significance than the cosmetic egalitarian practices, such as a common uniform. And women in particular seem to savour the chance to tie up loose ends; so they do not object at Matsushita in Cardiff to spending a few minutes at the end of the day in clearing up their work space: time which is included in their paid working hours.

All of the above suggests that the Japanese management style and the kind of work found in electronics factories seem to have been especially appropriate for working women in the British Isles. The question is whether they have been bamboozled. But I do not think so. Several of the women to whom I spoke had been employed in other workplaces and it was they, rather than the school-leavers, who were most eloquent in their positive assessment of working for a Japanese company. Thus our earlier question concerning whether women operators in Japanese plants fit in better because they accept a higher degree of domination may not really be relevant. The system works not because of paternalism, but because of the shop floor being a place to learn and improve on one's performance. The focus of a Japanese factory is on what goes on on the shop floor and the quality of the products, rather than on financial performance and corporate goals. And British and Irish women appreciate these factors, even though they have not in their childhood gone through a Japanese education system which places a lot of value on learning and in which both co-operation and intense competition to succeed are emphasized.

Before concluding this section it should be reiterated that a lot of what I have written applies only to shop-floor production staff, since the relationship of British and Irish managerial staff to their Japanese colleagues is far less satisfactory (Chapter 7). Whereas shop-floor staff can work well and take their leave with a light heart, managers feel under pressure to demonstrate the same sort of long hours as customarily worked by the Japanese, which would be particularly hard for married women; so it is perhaps no accident that the only women I met in executive posts in Japanese companies were personnel officers. Reports that the production staff at many Japanese plants are happy with the Japanese management style, while retaining an antagonistic attitude towards the British managers in their plants suggests that human relations are of some importance, despite my earlier arguments concerning organizational methods. Malcolm Trevor (1987, p.16) concluded that Japanese managers generally got on well with British operators and suggested that British 'blue-collar workers with their groupishness and solidarity are closest to the Japanese pattern', while British managers are more individualistic and therefore are less content with Japanese management systems. It may be that since it is the personnel manager's post which is usually localized, he or she is in the awkward and front-line position of having to negotiate and explain the management side. The Japanese retain their allure by remaining rather quiet and in the background.

In concluding, it is important to remember that certain characteristics of Japanese employment – lifelong on-the-job training and career paths for most regular employees in large companies – have not been transferred to Japanese plants in Britain and Ireland, though that may be partly because the plants are still too new and too small. (Ironically the same complaint can be made about how most of the Japanese women employed in major companies are left out in the cold without enjoying the real benefits of the internal promotion system.) Citing deficiencies in general education among British and Irish school-leaver recruits should not be a justification for failing to establish a regular career path. Indeed the responses of the women in Chapter 8 showed how much they appreciated being given training in skills and in QC statistical techniques. It is unfortunate that up to half of the supervisors at the Japanese plants in Britain and Ireland have been recruited externally, although the posts are first advertised internally. That situation may change once there are a sizeable number of employees with an appropriate length of service and enough experience. At the same time more external pressure may need to be applied to ensure that better opportunities and training are provided so as to improve further the quality of employment. At present the emphasis is on localization in terms of parts procurement, with some attention also to the overall numbers to be employed at a Japanese plant. But we have come to expect more from the Japanese than simply a certain quantity of secure employment opportunities. Women can at least find job security with a Japanese company in Britain and Ireland – insofar as the work does not conflict with child-rearing – but they also need to expect a career in order to motivate them to stay longer and be more ambitious.

It is also worth noting that wage features such as the biannual bonus system, which is the equivalent of a few months' salary, and steeply rising seniority payments have not been implemented in Britain and Ireland. There may be a limited attendance and production bonus, but often agreement with the union cannot be reached. The only way in which some sort of consideration is given to seniority is in the fact that annual wage increases are usually an equivalent percentage for all – rather than an across-the-board absolute rise – which thereby widens the absolute margin between pay scales. In Japan companies would in any case like to do away with seniority payments since the ageing work-force is increasing the labour cost of production substantially. It is unlikely, therefore, that Japanese companies would voluntarily introduce the seniority wage system overseas.

Nor certainly have the more controversial and possibly ephemeral features of contentment and total loyalty to the company, as typified by the singing of a company song, found many adherents in Britain and Ireland. Wolf Reitsperger's study, which was cited earlier, also found from explicit ratings of job satisfaction for British employees in Japanese and other plants that satisfaction was generally no higher in the Japanese plants, so there was not an exceptionally 'happy' work-force. At the close of Chapter 7, I posed the question of how loyalty was maintained in the Japanese electronics plants in the British Isles, since the women I met were intending to be long servers. The discussion since then should have shown that there is commitment not because of an ephemeral 'happiness', but because of an interest in the work, which has been engendered through the organization of flexible job assignments and the operators being given responsibility for inspection and recording their own output.

What have, therefore, been successfully inculcated in NEC Ireland and in Matsushsita in Cardiff are a perception of job security, pride in one's work and a certain measure of discipline, all three of which are mutually reinforcing. There is nothing remarkable in their transference to another culture since workers anywhere are as susceptible as the Japanese to a work ethic. Indeed it is misleading to use the word 'transfer'; what has merely happened is the reinforcement or release of latent favourable attitudes to work, which have also been shown by relatively low rates of turnover and absenteeism.

Implications for women

What is remarkable is that this reinforcement has been more successful in the case of women employees of Japanese companies than of men, despite the popular perception of women as being less committed to their work because of all their other responsibilities. I found that the older married women were usually more receptive than the school-leavers to the notion of zero defects and concentration on detailed work, including the final inspection of chips. Since, moreover, Japanese management methods are meant to depend on having a multi-skilled work-force, it makes no sense to let go of departing mothers-to-be who have demonstrated their flexibility and become experienced. The simple solution is that the Japanese companies in Britain and Ireland need to veer their attention away from employing raw school-leavers to find ways of re-employing their former female employees whose children are now older. And once there is an expectation that mothers will some day return to the shop floor, then not only will an additional investment in proper training programmes become justifiable, but also women themselves will become more ambitious and even more diligent workers in seeking promotion to further their careers.

10 | Post-industrial employment for women

The term 'post-industrial' is not intended to refer to some rural idyll far off in the future; its use covers the general shift towards the production and consumption of services at the same time as manufacturing industry becomes more highly automated and international. (Some more specific criteria have been proposed such as that, when over 50 per cent of employees are in the tertiary sector, the economy has 'softened' and entered the post-industrial age.) In Britain and Japan the post-industrial age has, therefore, already begun and some of its effects on women's employment are already evident with increasing opportunities for employment in services and in the subsidiaries of foreign companies. The questions to be explored, then, are whether the present evidence suggests that there will be an overall improvement in the conditions under which women work and how the participation of women in the labour force will change. Ultimately it would be good to speculate about whether the employment patterns for Japanese women and British women will converge or whether important differences will remain. It would be tempting in answering these questions simply to rely on projections of participation rates made by the ILO or OECD. Such projections, however, seem to be based on extrapolations of present trends without allowing for any radical changes in industrial and employment structures.

The future encompasses a lot. Here I will have to be selective, but the aspects on which this chapter will concentrate do interact and do hold lessons which can be transferred to some other topics which would otherwise have to be ignored. Thus in the case of Britain and Ireland, even though my main focus will be on employment prospects for women working in Japanese companies, the discussion about the implications of the changes in Japan's industrial and demographic structures are also relevant to what could happen in Britain. And, in reverse, the fact that British women are now somewhat more deeply embedded in the labour force than Japanese women does provide some lessons for speculating how women's employment in Japan might change.

Changes in industrial structure

One implication of overseas Japanese investment – and of the appreciating yen which accelerates that trend – is the hollowing out of Japanese industry, whereby production is increasingly located overseas with a possible concomitant decline in manufacturing employment in Japan. This process is beginning to take place not in the large companies investing in Britain, whose growth permits an increase in employment both at home and overseas, but in the small subcontracting companies, which had been supplying the parts to the major companies. And it is predominantly in such companies that middle-aged Japanese women have been finding employment.

Evidently employment adjustment will be needed and it will often be women who have to bear the burden of adjustment, since they are located in the more unstable secondary labour market. Ministerial outlooks for the industrial structure in the twenty-first century are reasonably confident that the number of jobs lost in some sectors of manufacturing will be more than compensated for by new jobs in high technology and knowledge-intensive industries, including micro-electronics, biotechnology and new industrial materials. Such prospects do not hold much hope for the present middle-aged female work-force. And in certain sectors, such as banking and clerical duties, the introduction of micro-electronic technology is associated with a small decline in female employment, despite the job creation effects of the increased flow of information. While jobs associated with micro-electronic technology could be subject to less sexual stereotyping than other kinds of work, the use of computers among some women clerical workers may herald a loss of skills and understanding of the object of their work. It should also be remembered that there is considerable anxiety concerning the effects of long-term exposure to video displays in the case of pregnant women.

The relatively high educational levels of young Japanese women today should permit them to participate in the newly opening non-routine jobs in the knowledge-intensive industries as long as society's strictures do not cause them to lack confidence. Thus Makoto Yamaguchi (1986, p.112) suggests, without much evidence, that Japanese women are 'negative in their attitude towards education and training' in the use of micro-electronic technology. But I judge that Japanese women do have the skills and the drive to tackle the new jobs and the transformation of their present jobs through automation. As we have seen in the electronics plants, women not only cope with highly automated processes, but also engage in recording and analysing their output for the sake of QC circles. And the possible scope provided by information technology for jobs for educated Japanese women, who are at present often underemployed in routine office jobs, is considerable. It could be that even the presently rather ineffectual 'office ladies' may be transformed into 'techno-ladies', as Jane Condon (1986, p.288) indicates is happening in the case of some enterprising women. In these circumstances it was appropriate that a symposium on the implications of science and technology on the status of women was held in Tokyo in August 1988. The fact that one paper by Sumiko Iwao reported that 60 per cent of Japanese women responding to a survey lacked confidence in using computers indicates the degree of social conditioning and the lack of a relevant education.

Japanese society could in any case clamp down on women's participation in the new technologies, because as employment opportunities are reduced in the heavy manufacturing industries which locate overseas, men may choose to enter the clerical world and other occupations which have been considered to be the province of women. But at least the fact that brute manual strength is no longer needed in most jobs should encourage more women also to move into a greater range of industrial jobs. Men moving into women's jobs – a trend with few precedents – does raise the status and wages associated with such jobs, but women may feel obliged to sacrifice their own jobs for the sake of employing the 'household heads'. Sadly, Japanese women are conditioned to make such sacrifices and historically have always done so, because they have defined their commitments in terms of the family not the workplace, despite their relatively high levels of participation in the labour force.

One way in which women may preserve a proportion of such jobs for themselves is through working at home using a computer terminal or a personal computer with a modem. That development should put a new dimension and higher status on the kind of work homeworkers could do while caring for small children. There is the drawback, however, that the kinds of social interaction which women often seek when taking on paid employment would be almost non-existent. More seriously, women would be unable to organize effectively to protect their employment conditions and the contracting companies could impose heavy workloads without having to provide any kind of job security. Working with a computer at home may thereby become downgraded close to the kind of status presently suffered by homeworkers engaged in assembling light-manufactured goods and in sewing. Generally, however, changes in industrial structure in Japan and Britain could lead by the mid-1990s to better bargaining positions for working women because of labour shortages in jobs which are unlikely to be 'appropriate for rugby players'.

Resistance to reducing working hours

To the limited extent that micro-electronic technology may displace workers, there is scope in Japan for employing the same number of workers simply by reducing the present long working hours in offices. Yet in Japan there is considerable resistance to this pleasant idea, which in particular would permit more married women to commit themselves to full-time work. I puzzled for some time over the following extract from an editorial in the *Asahi Shimbun* (26 September 1987):

> [It is] workers' labour consciousness and the strong perception of the division of labour by sex that make it difficult to reduce working hours.

There could be a variety of interpretations of this editorial stance. One is that men prefer to stay at the office in the evenings, because if they were at home they might feel obliged to help with some of the household tasks and thereby interfere with the division of labour in the home. Another even less benign interpretation would be that only if men were willing to off-load some of the more important and interesting work onto women, could working hours be reduced; but men will not do so. Indeed the very idea of 'job sharing' would be met with incredulity by most Japanese. Although the number of women working part-time increases dramatically every year, by no stretch of the imagination is their work appropriate for job sharing, since their jobs are mostly peripheral and unstable.

Is then Japanese society so rigid, that it cannot accommodate the idea of substantially more women holding managerial and supervisory positions? That would be a surprising conclusion in view of the fact that a substantial part of the reason for Japan's economic success has been the way in which the economic sectors have been flexible enough to adapt to changing conditions and to seize upon new opportunities. There is also, however, a powerful conservative streak in Japanese society, especially concerning the family and, in particular, the mother's role. The language in which even the Equal Employment Opportunity Law is couched with its emphasis on harmonizing a woman's paid work and her family life attests to that perception. A public opinion poll carried out by the Prime Minister's Office (1987) shows that close to 70 per cent of men would be unwilling to work underneath a woman supervisor; and there has been little change in this proportion in spite of the attention given to the supposed ramifications of the Equal Employment Opportunity Law.

Despite social attitudes, however, a barely perceived change is already underway in Japan as the total number of female administrators (sub-section chiefs and above) has doubled since the late 1970s – though from a very low base – as we have seen in Chapter 3. This change has only become possible because more women have offered uninterrupted careers with probable accompanying family and personal sacrifices. A more balanced and radical change could occur, once it were fully realized that not only women, but also men need to harmonize their careers with obligations to their family, beyond the merely financial. A shortening of working hours – or at least making working hours more flexible – for all workers would give men the opportunity to participate in family activities and women the opportunity of pursuing a career, which should permit the possibility of not just a dual-career family, but also a dual-parent family. The concern over the suffocating embrace of the *kyoiku mama* ('education mother'), who pours all her energy into furthering her children's studies, could then be quite simply relieved.

An impetus towards a more rational working life may come from the Ministry of Labour itself, although its proposals are fairly constrained. In its 1988 white paper on labour, the Ministry explicitly states that the quality of life for workers is very low. Not only are their annual working hours (including overtime) over 2,100, which is about 200 hours more than in Britain, but also they spend longer additional hours in commuting than in the West. But workers in the West would be surprised to hear that the goal is merely to try to reduce scheduled working hours to 1,800 hours – a 40-hour week with 20 days of paid holidays – by 1992 and to call for reduced overtime and a complete use of paid vacations. Under present labour shortages, even this limited target is not considered achievable, especially in the service industries and in small companies, where Japanese working women are usually employed. Moreover Haruo Shimada suggests that Japanese workers themselves do not realize the value of free time and prefer to work long hours simply in order to increase their ability to consume (*Japan Labor Bulletin*, March 1989). One would hope that a change in values towards spending more time with the family would occur, which would be to the benefit of all, if women were no longer peripheral members of the labour force, but became fully integrated at the managerial level.

Thus it is in any case not enough to seek slightly shorter working hours; what is needed is a wholesale change in attitudes, since the Japanese employee is at present expected to demonstrate an unswerving commitment to work, which is only really desirable for a minority of both women and men. The rest of the population would benefit from the implementation of more diversification in employment patterns – encompassing not only flexible working hours but also career breaks. Flexitime is now being introduced by some companies, including Hitachi, in the wake of the revised 1988 Labour Standards Law, but in other respects the law's relaxation of the definition of what are regular working hours is rather expected, as was discussed in Chapter 4, to compel women to work longer hours. In the case of career breaks, only a minority of Japanese women participates in the existing re-employment schemes (Chapter 5). Therefore such schemes need to be made more attractive by both the private sector and by public welfare policies so as to encompass better financial support and the full protection of pension rights. And, of course, there should always be the option for the father to take a career break instead of the mother.

Expanding service sector but poorer conditions

Rather than depending on government policy, working hours may become more flexible through the initiative of employers in the expanding service sector, which by its nature requires a less rigidly defined working day. Moreover, even in the eventuality that employment in some areas of manufacturing declines, the anticipated further growth of employment in services, as rising incomes lead to higher proportions being spent on leisure activities and health, is going to contribute more to female than to male employment. By the late 1980s the number of workers employed in social welfare, medical, hygiene and leisure-related services had risen almost 40 per cent over the number in 1975, according to the Ministry of Labour (1988). Indeed women's work in the service sector is particularly valued in Japan for reasons which would upset almost anyone concerned about women's rights; we have seen that much value is placed on their 'sense of fashion' and 'way of speaking' (Chapters 2 and 3), as well as presumably their rather obsequious manner towards customers.

The Ministry of Labour predicts that by 1995 service sector employment will have expanded by around 18 per cent since 1988 whereas there will be only a slight increase in manufacturing employment. Consequently the participation rate of women will rise, while that of men will actually decline as a larger proportion of men will be aged over 60 years and thus retired. Already the yearly growth in female employment at around 1.5 per cent exceeds that of male employment growth of just about 1 per cent. This trend then is the most important reason why women's employment growth in Japan has been greater than in Britain since the late 1970s, since the shift towards the service sector occurred earlier and less dramatically in Britain, where – it is also worth remembering – high levels of unemployment and the effective implementation of equal pay legislation have not reduced the demand and supply for female labour (Zabalza and Tzannatos, 1985). Therefore in both Japan and Britain women's participation in the labour force is going to increase, though with more diversification in employment patterns – including self-employment and casual work – than has been expected in the past.

The only trouble is that – as experience has shown in the USA, (Kelly and Bayes, eds., 1988, p.77) – it is particularly in the service sector that women are clustered at the lower job levels and they receive significantly less pay than their male colleagues. In France also the service sector is noted for its 'petty lay-offs' of women employees, with the consequence that the unemployment rate is much higher among women and those who do work are at the 'bottom of the heap' (*Le Monde*, 15 September 1987). In Britain the increased casualization of work among women since the 1980s is going to bring about a similar effect, in that conditions of employment could worsen and the average pay differential between women and men widen once more, especially since the 1986 Wages Act has reduced the coverage of Wage Councils and women aged under 21 years are no longer protected by minimum wage legislation. Already women's average hourly earnings as a percentage of men's has declined by over 1.4 percentage points from 74.8 per cent in 1981 to 73.4 per cent in 1987. And in Japan the average pay differential by sex has widened since 1975 by almost one percentage point as more middle-aged women have taken up paid employment in the secondary labour market (Table 1.4). Indeed in the case of Britain Jill Rubery (1988, p.122) concludes:

> Instead of a progressive improvement in both employment opportunities and terms and conditions of employment, women's employment may be experiencing a trend towards a more intensive form of labour exploitation for a substantial part of the female labour force.

Oddly enough, US women researchers (Koziara *et al*, eds., 1987, p.12) take a much more upbeat view:

> The future looks brighter than the past for working women . . . the advances made in the past two decades are unlikely to be

reversed . . . the next generation of middle-aged women are less likely to be in low-paying traditional jobs because young women have fewer children and stay in the work-force longer.

Perhaps the US perspective can be more optimistic because unemployment has been lower and less socially divisive than in Britain. As various government schemes come into play in Britain to subsidize employment for youths and the male unemployed and to remove minimum wage requirements, unskilled middle-aged women are likely to have to compete even for the worst-paid jobs. In Japan, where sex roles are more sharply defined and adhered to, men have been unlikely ever to want to take over the women's jobs, although there is a greater variety of jobs engaged in by both sexes (Chapter 3). But Japanese women will continue to be confined to low-status jobs, because under present employment patterns only a few of the present generation of young women will be able to embark upon real careers in internal labour markets. Therefore neither the predicted US nor British scene will be characteristic of Japan, although there will be the common points that only a minority of women will be in high-status jobs or in self-employment and that employment conditions for the majority of women could worsen, despite their likely higher rates of participation. Although self-employment and the associated informal labour market can, as we have seen, be an almost ideal option for some women, it will be a viable option only for a minority. Nonetheless it is an option which merits further discussion later on in the section on family life.

There are two important qualifications to this rather depressing analysis of employment opportunities. One is that as mentioned earlier in this chapter, not only could some Japanese men possibly seek to enter 'women's' jobs, but also people may begin to demand changes in the permanent employment structure, which has been thought to be the ideal in Japan. In that case, intermittent 'women's' jobs could be upgraded and their participation would be more compatible with family life. The other qualification concerns the nature of part-time work, which is at present associated with low-status, peripheral work. There is now a trendy word in Japan – *parlite* – to refer to part-time work which is also 'elite' in nature. While there are very few women who are presently employed on such terms, the kind of work that will be increasingly found in the post-industrial age may be more appropriate for *parlite* workers, who should be better positioned to move between part-time and full-time jobs.

Ageing of society

The particularly rapid growth in Japan of life expectancy from around 50 years in the 1940s to around 80 years in 1989 has brought about a keen awareness of the implications of a substantial increase in the proportion of the elderly, which will reduce the level of savings and bring an extra strain onto welfare programmes. Projections are made on how there will be fewer workers on average to support in effect each aged person in the twenty-first century compared to the present; the ratio of those in the productive age groups to those in the non-productive age groups in Japan is predicted to be only 1.5 by the year 2025. The projected ratio in Britain for the same year of 2.5 is less alarming, but is still a matter for concern. Another way to express the projections is that by the year 2025 every ten economically active citizens in Britain will be supporting nearly four pensioners, while in Japan they will have to support over six pensioners. (As with many predictions a simple extrapolation of present trends may be somewhat misleading.)

Such projections become much less dismal when a rise in the participation rate of women in the labour market is included in the estimates, since the burden of support is then reduced. There will in any case be a rise in the demand for labour associated with services for old people in providing meals, nursing and general care. And such services will under present social trends almost invariably be provided by women. Whether the services are rendered on a commercial basis or as part of public welfare, the effect will be an exacerbation in job segregation, unless an amazing number of men choose to enter the 'caring' jobs associated with women. And in the case where women are looking after their own aged relatives, their ability to take on paid employment will become even more constrained. Whereas absences from the labour market for the sake of child care can be reckoned to last for only a limited number of years, time spent on the care of the aged can be almost indefinite. Japan is thought to be a society where old people will be taken care of by their offspring; in fact, since life expectancy was relatively short until the 1950s, care of the aged would have only lasted for a few years at most after the old had given continuing years of work on the family farm or business. Under present conditions it is much less reasonable to expect women to take on without assistance the considerable burden of total care of their sick or incapacitated relatives.

The ageing of Japanese society is changing the employment structure in other ways as well. As the work-force becomes top heavy and the economic growth rate slows, companies are much less inclined to give their regular employees the implicit promise of assured employment until retirement age coupled with increasing salaries in line with seniority. Women have found it wellnigh impossible to fit into the permanent employment system, but now companies may themselves begin to take the initiative in offering flexible occupational careers, which could be taken up by women. Technological developments, including automation, reinforce these changes, because already-acquired skills and length of service become less important than dexterity and the ability to learn quickly – qualities which even some male chauvinists believe that women amply possess.

Another factor which might lead to changes is that Japanese companies are beginning to view the personnel practices of Western companies as a source of inspiration. After a decade during which the West praised the egalitarian employment practices of Japanese companies, the influential

Keizai Doyukai (Japanese Association of Corporate Executives) has now called for a shift towards individualism in the personnel management strategy of Japanese firms with more account taken of the ability and performance of individual employees in determining their salaries and promotion (*The Japan Times*, 2 February 1988). Although the interests of older male workers who can hold onto the positions of power will prevent a complete breakdown of the permanent employment system, there should be a blurring of the present rigid distinction in Japan between the primary internal labour markets, in which regular male employees are ensconced, and the secondary labour markets, where women are predominantly found. Already there is evidence that the number of those who change jobs is increasing each year. The changes from a breakdown of the permanent employment structure would include a narrowing of the present wide wage differentials between the two kinds of markets and the greater possibility of workers crossing the boundaries. Older male workers may have to join the secondary market, while young women may be able to join and then temporarily leave the primary market, in line with family cares. (I have deliberately used the word 'may', because in Japan – just as is possible in the case of new technologies – Japanese women may feel compelled by society or choose themselves not to take advantage of the changes in the permanent employment system, which has been such a powerful impediment to their career opportunities.)

Those Japanese women who do join the primary labour market are not likely to be numerous. In Britain there are indeed women who are increasing their level of qualifications and endeavouring to be stable participants in the labour market with the result that they are taking on the characteristics and benefits which used to be wholly associated with male workers. But they are still a minority. And Jill Rubery and Roger Tarling (1988, p.127) believe that the majority of British working women will find that their labour conditions deteriorate because of labour market factors and the 'unacceptable stresses to family organizations' imposed by full participation in the labour market. There is no escaping the fact that family considerations do presently constrain a woman's economic activity.

Family life and stress

So much for the macro-scenario of structural changes in the economy and in employment – but we have seen that a woman's ability and willingness to take on paid work depend on more than long-term economic trends. In particular, the double burden she bears is not so easily disposed of by the provision of day-care centres and home appliances. What is rather needed is a change in not only society's attitudes, but also companies' employment practices. It is not enough for there to be an Equal Employment Opportunity Law or even affirmative action policies, when there is stress and incompatibility between work and family responsibilities. For men in Japan the working hours are so long that home life has to be confined mostly to sleeping and one day's recovery a week, while for working women their hours of relaxation are almost negligible and they must bear the additional stress of being almost wholly responsible for the children's well-being and the family finances, even though there is little social disapprobation if their children are in day-care centres.

In Britain such disapproval is on a disturbing upswing. Data from the 1987 *British Social Attitudes* survey show that more than three-quarters of the British believe that mothers with children aged under five years should not go out to work even part-time; and wide media attention was given to a highly contentious book published by the Social Affairs Unit, called *Full Circle?*, which gave emotional support to such beliefs (*The Times*, 19 August 1988).

Admittedly there are some limits on how much most women can do. The recent appearance of the syndrome which is known in the US as CEBV (chronic Epstein Barr virus) and in Britain as ME (myalgic encephalomyelitis) is said to affect particularly women in their thirties; the unrelievable exhaustion and chronic flu symptoms are considered to have been exacerbated by women pushing their bodies too far in trying to live up to the superwoman image. Even where her partner is supportive of her career and takes on a share of the household tasks, the fact remains that it is the woman who has to fit maternity into the scheme of things and who almost always has to juggle schedules and responsibilities in order to ensure that home life runs reasonably smoothly for the whole family. The superwoman myth has led both women and men to believe that a woman can do just about everything while her partner wallows in his own career and leisure activities. In fact the notion of the superwoman who could combine a brilliant and uninterrupted career with bringing up happy and successful children is usually not feasible for a woman, unless she depends upon a domestic servant and, thereby, perpetuates not only the sexual division of labour, but also some of the unsavoury aspects of the class system.

Consequently there is talk of the 'new realism' under which women would willingly agree to return to the hearth. That would, however, be a great pity and not at all necessary, because compromises in terms of the number of hours worked, as was discussed above, and in ways of sharing and lightening household chores are quite feasible. Moreover the love and attention that mothers give to their children should be given no more merit than that which fathers also feel and want to express. The household in which the mother works permits the father to partake in and enjoy many more aspects of child-rearing. Where Japanese husbands of working mothers fall short on sharing household chores, they often make up for in their enthusiasm in entertaining the children; and there is increasing, though limited, support for the idea of establishing paternity leave systems.

Even so, while there is some scope for a rise in the participation rate of women in their late twenties and thirties in Japan and perhaps in Britain, the trough seen in Figure 1.1 of a reduced rate among young Japanese and British mothers is unlikely to be filled in, unless both paternity-leave schemes are widely established and also part-time work of less than 20 hours a week becomes better paid and part of a proper career structure. In that case the shape of women's participation according to age could begin to mirror the single plateau of the Scandinavian countries. However there are few signs in either Japan or Britain that the association of part-time work with unskilled and poorly paid jobs is going to change for the majority of women. As was indicated in the discussion on shortening working hours by job sharing, it is particularly hard to imagine Japanese companies agreeing to make their employment structure more flexible by including part-timers in positions of influence, because their total loyalty to the company, which is so prized in Japan, would be in doubt.

But there is one other alternative for the employment of mothers: to work in a family business or be self-employed. The informal sector in Japan, which has persisted in its traditional forms of small family-run retailers, manufacturers and tutoring services right through industrialization into the post-industrial age, has always provided plenty of opportunities for women to be economically active. In this respect, there could be potential for the British pattern of employment to converge towards the Japanese. Although there are legitimate fears that the further casualization of employment for women may lead to a deterioration in their labour conditions and status in the labour market, that need not be necessarily so, if women themselves start up their own small businesses.

Policy statements proliferate

One should not perhaps leave Japan without giving a nod to the government's proposals on how to improve the participation of women in both jobs and society. The

Women's Bureau in the Prime Minister's Office has produced a grandiose-sounding 'New National Plan of Action towards the Year 2000', whose ostensible intention is to create a society in which women and men can participate equally and to improve the status of women in Japan. The plan does at least recognize that there can be no meaning to equality of opportunity while the traditional sex roles under which women take care of the house remain in force. Therefore the plan includes statements about the kind of home economics that should be taught in schools to both boys and girls. The other proposals are fairly bland, but worthy – such as extending nursery facilities and re-employment systems and improving conditions for part-time workers. The Education Ministry and local governments have played a more constructive part by opening up 'Women's Centres' with information services, libraries and meeting rooms, though their actual impact is hard to judge.

The general thrust of such policy proposals seems admirable. Whether or not they will be fully implemented is an open question. The Japanese are sensitive to criticism that their women are treated as second-class citizens, while at the same time they do not really believe that there is much truth in the accusations, which are admittedly sometimes based on inadequate evidence and without reference to other industrialized countries. Japanese policy makers, therefore, hope to respond in a like manner by drawing up grand statements of intent, which may never be fully implemented because so much of women's employment takes place in the casual and informal sectors, part of which – the successfully self-employed – may have favourable work conditions. Meanwhile the nature of occupational segregation in Japan, though certainly not any more severe than in Britain, keeps women especially tied into a secondary labour market, most of which is characterized by unskilled and unstable work in small companies.

What I hope to have shown in this book is the overwhelming importance of these sectors for working women in Japan, which is where, therefore, action to improve conditions must be directed. In Britain as well, where the Conservative government's policies are directed towards encouraging small businesses and deregulation, middle-aged women are likely to be found increasingly in the kinds of casual or secondary sector jobs presently occupied by Japanese women. There are a few advantages in terms of flexible hours and the vague possibility of pursuing a career in spite of interruptions due to motherhood, but on the whole the implications for women include a widening of the average wage differential by sex and insecure employment. This prospect for women's employment in Britain can already be seen in Japan, which is therefore worthy of the attention of those who are concerned about the future of women and work in the British Isles.

More employment in electronics companies

When discussing the general shift in resources and employment towards the service sector in the post-industrial age, one should note the important exceptions. There are certain manufacturing industries which will continue to grow rapidly, both because of their association with leisure activities and also because they supply the automated machinery and devices which are increasingly demanded by other industries. The most obvious example is the electronics industry. Furthermore this industry is particularly appropriate for locating plants overseas, since the technology may be easily transferred and there is a pressing need for the Japanese to avoid trade friction in electronic products and components, most of which have a high profile in the marketplace.

Consequently employment prospects in the subsidiaries of Japanese companies such as Matsushita and NEC which are located in Britain and Ireland can only continue to improve – at least in quantitative terms – and there will be considerable job security, because of the expanding markets for their output. The question is whether the British and Irish women employed in these plants will also see a qualitative improvement in their employment conditions in terms of skill acquisition and career progression. One factor hampering their opportunities is the way in which Japanese companies locating overseas have tended to confine training programmes to the bare minimum and to keep their design and research facilities in Japan. In 1989 this situation shows signs of changing with announcements of plans for research laboratories following upon one another. NEC and Fujitsu – being aware of the criticism about a lack of technology transfer – are among the founding sponsors of the research and development facility to be called the Japan-European Technology Studies Institute (JETS), which will be established in Edinburgh (*Nihon Keizai Shimbun*, 16 April 1989). Nonetheless, at present JETS, which sounds at best like an academic research institute for exchanging technology and at worse like a public relations exercise for avoiding technological friction, will not have any impact on the training and careers of shop-floor employees of Japanese electronics firms. Not long after the announcement of JETS, Hitachi unfolded a plan to start two joint basic research projects with universities in Britain and Ireland. Although the kind of research to be conducted – in high-speed semiconductor devices and high-level language for super-computers – seems to bear no relevance to women on the shop floor, there may one day be some externalities in the offering of training courses and certification of skills.

The factor of a relative lack of training could be just as constricting to men as to women, except that men are more likely to aim to become supervisors and thereby be entitled to further training. Many of the women on the shop floor have shown a remarkable aptitude for the job and also for Japanese working methods to the extent that their promotion prospects should be better than those of their male colleagues. Yet we have seen that the ratios of female supervisors to male are still relatively low. Part of the reason lies in their shorter length of service because of their withdrawal from the work-force for child-rearing. That drawback could to some extent be remedied with appropriate re-employment schemes and child-care facilities.

Yet in Japan where such schemes are theoretically in existence and where child-care facilities are extensive, there are invariably no women supervisors in the large electronics companies. Thus in both Japan and in the British Isles – but to a greater extent in Japan – the scarcity of female supervisors has been seen to be partly a function of some women's reluctance to be promoted, which in itself reflects the attitude of society. Japanese society in general has yet to recognize all the benefits of permitting, let alone encouraging, women to be in the mainstream of economic activity, unless they are in the professional and technical categories.

Attitude of society will determine working conditions

Will there be any change in the attitudes of not only women, but also society to their promotion and hence their working conditions in the post-industrial age? The changes would have to be more far-reaching than a simple recognition of the need for equal opportunity; there would need to be considerable adjustments in the division of labour within the home and in the education system, including the ways in which parents bring up their children. Such changes seem to be already under way in Britain. But there have been some recent reverses and while alternative career tracks are being planned for mothers in high-status careers, women on the shop floor are still being treated as expendable.

In the case of Japan many mothers still relish being full-time housewives, since the alternative often requires hard work which is badly paid, because society does not yet place much value on their work. Since the hours for regular workers are too long for most mothers, their commitment to outside work will depend on there being shorter working hours. Ultimately working conditions and promotion prospects for women can only improve when there is a much better integration of part-time and full-time work which would extend to not only elite workers, but also to women on the shop floor.

Partly because of labour shortages in Japan's service sector and because of women's educational level being relatively high, there could be more potential than in the British Isles for post-industrial Japanese society to place a higher value on the economic activity of women. In that case, since both good day-care facilities and an informal sector for employment are already established in Japan, the participation rate of Japanese women and their working conditions may surpass those of British women in the late 1990s. Meanwhile a more positive view towards women's employment in Britain could be hampered by higher unemployment levels and by cutbacks in the public sector, in which women have tended to find good employment opportunities.

But even if there were substantial changes in the view of society – whether in Japan or the British Isles – the outcome may not be as radically different as many would like to see. What society needs to ensure is that managerial expectations do not deter the aptitude and potential ambition of women on the shop floor of Japanese electronics companies, whose success is increasingly leading to their imitation by other companies. If a sizeable body of female production workers could embark upon real careers which incorporated a couple of breaks, one important outcome would be a better articulation of work and home interests for both women and men in the post-industrial age.

Bibliography

Allen, S. and Wolkowitz, C. (1987), *Homeworking, Myths and Realities*, Macmillan Press, London.

Aoki M. (ed.) (1984), *The Economic Analysis of the Japanese Firm*, North-Holland, Netherlands.

Bando, M. (1986), *Japanese Women, Today and Yesterday*, Foreign Press Centre, Tokyo.

Beechey, V. (1987), *Unequal Work*, Verso, London.

Beechey, V. and Perkins, T. (1987), *A Matter of Hours*, Polity Press, Oxford.

Berg, B.J. (1986), *The Crisis of the Working Mother – Resolving the Conflict between Family and Work*, Simon and Schuster, New York.

Bernstein, G.L. (1983), *Haruko's World*, Stanford University Press, California.

Clark, R. (1979), *The Japanese Company*, Yale University Press, New Haven.

Cole, R.E. (1979), *Work, Mobility and Participation – A Comparative Study of American and Japanese Industry*, University of California Press, Berkeley.

Condon, J. (1985), *A Half Step Behind – Japanese Women of the 80s*, Dodd, Mead and Company, New York.

Cook, A.H., Lorwin V.R. and Kaplan Daniels A. (eds.) (1984), *Women and Trade Unions in 11 Industrialized Countries*, Temple University Press, Philadelphia.

Cook, A.H. and Hayashi, H. (1980), *Working Women in Japan – Discrimination, Resistance and Reform*, Cornell University Press, New York.

Denki Roren (1985), *Fujin Kumiai-In Anketo Chosa* (Survey of Women Unionists), Chosa Jiho No. 205, Tokyo.

—— (1986), *Jukkakoku Denki Rodosha Ishiki Chosa* (Survey of Electronics Workers in Ten Countries), Chosa Jiho No. 212,

Tokyo.

—— (1987), *Seinen, Fujin Tantosha, Fujindai Hyosha Godo Kaigi* (Reports and Material for General Meeting of the Youth's and Women's Sections), Tokyo.

Dore R.P. (1973), *British Factory – Japanese Factory*, University of California Press, Berkeley.

—— (1987), *Taking Japan Seriously*, The Athlone Press, London.

Dunning J.H. (1986), *Japanese Participation in British Industry*, Croom Helm, London.

Franko L.G. (1983), *The Threat of Japanese Multinationals – How the West Can Respond*, John Wiley & Sons, New York.

Hataraku Fujin no Kai (Working Women's Assoc.) (1987), *Obasan wa Okotta-zo!* (We're Really Angry!), Minerava Shobo, Tokyo.

Hill A.M. (1984), 'Female Labor Force Participation in Japan: An Aggregate Model', *Journal of Human Resources*, No. 2, University of Wisconsin.

Higuchi K. (1985), *Bringing Up Girls*, Shoukadoh Booksellers, Tokyo.

Hirota H. (1988), *Japanese Women Today*, International Society for Educational Information, Tokyo.

Hunt A. (ed.) (1988), *Women and Paid Work*, Macmillan Press, London.

Imai M. (1986), *Kaizen: The Key to Japan's Competitive Success*, Random House, New York.

International Labour Office (1986), *Economically Active Population 1950–2025*, ILO, Geneva.

—— (1988), *Year Book of Labour Statistics*, ILO, Geneva.

Ishida H. (ed.) (1986), *Josei no Jidai – Nihon Kigyo to Koyo Byodo* (The Age of Women – Japanese Industry and Equal Employment Opportunities), Kobundo, Tokyo.

Japan Institute of Labor (monthly), *Japan Labor Bulletin*, Tokyo.

—— (1984), *Wages and Hours of Work*, Industrial Relations Series No. 3, Tokyo.

—— (1986), *The Problems of Working Women*, Industrial Relations Series No. 8, Tokyo.

Jenson J., Hagen E. and Ceallaigh R. (eds.) (1988), *Feminization of the Labour Force, Paradoxes and Promises*, Polity Press, Oxford.

Joshi H. (1988), *The Cash Opportunity Costs of Childbearing: An Approach to Estimation Using British Data*, Discussion Paper

Series No. 208, Centre for Economic Policy Research, London.

Jowell D., Witherspoon S. and Brook L. (eds.,) (1987), *British Social Attitudes – The 1987 Report*, Social and Community Planning Research, Gower, London.

Kaji E. (1986), 'Herded into the Labor Market', *Ampo*, Vol.18 (2–3), Tokyo.

Keizai Koho Center, (1989) *Japan – An International Comparison*, Tokyo.

Kelly R.M. and Bayes J. (eds) (1988) *Comparable Work, Pay Equity and Public Policy*, Greenwood Press, New York.

Kessler-Harris A. (1982), *Out to Work. A History of Wage-Earning Women in the US*, Oxford University Press, New York.

Koike K. (1988), *Understanding Industrial Relations in Modern Japan*, Macmillan Press, London.

Koziara K.S. *et al* (eds.) (1987), *Working Women: Past, Present and Future*, Industrial Relations Research Association, BNI, Washington.

Kusaka K. (1989), 'The Power of Japanese Women', *Economic Eye*, Vol.10, No.1, Keizai Koho Center, Tokyo.

Lebra J., Paulson J. and Powers E. (eds.) (1976), *Women in Changing Japan*, Stanford University Press, California.

Lebra Sugiyama T. (1984), *Japanese Women, Constraint and Fulfillment*, University of Hawaii Press.

Lewenhak S. (1977), *Women and Trade Unions*, Ernest Benn Ltd., London.

Marsden D. *et al* (1985), *The Car Industry – Labour Relations and Industrial Adjustment*, Tavistock Publications, New York.

Mito T (1984) 'Japanese Management Principles and Seniority Systems', *The Wheel Extended*, Vol.14, No.1, Toyota Motor Co., Tokyo.

Murase H. (1984), *Kaiketsu Hausu Hazubando* (Marvellous house-husband), Shobunsha, Tokyo.

Nakajima K. (1986), 'Micro-Electronics: For Women the Technology of Oppression', *Ampo*, Vol.18 (2–3), Tokyo.

National Institute of Employment and Vocational Research (1988), *Women Workers in Japan*, Report No.4, NIEVR, Tokyo.

Okimoto D.I. and Rohlen T.P. (eds) (1988), *Inside the Japanese System – Readings on Contemporary Society and Political Economy*, Stanford University Press, California.

Organisation for Economic Cooperation and Development

(1985), *The Integration of Women into the Economy*, OECD, Paris.

—— (1986), *Employment Outlook*, OECD, Paris.

—— (1987), *Employment Outlook*, OECD, Paris.

—— (1988), *Employment Outlook*, OECD, Paris.

Oliver N. and Wilkinson B. (1988), *The Japanization of British Industry*, Blackwell, Oxford.

Osawa M. (1988) 'Working Mothers: Changing Patterns of Employment and Fertility in Japan', *Economic Development and Cultural Change*, Vol.36, No.4.

Pascale R.T. and Athos A.G. (1981), *The Art of Japanese Management*, Simon and Schuster, New York.

Patrick H. (ed.) (1976) *Japanese Industrialization and its Social Consequences*, University of California Press, Berkeley.

Paukert L. (1984) *The Employment and Unemployment of Women in OECD Countries*, OECD, Paris.

Plath D.W. (ed.) (1983), *Work and Lifecourse in Japan*, State University of New York Press, Albany.

Robins-Mowry D. (1983), *The Hidden Sun – Women of Modern Japan*, Westview Press, Boulder, Colorado.

Rubery J. (ed.) (1988), *Women and Recession*, Routledge & Kegan Paul, London.

Sasaki T. (1987), *Nihon Denshi Sangyo no Kaigai Shinshutsu* (Japanese Electronics Industries Overseas), Hosei University Press, Tokyo.

Sato K. (1984), 'Working Women Pose No Threat', *Japan Echo*, Vol.XI, No.4, Tokyo.

Schroedel J.R. (1985), *Alone in a Crowd – Women in the Trades Tell their Stories*, Temple University Press, Philadelphia.

Shinotsuka E. (1989), 'Japanese Women's Limited Job Choices', *Economic Eye*, Vol.10, No.1, Keizai Koho Center, Tokyo.

Shirai T. (ed.) (1983), *Contemporary Industrial Relations in Japan*, University of Wisconsin Press.

Sievers S.L. (1983), *Flowers in Salt – The Beginnings of Feminist Consciousness in Modern Japan*, Stanford University Press, California.

Takagi S. (1986), 'Women on the Labor Front', *Ampo*, Vol.18 (2–3), Tokyo.

Takahashi N. (1976) 'Women's Wages in Japan and the Question of Equal Pay', *Women Workers and Society*, International Labour Office, Geneva.

Takamiya S. and Thurley K. (eds.) (1985), *Japan's Emerging Multinationals*, University of Tokyo Press.

Tanaka K. (1987), *Changing Life Cycle Employment of Japanese Women*, Annual Meeting of Association for Asian Studies (unpublished paper).

Thurley K. *et al* (1980), *The Development of Personnel Management in Japanese Enterprises in Great Britain*, International Centre for Economics and Related Disciplines (ICERD), LSE, London.

Thurley K. *et al* (1981), *Japanese Management in Western Europe*, ICERD, LSE, London.

Toyo Keizai (annual), *Kaigai Shinshutsu Kigyo Soran* (Digest of Japanese Subsidiaries Overseas), Tokyo.

Trevor M., Schendel J. and Wilpert B. (eds.) (1986), *The Japanese Management Development System*, Policy Studies Institute, Francis Pinter, London.

Trevor M. (ed.) (1987), *The Internationalization of Japanese Business*, Campus, Colorado.

—— (1988), *Toshiba's New British Company*, Policy Studies Institute, London.

Watanabe Y. (1984), 'The Role of Academic Background in Japanese Society', *The Wheel Extended*, Vol.14, No.1, Toyota Motor Co., Tokyo.

White M. (1987), *The Japanese Educational Challenge*, The Free Press, New York.

White M. and Trevor M. (1983), *Under Japanese Management – The Experience of British Workers*, Policy Studies Institute, Heinemann, London.

Wickens P. (1987), *The Road to Nissan – Flexibility Quality Teamwork*, Macmillan Press, London.

Woronoff J. (1981), *Japan's Wasted Workers*, Lotus Press, Tokyo.

Yamaguchi M. (1986), *A Cross-Cultural Study of Women's Vocational Aspirations and Education in England and Japan*, Shigakuken, Tokyo.

Yokakaihatsu Centre (1987), *Kigyo ni okeru Rodojikan to Yokakyoju Kankyo ni kansuru Chosa* (Survey on Labour Hours and Leave Provisions), Tokyo.

Zabalza A. and Tzannatos Z. (1985), *Women and Equal Pay: The Effects of Legislation on Female Employment and Wages in Britain*, Cambridge University Press.

Government publications

JAPAN

Economic Planning Agency (1983), *Annual Report on the National Life for Fiscal 1983*.
—— (1987), *Atarashii Josei no Ikikata wo Motomete* (The Life Cycle of Modern Women).
—— (1988), *White Paper on the Life of the Nation*, Foreign Press Centre.
Management and Coordination Agency, Statistics Bureau (annual), *Rodoryoku Chosa Nenpo* (Labour Forces Survey).
—— (annual), *Kakei Chosa Nenpo* (Family Expenditure Survey).
—— (annual), *Japan Statistical Yearbook*.
—— (1968, 1982, 1987), *Shuugyo Kozo Kihon Chosa* (Survey on Employment Structure).
Ministry of Education (annual), *Gakko Kihon Chosa* (Survey on Schools and Colleges).
Ministry of Education (1987), *Gendai no Katei Kyoiku* (Education in the Contemporary Home).
Ministry of Finance (1989), *Direct Overseas Investment Recorded in FY1988*, Foreign Press Centre.
Ministry of International Trade and Industry (1987), *Chuusho Kigyo Hakusho* (White Paper on Small- and Medium-Sized Companies).
Ministry of Labour (annual), *Chingin Kozo Kihon Tokei Chosa* (Statistical Survey on the Structure of Wages).
—— (annual), *Fujin Rodo no Jitsujo* (The Situation of Working Women).
—— (biannual), *Koyodoko Chosa* (Survey on Employment Trends).
—— (monthly), *Rodo Tokei Chosa Geppo* (Monthly Labour Statistics and Research Bulletin), with *Maitsuki Kinro Tokei Chosa* (Labour Survey Statistics).
—— (1985a), *Pato Taimu Rodo Jittai Chosa* (Survey of Part-Time Workers).
—— (1985b), *Shokibo Jigyosho no Chingin, Rodojikan oyobi Koyo* (Wages, Hours and Employment in Small Companies).
—— (1986), *Joshi Hogo Jisshi Jokyo Chosa* (Survey of Effectiveness of Protective Measures for Women).
—— (1987), *Joshi Rodosha no Koyokanri ni kansuru Chosa* (Employment Management for Female Employees).

Bibliography

—— (1988), *Koyo Taisaku Kihon Keikaku* (Employment Policies and Plan for 1988 to 1993), Okurasho, Tokyo.

—— (1988), *Ikuji Kyugyo Seido Jittai Chosa* (Survey on Child-Care Leave System).

—— (1989), *Rodo Hakusho* (White Paper on Labour).

Prime Minister's Office (1972, 1975, 1979), *Fujin ni kansuru Ishiki Chosa* (Survey on Attitudes towards Women).

—— (1981), International Survey on Youth, [Results reported in Economic Planning Agency (1983)].

—— (1983), *Fujin Mondai ni kansuru Kokusai Hikaku Chosa* (International Comparative Survey on Women's Issues).

—— (1984, 1987), *Fujin ni kansuru Seron Chosa* (Public Opinion Survey on Women).

—— (1986), *Public Opinion Survey on the Family and the Home*, Foreign Press Centre.

—— (1987), *Seireki 2,000-nen ni mukete no Shinkokunai Kodo Keikaku*, (New National Plan of Action for Women towards the Year 2000).

—— (1989), *Fujin no Genjo to Shisaku* (White Paper on Women).

Tokyo-to Meguro-ku (1988), *Kusei Yoran* (Ward Directory), *Koho Meguro* (Meguro Report).

BRITAIN

Equal Opportunities Commission (1987), *Women and Men in Britain: A Statistical Profile*, HMSO, London.

—— (1988), *Women and Men in Britain: A Research Profile*, HMSO, London.

Central Statistical Office (annual), *Social Trends*, HMSO, London.

Department of Employment (annual), *Family Expenditure Survey*, HMSO, London.

—— (annual), *New Earnings Survey*, HMSO, London.

Appendix

Questionnaires

Copies of the two questionnaires in Japanese are available from Mary Saso by contacting her through the publisher.

Questionnaire for an Employee

Thank you for participating in this survey, the results of which will be used in a book about women working in Japanese companies. I will ensure that your privacy will be respected and that you will not be at all inconvenienced by your participation.

If there are any questions that you would prefer not to answer, you may leave a blank space. For those questions with a choice of answers, please just place a tick across your choice.

1) Personal details

1-1 Name (may be omitted):

1-2 Age: _____ years

1-3 a) female   b) male

1-4 a) single   b) married

1-5 At what age did you complete full-time education?
   a) 16 years   b) 18 years   c) 21 years and over

2) Working hours

2-1 At what time do you usually –
   1)   – get up in the morning?   _____ am
   2)   – leave home?   _____ am
   3)   – return home?   _____ pm
   4)   – go to bed?   _____ pm

2-2 How long does it usually take you to get to work?
   a) less than 15 minutes   b) less than 1 hour   c) more than 1 hour

277

2-3 At what time do you begin and finish work?
 From _____ am to pm
     * *If you work on shifts:*
     Early shift:
     from _____ am to _____ pm   no. of days per month _____
     Late shift:
     from _____ am to _____ pm   no. of days per month _____
     Night shift:
     from _____ am to _____ pm   no. of days per month _____
2-4 How many hours overtime on average do you work each month?
     _____ hours

3) The following questions are about your job.
3-1 For how many years have you been working in this company?
     _____ years
3-2 What type of employee are you?
     a) full-time   b) part-time   c) temporary
3 3 How many days holiday –
         – are you entitled to each year? _____ days
         – do you take each year? _____ days
3-4 What kind of work do you do?
     a) clerical   b) production/assembly   c) design/planning
     d) inspection/supervision   e) general affairs   f) other _____
3-5 Do you have any special skills?
         1) national certificates/qualifications: _____
         2) company certificates/qualifications: _____
3-6 Do you participate in job rotation in the workplace?
     a) no   b) yes   c) sometimes
3-7 Are there any quality control (QC) circles in your workplace?
     a) no   b) yes
         * If there are QC circles, do you belong to one?
         a) yes   b) no   c) used to belong
3-8 Do you feel you can speak freely with the managers?
     a) no   b) yes   c) don't know
3-9 Is there a suggestion system at your plant?
     a) no   b) yes
         * If so, do you make suggestions?
         a) yes   b) sometimes   c) never
3-10 1) Are you sometimes given on-the-job training in your workplace?
         a) no   b) yes
     2) What other kinds of training have you received? _____
     _____
3-11 Is there anything different about working for a Japanese company
     rather than any other kind of company?
     a) no   b) yes

* If so, what are the main differences?

___

4) The following questions are about the future of your job.

4-1 Are you worried about operating increasingly automated processes?
   a) not at all worried   b) very worried
   c) don't know   d) will operate under certain conditions
       * If possible, please give a reason for your answer:

___

4-2 In general, what is your job like? *(Please choose one answer from each line.)*
   1-   a) easy   b) not really easy   c) difficult
   2)   a) tiring   b) not too tiring   c) pleasant/enjoyable
   3)   a) satisfying   b) normal   c) boring
       * What kind of job would you like to do in the future?

___

4-3 Have you ever considered changing your place of employment?
   a) no   b) yes
4-4 Did you move to this company from another company?
   a) no   b) yes
4-5 Do you have good prospects for being promoted?
   a) no   b) yes   c) don't know
4-6 Would you accept promotion into a supervisory position?
   a) no   b) yes   c) don't know
4-7 Would you accept being moved into a different department?
   a) no   b) yes   c) don't know
4-8 Are you worried about ever being made redundant or laid off?
   a) no   b) yes   c) don't know
4-9 What are your plans for the future? *(You may choose more than one answer.)*
       a)   to work until retirement age
       b)   to retire early
       c)   to be promoted
       d)   to get more qualifications
       e)   to stay in my present position
       f)   to move to another position

5) The following questions are about trade unions.
5-1 Do you wish to be a member of a trade union?
   a) no   b) yes   c) not sure
5-2 Are you actually a union member?
   a) no   b) yes   c) used to belong, but left
5-3 If there is a union at your company, do you think that it is sympathetic to working women?
   a) no   b) yes   c) fairly sympathetic   d) no union

5-4 Do you think that you could depend on a union to improve your wages and working conditions?
a) no   b) yes   c) don't know

6) The following questions are concerned with women in the workplace.
6-1 Have you ever worked under a woman supervisor?
a) no   b) yes
6-2 Do you accept the idea of working under a woman supervisor?
a) no   b) yes   c) don't know
6-3 Do you think that women can work as well as men in your workplace?
a) no   b) yes   c) don't know
    * *Please give a reason for your answer*
6-4 What do you think are the main problems that women face in the workplace?

---

7) The following questions need only be answered by women.
7-1 Until when do you wish to continue working?
    a)   until retirement age
    b)   until I have children
    b)   to stop while the children are small, but then start again
    c)   until I find good part-time work
    d)   not sure or other: _____

Questions 7-2 and 7-3 need only be answered if you have a child/children.
7-2 How many children do you have and what are their ages?
    1) Number of children: _____   2) Ages: _____
7-3 How are/were your children who are/were not yet at school taken care of?
    a) in a day nursery
    b) by grandparents or other relatives
    c) by a childminder
    c) other: _____
7-4 When do you usually do –
    1)   – shopping for food? _____
    2)   – cleaning the home? _____
    3)   – washing clothes? _____
7-5 If you are married, how much time does your husband give at home –
    1)   – to helping with the housework?
        a) considerable time   b) a little time   c) no time at all
    2)   *(if you have children)* – to taking care of and entertaining the children?
        a) considerable time   b) a little time   c) no time at all

7-6 For what reasons have you chosen to be employed? *(You may choose more than one answer.)*
    a)   to earn money for paying off a house mortgage
    b)   to earn money for buying essential items, such as food
    c)   to earn money for spending on luxuries (e.g. travel)
    d)   to continue my career and become more skilled
    e)   because I would be bored at home
    f)   other: _____

7-7 What do you think are the main problems in combining the roles of a worker and a housewife/mother? _____

Thank you very much for your co-operation and the time you have given.

Questions Relating to Women Working in Japanese Companies
(submitted to personnel officers)

1.   What is the average length of service for:
    production workers   managerial staff?
    i. female _____   i. female _____
    ii. male _____   ii. male _____

2.   What is the crude annual turnover (separation) rate?
    i. female employees _____   ii. male employees _____

3.   What is the absenteeism rate?
    i. female employees _____   ii. male employees _____

4.   In the following categories, what percentage of the total are women?
    i.   production workers _____
    ii.   group leaders _____
    iii.   supervisors _____
    iv.   clerical staff _____
    v.   managerial staff _____

5.   i.   Approximately what proportion of the pay packet for production workers is made up of a merit payment/bonus? _____
    ii.   How is the merit payment determined? _____
    iii.   On average how does a female employee's merit payment compare to that of a male employee? _____

6. What training programmes, including on-the-job training are available for production workers?

Index